A CENTURY
OF
TROUBLES

A CENTURY OF TROUBLES

1600-1700

STEVIE DAVIES

For Emily, Grace and Robin
My lovely three

First published in 2001 by Channel 4 Books, an imprint of Pan Macmillan Ltd,
Pan Macmillan, 20 New Wharf Road, London N1 9RR, Basingstoke
and Oxford.

Associated companies throughout the world

www.panmacmillan.com

ISBN 0 7522 6168 X

9 8 7 6 5 4 3 2 1

A CIP catalogue record for this book is available from the British Library.

Design by DW Design, London

Colour reproduction by Aylesbury Studios

Printed and bound in Great Britain by Bath Press

This book accompanies the following television films made for Channel 4.

Gunpowder, Treason and Plot made by Wall to Wall
Producer: Ben Goold
Director: Andrew Chater

Cromwell: New Model Englishman made by Wall to Wall
Producer: Ben Goold
Director: Paul Sen

The Great Plague made by Juniper Communications Limited
Producer: John Toba
Director: Justin Hardy

The Great Fire made by Oxford Film and Television Limited
Producer/Director: James Runcie

CONTENTS

INTRODUCTION

T he seventeenth century was a period of convulsive political and social change. When Queen Elizabeth I died in 1603, she left to her Stuart successors a Protestant state in which profound conflicts were kept in a condition of precarious balance. Only sixty years earlier her father, Henry VIII, had broken the tie between the English Church and the papacy, dissolving the monasteries, whose wealth he appropriated for the Crown and divided among a new Protestant elite. He had been the first English monarch to be addressed as 'Majesty', and the first Defender of the Faith and supreme Head of the Church. The Tudors asserted an absolute rule over Church and State, which the Stuart dynasty in the seventeenth century would find severe difficulty in sustaining.

When James I acceded to the throne of England, he would inherit not only the Reformed Church instituted by Henry VIII but the continuing reverberations of the aftermath of Henry's rule in the catastrophic reign of his Catholic daughter, Mary I (1553–8). Throughout the seventeenth century she was recalled with fear and abhorrence as 'Bloody Mary', for her burning of 300 Protestant martyrs at Smithfield. These burnings had been recorded by John Foxe in his *Book of Martyrs*, a book that all seventeenth-century Protestant households kept beside their Bibles. Hugh Latimer's last words to his friend Nicholas Ridley, chained in torture on the slow-burning fire, are reported as, 'Be of good cheer, Master Ridley... we shall this day light such a candle, by God's grace, in England, as I trust shall never be put out.' The seventeenth century, with its all but hysterical fear of the Catholics and 'popish plots', bore out Latimer's prediction. Catholics in Elizabethan England were a persecuted minority, whose practices were illegal and whose priests were banned and subject to the death penalty if detected.

Religious faith and political loyalty were intrinsic to one another. Under the Stuart kings' strife between king and Parliament issued in a dispute between Charles I and his Parliament, which culminated in the fratricidal Civil Wars of 1642–8. This was also a religious war, in which Puritans (who believed in a simplified, unritualized religion of the heart) and moderate Anglicans attacked the 'High Church' policies of Archbishop William Laud as a tyranny of the spirit. The execution of Charles I as a tyrant, shocking to most citizens of all persuasions, was the turning point of English history. For the first time Parliament asserted a right to act as representative and legal ruler of the nation. Cromwell dominated these years, both in the Commonwealth and as Lord Protector, a powerful, complex and inscrutable force. When the chaos that succeeded his death in 1658 was resolved in 1660 by the restoration of the Stuart dynasty in Charles II, the Crown was never quite as strong as before, nor Parliament as weak. But the religious strife that had precipitated the wars did not die away: it broke out in new fears, and suspected treasons.

The Reformation's battle against popery, associated in the public mind with imperialism and tyranny, was a continuous process of struggle against an enemy thought of as supernaturally devious and powerful. The Pope and the Jesuits (the 'Society of Jesus', dedicated to overturning the Reformation, who sent undercover priests into England) were imagined to be sedulously working to undermine the Protestant monarchy and Church, from generation to generation. The seventeenth century was characterized by an inflamed Protestant pathology, which divined Catholic conspiracies, plots and treasons in every riot and struggle. Seventeenth-century Protestantism read its own experiences – the Gunpowder Treason, the Irish uprising, the Civil War, the Great Fire of London and the spurious Popish Plot of 1678 – in the light of a traumatized dread that demonized Catholics as the enemy within.

Such was the anti-Catholic hysteria in this century that, according to Thomas Barlow in *Popery* (1679), Jesuits were behind every treason plotted in England, all being replays of the Gunpowder Plot, 'a black and unparalleled villainy, worthy [of] Rome and a Jesuit; the Blowing up of a whole Parliament, King, Lords, and Commons, the Murdering of a whole Kingdom'. After James I's reign, Barlow went on, 'their designs slept not', for it was Jesuits who invented the 'Traitorous Conspiracy to Murder Charles the First'. This was, he said, a fact 'notoriously known to be true'. Thus the Puritan Parliamentarians who had attacked the bishops as 'popish lords', and executed the king in 1649, were actually deemed to be front men for a Jesuit council in London, with orders straight from the Pope. The Puritan revolutionaries Oliver Cromwell and John Milton were madly unmasked as Catholic agents. Foreigners (bound to be Catholics) were lynched for 'lighting' the Great Fire of

London. In the reign of Charles II, the arch-liar Titus Oates disclosed a byzantine popish assassination plot against the king, causing mass hysteria and hallucination, as folk were awoken at night by phantasmal night-riders, armies of Catholic assassins. Many innocent Catholics were executed for non-existent conspiracy. After the Catholic James II had been expelled in 1688 and a Protestant King William III installed in what came to be known as the 'Glorious Revolution', the horror of papism, which saw all plots as exponential unfoldings of the one almighty Plot, did not so much die down as face outward to Catholic Europe, with which England was at war for decades. Yet the very people who feared papist intrigue lived amicably alongside Catholic neighbours, ate with them, did business with them and knew that they were ordinary people much like themselves. Anti-Catholic fear was comparable with anti-Semitism and the Communist witch-hunts at a later period.

Throughout the century both king and Parliament perpetuated an ancient dispute about their respective rights, the Crown upholding its prerogative and Parliament jealously protecting gentry property rights. Whereas in 1600 there was no party system and Parliament was subordinate to the monarch, having limited powers and in session only at the king's summoning, by 1700 the party system was evolving, the electorate had grown as wealth spread, and Parliament had secured major rights and liberties. Historical precedent and its interpretation were vital to the issue of the legitimate royal succession, which began and ended the era.

The politics of the period were also characterized by xenophobia. To the west lay Ireland, split between oppressed Catholics and the 'old English' colonists and the newer Scots planted there by James I, all of which groups were plagued by internecine feuds and factions. To the north Scotland seethed with internal conflicts of clan blood feud, Presbyterian and Catholic loyalties. The dominant Presbyterians were a Protestant sect with a strong internal discipline, based on the Calvinist doctrine of the elect and ruled by a general assembly of elders and ministers. For the English, Scotland and Ireland were foreign countries, whose customs and religion they deplored and whose language they construed as gibberish. The century saw a long and bloody series of campaigns to crush Ireland's Catholics, by colonialism, oppressive laws and taxes and by violence, sealed in the blood of Cromwell's vengeance of 1649–50 at the massacres of Drogheda and Wexford and William III's Battle of the Boyne in 1689. When the Scots King James VI came down to be James I of England, he seemed to the English to speak an uncouth foreign language, practising unhygienic foreign customs and importing guttural foreigners to pick the plums of office.

Protestants nervously observed the growing imperialism and absolutism of Catholic France under Louis XIV. But Protestantism, itself a separated religion, had split into sects which again split, begetting radical sects which might be as small – and as potent – as one single person. The poet John Milton could speak of himself as a church of one; a nation of one: 'One's native land is wherever it is well with one.' While a fashionable aphorism held that the great Catholic reformer Erasmus 'laid the egg that Luther hatched', it was equally true that the Church of England, or more properly that incendiary book, the Bible in English, hatched in the mid-century its own brood of Baptists, Independents, Fifth Monarchists, Quakers, Seekers, Muganletonians, the 'dreaming saints' of the Revolution. In an age when religion and politics were twin trees twisted round one another from one cloven root, sedition was seen, from one angle, as an upstart bishop in a mitre (William Laud, Archbishop of Canterbury under Charles I) and, from the other, as a seditious leather-clad weaver's son (George Fox, the founder of Quakerism) or an itinerant tinker (John Bunyan, the Baptist minister and author) with nothing but a Bible in his hand and inspiration on his tongue.

By the end of the century, Isaac Newton and Robert Boyle had eclipsed alchemy and astrology; classicism had left behind the Elizabethan vernacular architecture of black-and-white timber-framed buildings with quaintly crazed asymmetries and leaded panes that might be flawed and 'nookshotten', set awry. Wren's St Paul's Cathedral, replacing that burnt in the Great Fire, proposed in the complex technology of its dome an age in which reason and religion might advance hand in hand. The foundations of modern science had been laid, from William Harvey's discovery of the circulation of blood, to Newton's proposal of the theory of gravity. Logarithms, the differential calculus, the microscope, the spring balance, the marine barometer and the air pump were invented. The forceps were introduced by the Chamberlen family, who jealously kept the device secret for decades – thereby doubtless saving the lives of many women, since the 'men-midwives' of the next century were to introduce sepsis with their unsterilized instruments. Leisure pursuits also changed. Golf was introduced by King James from Scotland; Charles II and his brother James came back from the Netherlands keen yachtsmen, and ice-skating became a fashion. A ghost from 1600 would not have recognized the London of 1700, for after the Great Fire of 1666 had destroyed 80 per cent of the city, it was rebuilt according to the most up-to-date designs, often recycling the old materials.

From the padded, farthingaled, ruffed rotundities of Elizabethan styles the century had passed through the fluent, artistically natural styles of the Caroline court, all silk and lace; through the dark periwigs, petticoat breeches and leggy elegance of the male in the court of King Charles and sleepy-eyed sensuality of silken décolletage painted by Lely, to the powdered, uniform perukes and new fabrics of the Williamite age. A revolution of dyes and fabrics made possible the apricot, canary-yellow and purple satins of the cavaliers. The court of Charles II was characterized by prodigal spending, lavish consumerism and, until 1680, empty pockets. In the age of William III, the Bank of England and the creation of the national debt would revolutionize finance, and England became a world power, the financial capital of the world. A hard-won political settlement modestly increased Parliament's standing in relation to the crown, an Act of Toleration pacified Dissenters and in the Glorious Revolution the last Stuart king 'vacated' the throne in 1688.

The antiquarian, John Aubrey, enjoyed gleaning the memories of old folk, who could tell him about a time before tobacco, brought home by Sir Walter Raleigh with potatoes, which were held to be aphrodisiac. He had spoken with old men in Somerset who, in 1668, remembered a time before carrots, and an octogenarian recalled that cabbages were once a delicacy from Holland. By the end of the seventeenth century the landscape of England had greatly changed. After 1650, farming techniques had been modified in many areas, generally the richer estates. Clover, lucerne and sainfoin, and other nitrogen-fixing crops introduced from the Low Countries, reduced the time when land must lie fallow; water meadows were flooded in winter and drained in spring, so that early spring grasses allowed animals to survive the winter and produce manure for fertilizer. Turnips (introduced early in the century) and new feed crops, along with experimental animal breeding, produced hardier strains. Land was cleared and drained. The famous 'Norfolk' system of crop rotation (turnips, barley, clover, wheat) was being used, with spectacular results in yield, long before the eighteenth century. In the rich pasture of the south of England there were cherry orchards and hop fields. Mining was opened up in the north-east, Wales and Cumberland, while smelting of iron, lead, tin and copper expanded. Textiles, once the mainstay of English exports, had declined, while other manufacturing industries expanded. Throughout the seventeenth century, deforestation continued, as forests were hacked back for fuel and timber: the woodlands that had once covered England, memorialized in Shakespeare's Arden, were remorselessly driven back. Meanwhile, after the Civil War, old customs waned and died. Aubrey recalled the country people propitiating the fairies, perpetuating customs such as bridecake at weddings, over which the bride and groom would kiss.

It was the age of stop-press news, seeing a revolution of printed matter, news-sheets, broadsides, pamphlets and ballads, which could be brought out in vast print-runs overnight. Shorthand, codes and invisible ink were invented. The price of books tumbled and literacy increased over the century. By 1700 the public's appetite for reading material was fed by recognizably modern news-sheets, containing political propaganda, or topics of a more lurid and popular nature. Advertisements for every kind of product from 'Mr Stringer's Lemon Elixir' to novel imports such as rum, port, gin, champagne, sugar and peppermint were printed in the newspapers, which, having started as weeklies, had become daily papers, only to divide again into morning and evening editions. Whereas in 1600 a gentleman might not care to publish at all but circulate his poetry in manuscript form (and few ladies dared to challenge the prohibition on ladies immodestly publishing), by 1700 a new generation of professional journalists, novelists, dramatists and writers of manuals on everything from home medicine and beauty to cookery and marriage could make a living. Libraries and museums flourished, mainly in the centres of learning and privilege. The Bodleian at Oxford dates from 1610 and Wren's Library at Trinity College, Cambridge, was built in the last decades of the century.

The century was outstandingly rich in personal writings, for memoirs, diaries and autobiographies were confessional forms especially important to Protestants. The diaries of Samuel Pepys and John Evelyn, the *Journals* of George Fox and the autobiography of John Bunyan (*Grace Abounding to the Chief of Sinners*) give a vivid sense of individual and group experience. Biography, such as John Aubrey's brilliant *Brief Lives*, and histories such as Gilbert Burnet's *History of My Own Time*, open vivid windows into the age, and the way it thought about itself.

'We in England,' wrote William Harrison in *The Description of England* (1577), 'divide our people commonly into four sorts, as gentlemen, citizens or burgesses, yeomen, and artificers or labourers.' While the 'major gentry' included king and nobles, the minor were gentlemen, defined by the ability to live 'without manual labour' and the ability to purchase a coat of arms, as did Shakespeare, a glover's son. The gentry constituted the elites who controlled local government, acting as JPs and civic leaders, in a complex dynastic network. Beneath this group came yeomen, 'freemen born English' with a certain income from land. Lowest on the scale Harrison names 'day labourers, poor husbandmen, and some retailers… as tailors, shoemakers, carpenters, brickmakers, masons, etc'. From this class were drawn local officials such as churchwardens and constables. Gentlemen were entitled to be addressed as 'Master', while a yeoman was merely 'Goodman'. A language of deference articulated this hierarchy: 'thou' was used to an inferior and 'you' to a superior (except, confusingly, in the case of God or an intimate, who were both 'thou'd'). This system was in stressful flux, as affluence bought gentle status and the perquisites of rank, while others toppled down the social scale. Oliver Cromwell for some years fell out of the gentry, economically straitened so that he had to work land with his own hands.

The lowest ranks lived in a poverty that would not improve in the first half of the seventeenth century. The population of England almost doubled between 1540 and 1640, with London swelling from around 40,000 inhabitants in 1500 to nearly a quarter of a million a century later. In the next forty years it exploded to 400,000 people, becoming the largest city in Europe. The city was a hybrid of affluence and poverty, with people living in squalor, in lean-to tenements, packed tight in filthy conditions that made it all year round a breeding ground for disease and, in summer, plague. Although there were improvements in the city after the Great Fire in 1666, essentially London remained an overpopulated development of the medieval city, its streets depositories of sewage and waste that the rakers ineffectually cleansed each night. When the asthmatic William III invaded from the cleanly Netherlands in 1688, he soon withdrew to Hampton Court.

London was a magnet. To it flocked the rural poor and dispossessed, young people seeking apprenticeships or service, or cocky with high hopes of shedding their ties and inhibitions. In the city, infant mortality was high; law and order hard to maintain. The pressure of population on the market, in the context of a 'mini-ice-age' during this period, caused steep price rises in food, racking of rents and mass unemployment. Real wages in the seventeenth century had declined by half. Poor diet weakened people's constitutions and they fell victim to diseases such as tuberculosis, smallpox, scurvy, and the endemic bubonic plague borne by the fleas of rats. The Great Plague of 1665 was only the climax of a disease that claimed lives annually.

Innumerable people fell outside the social hierarchy, casualties of a system that could not cope with the multitudes of destitute it created. The labouring poor in rural areas, whose wages were fixed at less than subsistence, lay at the mercy of the seasons, the harvest, weather which was, throughout the period, undependable. In the 1590s, in 1623 and the later 1640s, harvest failure pushed up food prices. Incomes lowered as industry became depressed. The poor scanned the unreliable skies for weather that would keep them fed and sheltered. In lean years, hundreds would take to the roads.

Destitutes were analysed by the Elizabethan Poor Law in two categories: the 'deserving poor' and 'the thriftless poor', otherwise known as 'sturdy beggars', the 'dregs and scum', 'dunghill knaves', a criminalized underclass of vagrants. In a hierarchical society bound by deference, a shiftless, shifting mass of paupers constituted a threat to order and property. At the parish level, the Elizabethan Poor Law system represented a genuine attempt to provide community care for the unemployed and helpless, by charging a rate on parishioners. But the starvation and misery of the uprooted was compounded by the corrective element in the Poor Law system that punished 'masterless' strangers, by whipping those over seven years of age, issuing them with passports and bundling them back to their parish of origin. Of their experience is known only what the Quarter Sessions record: their names, offences, punishment and place of origin. The Register of Passports for Vagrants in Salisbury records:

> 25 March 1620
> Margaret Cheke, wandering with a lewd fellow named Martin Drake, was punished. Assigned 6 days to go to Benwell, Somerset, where she says she was born.

> 25 November 1635
> Nathaniel Leeche, a poor child, about 9 or 10 years of age, likely to perish and die in the streets with cold, was taken begging and crying. Passport to Lyndhurst, Hants, where he says he was born.

Local authorities did all possible to keep pregnant girls on the move. The heart-rending case of an Irish girl harried to her death through the hills of north-west Somerset by officials determined that the birth should take place in another parish was extreme but not atypical. An inquiry revealed that the girl had been bamboozled into thinking, when she was 'hardly able to go', that she would find haven in half a mile. Very near to term, she struggled on until, in labour, she begged 'for a little straw that she might rest... for she was then lying upon stones before the door of the head tithingman's house'. It was not uncommon for women to give birth in the road or in a ditch.

The vagrant subculture at once appalled and fascinated their 'betters'. Autolycus, the 'snapper-up of unconsidered trifles' in Shakespeare's *The Winter's Tale* (1611), thief, cheat, pickpocket, balladeer and wit, has all the punchy aggression and verve that the respectable perhaps half-envied in the footloose vagabonds who filched linen drying on hedges, pilfered chickens, shared women and paid no dues. A literature had grown up cataloguing the rogues' lewd and bawdy cant. Harrison lists rufflers (thieving beggars), uprightmen (gang-leaders), hookers (stealing through windows with hooks), rogues, wild rogues (born of rogues), praggers or prancers (horse-thieves), abtams (feigned lunatics) and dummerers (sham deaf-mutes). Their women were 'bawdy baskets' (peddlers), morts (prostitute–thieves), doxies (the leader's moll) and dells (apprentice doxies). When the diarist Simon Forman saw *The Winter's Tale* in May 1611, his notes show how hugely entertained he had been by the antics of Autolycus, but at the end of his detailed and chortling reminiscence, he reminded himself: 'beware of trusting feigned beggars or fawning fellows'. Their existence pointed up a threatening fact of life in a society of such drastic inequality: an underlying hostility between rich and poor. Food riots and anti-enclosure riots were common throughout the first half of the seventeenth century.

If the poor were not respected as members of the political nation, neither were women. They had no existence in law, being 'covered' by the legal being of fathers or husbands. They inhabited a world where authority was overwhelmingly male – God, Parliament, electorate, magistracy, Church, army, judiciary. Special punishments and implements existed for unruly women: the ducking stool and brank for scolds (the brank being a metal cage that locked over the head forcing into the mouth a bit, two or three inches long, with or without pins at the end). In rituals of shaming, a woman 'of masculine tongue' would be 'ridden' round the marketplace or town centre in a carnival atmosphere. The brank or bridle was a fearsome deterrent, which could shatter a woman's teeth or jaw. Between 1560 and 1640 court records suggest an intensifying concern with women running out of control. Only one account of wearing the brank survives, that of the militant Quaker Dorothy Waugh, who had begun as an illiterate Selby serving girl, for public preaching in Carlisle in 1656. She described it as 'a stone weight of iron... and three bars of iron to put over my face, and a piece of it was put in my mouth, which was so unreasonable big a thing for that place as cannot be well related'. The scold was next door to the witch. At the beginning of the century, witchcraft was still a crime punishable by death but King James, author of *Demonology*, and coming from a country a fifth the size of England, which burned four times as many witches as its neighbour, with a far smaller population, became sceptical. While in 1600 most people believed in witchcraft, by 1700 most did not. The last witch was executed at Exeter in 1685.

During the century, the institution of marriage, the centre of social order, came under seismic strain. Although a husband and father possessed what legally amounted to tyrannical power, he rarely used it coercively. Companionate marriage was a major Puritan ideal: it brought the two 'yoke-fellows' together as near-equals. Many private testaments, from that of the Essex minister Ralph Josselin to that of the London turner, Nehemiah Wallington, reveal marriages in which childcare was shared, the husband showing tender regard for girl-children as much as for boys and becoming inconsolable when a child died. In 1648, Josselin lost his baby Ralph: 'we gave him breast milk at last, and little else'. He lost his daughter Mary in 1650: 'My Mary voided six worms more this day... "Oh Mother," said she, "if you could but pull out something handsomely here" (and lays her hand on her stomach) "I should be well."' The eight-year-old died three days later, 'our first fruits', the father says. 'I kissed her lips last, and carefully laid up that body' in the coffin. Wallington reported his daughter Elizabeth's last prattling speech to him, in bed, snuggled down between her parents: 'Father, I go abroad tomorrow and buy you a plum pie.'

At the same time, social forces worked to separate men and women into specific and God-given roles. In 1620 King James I issued a directive to all clergy to 'inveigh against the insolency of our women, and their wearing of broad brimmed hats, pointed doublets, their hair cut short or shorn, and some of them stilettos or poniards'. Milton's 'He for God only, she for God in him' in *Paradise Lost* expressed the traditional distinction.

The century showed a tension between respect and contempt for women, a double-bound situation from which aristocratic women could more easily assert themselves in writing and publishing, painting, study, travel, investment and building. For a brief period during the revolutionary years ordinary women would emerge as radical activists. Mary Cary and Anna Trapnel the Fifth Monarchists; Katharine Chidley and Elizabeth Lilburne, the Levellers; the Quaker leader Margaret Fell and her seven magnificent daughters; Elizabeth Hooton, Mary Fisher and thousands of other Quakers would seize the God-given authority offered by the belief of Friends in the Inner Light, to challenge traditional truths and values. Imprisoned, whipped, stocked, branked, fined, Quaker women would hold out into the Restoration age, when the movement entered its quietist and pietist phase. Margaret Fell wrote *Women's Speaking Justified* (1667) in Lancaster Gaol. After the Revolution, a few women – Aphra Behn, the poet, dramatist and government agent, Bathsua Makin and Mary Astell the educationalists, Mary Beale the painter, Constance Pley, a ship's outfitter, businesswomen and printers – would inch forward the boundaries of women's activity. For most, however, there remained limitation and illiteracy. Female literacy was the lowest of all social groups. While 15 per cent of labourers and 21 per cent of husbandmen could sign their names, as against 56 per cent of tradesmen and 65 per cent of yeomen, 89 per cent of women of all classes had to sign with a cross.

But life for all ranks involved hardships. The children of the nobility were nearly as likely to die in infancy as those of the yeoman, for doctors' prescriptions were lethal. The poor woman, if she got enough to eat, breast-fed her child. Queens' children might well be denied by addled physicians the nourishment and immunity of breast milk and condemned to gruels and noxious medicines. Disease was ubiquitous and although the very rich could flee, most were open to infection from even the most everyday afflictions and their remedies, as well as death by accidents. The diary of Ralph Josselin is a litany of near-miss accidents ('Mrs Church throwing out a basin of water, threw her self out of the door', 'Mary was struck with a horse', 'Marie's neckcloth fired with a candle and she blew it, which increased the flame, my man damped it'). Anxiety about illnesses haunted Josselin through the decades, for the smallest cut might go septic. His devouring anxieties include a bee-sting in his nose, his wife's prolapsed womb, colds, agues, fits, toothache, painful gums and a suppurating navel that troubled Josselin for several months, as well as the diseases that carried off five of his ten children. He charted the looming epidemics of smallpox and plague as they spread through neighbouring parishes and thanked God for his signal favour in sparing the Josselins. Medicine, based on the false classical theory of humours adopted from the Ancient Greek physician Galen, did not significantly improve throughout the century. Adam Martindale's daughter Hannah, paralysed in her lower limbs, had her blood let (the normal remedy for all illnesses), and was made to sit in 'warm cow-bellies new killed' (which had helped other girls seemingly in the same condition). She was administered 'powder of swine-claws, which had restored a woman fifty years old'. The toxic remedies of physicians were often avoided by going to an alchemist or, more sensibly, the neighbourhood 'cunningwoman', whose skill in herbal remedies might prove more efficacious.

The political throes of the seventeenth century affected rich and poor, throughout the kingdom. Mental stress caused by the Civil Wars showed in hysterical or morbid streaks that afflicted both individuals and society as a whole. Richard Baxter testified to this in his loving memorial to his young wife, *The Breviate of the Life of Margaret Charlton* (1681). Margaret, a resourceful, outspoken woman, suffered from morbid terrors (what might now be called post-traumatic stress disorder) all her life. Into her private world at Apley Castle near Wellington, history had burst in the form of soldiers 'while she was in it, and part of the housing about it burnt, and men lay killed before her face. And all of them threatened and stripped of their clothing so that they were fain to borrow clothes.' This shock was compounded by subsequent experiences of catastrophe, both natural and manmade: a fire next door to her lodgings; the burning alive of a merchant and his entire family; a panic at St Dunstan's Church in the Fleet when Baxter was preaching, in which the weight of the roof began to crack a load-bearing beam and the congregation, believing that the church was falling down, threw themselves from the galleries; 'her mother's death; the great plague; the burning of London... the many fires and talk of firing since; the common rumours of murder and massacres'. The list continues. Spasms of panic gripped the community throughout the century: fear of Catholic plots, arson, uprisings, Irish invasion played out a pathology of anxiety and strain which, begotten by the Reformation, was fuelled by catastrophes caused by urban conditions and demography like the Great Fire, interpreted by mass frenzy and bad memories.

At the same time, the seventeenth century was an age which left incomparable works of art and architecture, monuments of philosophy and pictures that act like windows into its life. The artists Rubens, Van Dyck and Lely show the Stuart court as it wished to be seen, but there were miniaturists too, such as Samuel Cooper, who painted the face frankly, to the life, 'warts and all', in tiny portraits that give the modern viewer a pang like that of recognition, as the eyes of the past meet our own. King Charles II's period of exile on the continent gave to all the arts in Restoration England a greater cosmopolitanism: the music of Pelham Humfrey and Henry Purcell reflected both Italian and French influences and opera became a popular form among the English elite.

In 1600 England had possessed few significant colonies abroad, but by the end of the century was a world trading and military power. Its merchants, who had founded the East India Company to trade in the Spice Islands and the Royal African Company, to profit from slavery, traded around the globe as markets in the colonies of Virginia and Massachusetts Bay, Nova Scotia and Barbados were opened up. The amassing of enormous fortunes by individuals and groups accompanied a radical change in culture, fed by England's emergence as an empire. The fad for those exotic imported drinks, chocolate, tea and coffee, in the latter years of the century not only supplanted beer but changed the culture itself. At coffee houses in London, the beverage was drunk by gentlemen, merchants and politicians, as they engaged in discussion of the new political parties, 'Whigs' and 'Tories', as well as in elegant discussion of culture and science. The coffee houses and gentlemen's clubs became dynamic but urbane centres of political and intellectual activity.

As the century drew to a close, two revolutions had clarified and settled the role of the monarch within the English state. The Stuarts had ascended to a bankrupt, religiously troubled and insecure throne: they were to leave King James I's great dream of a United England and Scotland fulfilled. They left the Anglican church rationalized and Nonconformists officially tolerated, and a modernized system of finance, together with a patriotic pride and the laying of the antique ghosts of fear of Spanish invasion and – after the reign of Anne – of French domination. The Civil Wars and Interregnum had become a bad dream in the public mind, which acquiesced in a judicious modification and acceptance of a constitutional monarchy. If radical dissent went underground, it was however only waiting and not asleep. The emancipation movements of the end of the eighteenth century were as much the child of the English Revolution as of the Age of Reason.

CHAPTER 1

KING
JAMES
I

As James VI of Scotland, cousin to the late Queen Elizabeth I, rode down into England in 1603 to take his throne, the English people flocked to greet him and his court all along the route. He was elated by his reception. Now thirty-six, the son of the executed Mary Stuart had had a loveless childhood and youth. The pawn of rival clans, he had been raised in a crucible of violence and terror – an experience that marked him for life. Yet he emerged strengthened, canny and wise to political arts, a 'Solomon', as his Scots court poet, Alexander Montgomerie had said, 'so sapient a young and godly king'.

It was as Solomon judging between the two mothers in the biblical story that the fourteen-year-old was welcomed into Edinburgh in the autumn of 1579, in a tableau presented by the city. Three thousand horsemen accompanied the young Solomon from Stirling to his court at Holyroodhouse, the 'whole nobility and gentlemen' of Scotland. And it would be as Solomon that his son Charles I would commemorate him, in the great baroque Rubens ceiling of Inigo Jones's Palladian Banqueting House at Whitehall. James would nourish a lifelong abhorrence of war: he would aspire to the title *Rex Pacificus*, King of Peace. For his English and European peacemaking role, the feuding, fratricidal enmities of Scotland provided a cruel testing-ground.

JAMES'S EARLY YEARS

James had been endangered even while in his mother's womb. Daggers threatened a heavily pregnant Mary as her favourite, David Riccio, was butchered before her eyes in March 1566. Eight months after James's birth, his father, Henry Stewart, Earl of Darnley, was strangled and blown up in the old house outside Edinburgh known as Kirk o' Field. James, Earl of Bothwell, reputedly Mary's lover, was tried and acquitted in a patently rigged trial, and Mary married him in May 1587. Defeated by rebel lords, she was forced to abdicate in favour of her baby son and fled across the border, only to find herself imprisoned by Elizabeth. The child was now embraced by the untender mercies of four successive regents, the Earls of Moray, Lennox, Mar and Morton. Moray, his uncle, was assassinated in 1570; the Earl of Lennox, his paternal grandfather, for whom James felt affection, was killed in an affray the following year, and the appalled five-year-old boy watched his mortally wounded body carried out. The new regent, Mar, his guardian, and his wife then had physical care of James: Lady Mar was stern and strict, right down to his bed-linen, which was black. Mar died of natural causes in 1572, and the last regent, Morton, James's ruffianly second cousin, was executed for the murder of Darnley in 1581.

The first tenderness in James's life came with the visit of his Franco-Scots cousin, Esmé Stuart d'Aubigny, in 1579. James was thirteen and the sleek, fashionable young Esmé awakened in him adoration and probably an erotic love. With the terrible logic that dictated James's early years, this attachment was blighted when the young king was kidnapped by the Earl of Gowrie and a Presbyterian faction in 1582. He was imprisoned at the earl's estates in Ruthven, Perthshire, and forcibly separated from his French Catholic favourite. Esmé, now Duke of Lennox, was made to return to France, and shortly died. James was forced to curse and vilify him. Bereft, he wept uncontrollably, while the Master of Glamis rasped that it was 'better that bairns should weep than bearded men'. These words were observed to 'enter so deeply into the King's heart that he did never forget them'. James escaped his Ruthven prison after ten months.

Lennox had not only brought solace to James's barren craving; he had also brought a taste for France and its culture. James's court would seek to graft European Renaissance culture on to the gaunt splendour of native Scottish building, insofar as Scotland's and the king's poverty allowed. James, in the grief of his detention, eased his loss by composing poetry in the mannerist mode, *Ane Metaphoricall Invention of a Tragedie called Phoenix*, a long poem in which he encoded the name ESME STEWART DWIKE in acrostics, ingeniously adapting the rugged Scots language to the grace of continental traditions. At the dour court of Scotland, the colourful, Parisian fashions had been a dazzling window on to a world less sour and emotionally cold.

James's experiences of Presbyterianism had been dire, since Calvinism sought to impose rule by the Church, not by the king. When safely on his English throne, he recalled how he had reigned in Scotland as 'a King without state, without honour, where beardless boys would brave us to the face'. He never forgot the insults dealt the monarchy by the Presbyterians. James favoured episcopacy, and when the Presbyterian leader and academic Andrew Melvill disparaged him as 'God's silly vassal', he could retort with the tersely prophetic axiom: 'No bishop, no king.' Neither did he forget the murderous tussles of the lords in Scotland, who viewed the king as simply 'the first among equals'. James's insistence on the Divine Right of Kings, their godlike status, had grown from his need to militate against the encroachments of the Kirk and the anarchy wrought by brawling Scottish nobles. It was a response to his early impotence, as he was snatched and passed like a bag of gold from faction to faction.

The glamorous and unscrupulous Esmé Stuart, James's Franco-Scots cousin, was the adolescent king's first love.

His world-view was conceived in a lawless matrix of deep human pain, expressed in one of his most accomplished poems, written at the age of fifteen:

> Since thought is free, think what thou will
> O troubled heart to ease thy pain
> Thought unrevealed can do no ill
> But words passed out turn not again
> Be careful, aye, for to invent
> The way to get thine own intent…
> > With patience then see thou attend
> > And hope to vanquish in the end.

This is a bitter knowledge for an adolescent. The poem communicates an introspective solitude, which has learnt the cost of candour in a world of plot and counter-plot, betrayal and violence. Throughout James's life, however, a pattern of passionate homoerotic ardour would characterize his love for his favourites, making him vulnerable and needy. Knowing Esmé Stuart also initiated a tolerance for Catholics, although James himself was, and remained, a Calvinist to the bone.

The king was the pupil of the formidable Scots theologian, George Buchanan, then in his sixties and signally lacking in the milk of human kindness. James was terrified of him. 'They gar [made] me speak Latin ere I could speak Scots,' he was to recall. But the nurture of his young mind was perhaps the nearest thing to care he knew, and he thrived on theology, languages and classics. James grew up donnish and academic, thrilled to find himself so intellectually able. Buchanan also fed him a daily diet of Knoxian contempt for his absent mother, as a 'fornicatress, adultress, murdress'. The vituperation heaped on Mary as a Roman Catholic whore was a form of psychological abuse from which he did not emerge unscathed. A very early letter to her beginning 'Lady Minnie' (Lady Mummy) thanks her for a gift of fruit and wonders if he can have some more. But she had abandoned him and in due course he abandoned her, allying himself – in return for a humiliating pension of £4,000 a year and the hope of being named heir to the throne of England – with the childless Queen Elizabeth.

Mary Queen of Scots was executed in 1587, after the Babington Plot was foiled. (Anthony Babington, Mary's page, had engineered with her a Catholic plot to secure her release; Elizabeth became convinced that it would be dangerous to keep her cousin alive.) James's attitude to his mother's death was ambiguous. In 1586 he had counselled Elizabeth against Mary's execution, arguing cogently that regicide was against the law of God, more particularly in that the victim is 'alike in estate and sex to her that so uses her' and close blood-kin. 'What monstrous thing is it that sovereign princes themselves should be the example-givers of their own sacred diadems' profaning!' Where Mary's neck lay now, Elizabeth's might tomorrow, the one an unholy precedent for the other. When Elizabeth wrote denying complicity in the execution, however, James refused to allow the bearer of the letter to cross the border. He replied to the letter with sardonic acquiescence and continued to pursue his strategy of peaceful – and hopeful – coexistence.

James's escape from his Protestant captors in 1583 gave the sixteen-year-old a taste of autonomy, which he used with the cunning of an endangered man who lives by his wits to play off the Scottish factions against one another. As 'the child is father of the man', so the young King James VI was father of the mature King James I of England. A characteristic gesture, which explains the role of mediator he assumed as English king, was the publicity coup he stage-managed in Edinburgh in 1587. After a meeting of the Convention of Estates (clergy, nobility and burgesses), in which the usual vituperative tirades passed for dialogue, he ordered a 'love-feast': forcing the feuding lords to walk hand in hand through Edinburgh's main street, to symbolize their reconciliation. Though he had quelled risings by force, James's favoured method was mediation and manipulation. But these were hard to achieve in a lawless Scots world where he had no standing army – as the exploits of the 'Wizard Earl', Frances Bothwell, amply demonstrated.

After the Babington Plot, Queen Elizabeth I reluctantly took the decision to execute her
Catholic cousin, Mary Queen of Scots.

Bothwell associated himself with anti-Catholic policy, and set himself against James's right-hand man, John Maitland of Thirlestane. He was believed to have encouraged a group of women known as the 'Berwick witches' in their satanic plot against the king's life – tossing dead body-parts and cats into the sea in order to cause storms on his wedding crossing to Denmark in 1589. James was panic-stricken, both at the thought of his openness to malign supernatural powers and at the earl's escape from Edinburgh Castle. James entered a hell of anxiety, ordering Maitland to investigate the whole matter:

Try, by the mediciners' oaths, if Barbara Napier be with bairn or not. Take no delaying answer. If ye find she be not, to the fire with her presently and cause bowel [disembowel] her publicly. Let Effie Makkaillen see the stoup [stake] two or three days and upon the sudden stay her in hope of confession if that service adverts. If not, dispatch her the next ouke anis [next week sometime] The rest of the inferior witches, off at the nail with them [finish them off].

For three years, James was led a terrifying dance by Bothwell, who on one occasion apprehended him coming out of the privy, to feign surrender, which James feigned to accept. Another time, Bothwell smashed into Holyrood, chasing James to a distant tower and setting fire to it, while attempting to break down the door with hammers. It is against this background that James's supposedly 'neurotic' temperament should be viewed.

JAMES ANGLES FOR THE ENGLISH THRONE

All the while James worked to consolidate the royal power and to reduce that of the nobles, leaning to the side that most threatened at a given time. But even as he worked on the web of intrigue, he looked obsessively southwards to the civilized security of England. After his wedding to the Danish Princess Anne in 1589, he had more to offer the English: a royal family would guarantee dynastic stability. His son Henry was born in 1594, and Elizabeth herself was godmother.

When it became clear that Elizabeth's health was failing, James entered into coded correspondence with, among other English magnates, her Principal Secretary, Sir Robert Cecil, promising to 'rule all my actions for advancing my lawful future hopes by your advice even as ye were one of my own counsellors already'. Cultured, deep-thinking and massively conscientious, Cecil was concerned to effect a smooth transition of rule, avoiding civil turmoil between rival claimants. James's letters began, 'My dearest and trusty 10' and ended, 'Your constantly assured friend 30'. In this risibly transparent code, the Queen was 24 and the Earl of Northumberland 'My dear 3'.

After the failure of the Earl of Essex's rebellion in 1601 (Elizabeth's former favourite, Robert Devereux, attempted a palace coup against her, for which he was executed), Cecil and James agreed a draft proclamation of the succession. To Cecil, James was easily the most acceptable of the numerous claimants to the English throne: he was Protestant, male, married, fertile (with two sons by now, thus securing the dynasty), assiduous and shrewd. Groups came riding north to take the measure of James and to lobby him as heir-in-waiting. One of the most significant visitors, in the light of the religious schisms in England, was Thomas Percy, poor relation of the Earl of Northumberland, England's leading Catholic aristocrat in the 1590s and a secret correspondent of James. Percy was sent to discover whether James would tolerate Catholics, should he come to power. He came home buoyantly pleased.

Since 1585, England had been at war with Catholic Spain. Roman Catholics who would not conform by attendance at Church of England services and participation in the communion ('recusants') were treated as enemy aliens, fined and disqualified from civil life. The mass (obligatory to Catholics) was a felony; priests were illegal and liable to imprisonment and execution. Rumours percolated south that James, who had been censured by the Kirk for being soft on Catholics, might well convert to Catholicism. Thomas Percy returned from his mission with heady hopes for a genuine toleration. James had smiled upon him, nodded much, expressed sympathetic understanding, and gave it to be understood that his intentions toward Catholics were not only benign but in some unstated way supportive.

At this point, James needed to build support in every section of the English elite. He acted like a quicksilver mirror to all comers, angling back the image each most wanted to see. He made reassuring noises to English Catholics and Catholic powers such as Tuscany, France and Spain. He showed impeccable Reformation credentials to the English Protestants. If he could appear all things to all men, he could court maximum support, if and when the throne was offered. In this he was not precisely cynical, though he has been called 'flaky' and gained a reputation for deviousness. If the Catholics in England were eager to hope, James was eager to please, and inclined to tolerate peaceable diversity of opinion. His policy of 'divide-and-rule' had been outstandingly successful in Scotland, and there is no reason to doubt that the prudential policy he placed before Cecil in 1603 was sincere:

> I will never allow in my conscience that the blood of any man shall be shed for diversity of opinions in religion, but I would be sorry that Catholics should so multiply as they might be able to practise their old principles upon us… I would be sorry by the sword to diminish their number, but I would be also loath that, by too great connivance and oversight given unto them, their numbers should so increase in that land as, by continual multiplication, they might at last become masters…

The watchful, balancing grammar of this important letter ('I will never'/'but I would'), and its concern for the mathematical balance of Protestant majority against Catholic minority, typifies James's pragmatism. The old Catholic families were one thing, but mass conversions were another. The hope conveyed to suffering Catholics by Thomas Percy and Northumberland was to be thwarted. In this disappointment may have lain the seeds of the Gunpowder Plot, a template for the religious convulsions that rocked the throne of the Stuarts, executed James's younger son and expelled his grandson, the second James.

JAMES'S ACCESSION

Sir Robert Carey, who had frequently acted as messenger between Queen Elizabeth and King James, was determined to win the race to the king with the news of her death. He requested James not to budge from Edinburgh, and in his *Memoirs* described how he galloped hell-for-leather to Scotland in three days flat, making such progress that 'I might well have been with the King at supper time: but I got a great fall by the way.' The horse then kicked Carey's head, so that what with his bleeding wound and bruises, he was forced to slow down and reached the king only after bedtime. James, as Carey had hoped, received the news with a golden vow of preferment (a pledge which, he grumbled, was never redeemed).

The rest of the court was nearly as sedulous in racing northwards to swear allegiance and receive the royal favour, so that as James rode down, he was met along the way by Englishmen protesting fervid loyalty. Leaving on 3 April, James moved by easy stages in thirty-seven days from city to city, great house to great house, viewing for the first time his new kingdom. At the Berwick border he was treated to a special effects vision of an 'enchanted castle' wreathed in smoke, which cleared to give entrance to his new kingdom. At York, the northern capital, he visited the minster, refused a coach and came face-to-face with Sir Robert Cecil, whose office he confirmed.

As the English flocked to line his triumphant route south, they saw a man of middle height with a reddish beard, a powerful rider so that his bandy legs (from rickets in childhood) were not evident. He rode buoyantly through his cheering subjects, exuding intense gratification. On the way he conferred honours and knighthoods on the gentry who came to bend the knee – 237 knighthoods and hundreds more in the next four months, to English astonishment. This was the beginning of the so-called 'inflation of honours' that characterized James's reign, reckoned by many to cheapen honours but by James to represent the royal bounty.

From York he advanced to Doncaster, lodging at an inn called The Bear, whose owner found himself the leaseholder of a manor house when the king departed. On 21 April, James was in Newark, where he gave an amnesty to all the prisoners in the castle, but had a cutpurse who had plagued his retinue summarily executed. Thomas Cecil, second Lord Burghley, received him two days later at Burghley House, the first of many glorious buildings that were to make James swoon with envious gloating. Fulsome pageants and masques were staged along the way, and poets wore out their quills in praise poems – such as the seventy-three verses of a *Panegyric Congratulatory* by Samuel Daniel.

From Sherwood Forest Robert Hood and huntsmen in Lincoln green popped out, a 'woodsman' delivering an oration. At Hinchingbrooke he was entertained by Sir Oliver Cromwell, uncle of the toddler Oliver: 'Marry, mon, thou hast treated me better than any since I left Edinburgh!' James is supposed to have exclaimed. Solomonic and Arthurian impersonations met him at every turn. But it was at Burghley's second house, Theobalds, that James realized the true extent of the opulence possible in his new kingdom. In a great hall was a planetarium covered with the starry zodiac, across which a mechanical sun moved by day. Imitation trees ringed the walls, with real bark and artificial birds' nests, to which living birds were lured when the windows were opened to the pleasure gardens. James stood and lusted. Later he would acquire Theobalds from its owner. In Scotland James had been little more than a feudal chieftain: now, admiring the rich farmlands of southern England, the venerable towns, he looked forward to reigning in splendour over a nation rich in commodities and commerce. He would uphold the principles of divine right in a land grateful for release from the tight-fisted, formal, female and, finally, insecure rule of the Virgin Queen. He especially admired the game parks, for he was a passionate hunter, and had ten years previously emptied the forest of Falkirk of male fallow deer, which had had to be restocked from England.

In his speech to his first Parliament in 1604 James was to recall, with a warmth that already seems to have acquired the glow of nostalgia, the glorious welcome he had received:

> Shall it ever be blotted out of my mind how at my first entry into this kingdom the people of all sorts rid and ran, nay, rather flew to meet me, their eyes flaming nothing but sparks of affection; their mouths and tongues uttering nothing but sounds of joy; their hands, feet, and all the rest of their members in their gestures discovering a passionate longing and earnestness to meet and embrace their new Sovereign?

At the end of his triumphal progress, James entered London. The city had been suffering a visitation of plague, of which thousands died that summer. But even plague did not stop him from making straight for Westminster, to devour the fruits of success. On 25 July, with the poor dying around them, the King and Queen were crowned. People did not especially object that Anne, who was a Catholic convert, refrained from taking Holy Communion.

Munificent by nature, James looked forward not only to having wealth but to spending lavishly, on a scale Scotland had never allowed. But Elizabeth's legacy to her successor was a debt of £400,000, and the country was still notionally at war with Spain. James swiftly concluded a peace treaty with Spain; the Irish Rebellion of the 1590s, led by Hugh O'Neill, the Earl of Tyrone, ended in 1603 with his surrender. The problem of how to raise money to fund both his necessities and his luxuries (which he did not distinguish with any great strictness) was to dominate James's reign and that of his son, Charles I. To raise significant sums of money, an English king was obliged to summon Parliament. The Tudor and Stuart system of financial administration was inefficient, archaic, and unfitted to support the royal court. The patronage system required wealth to keep its wheels oiled: individuals chosen by the sovereign controlled access to his person, milked their position and were paid by clients in the country to represent their interests to the king. Reciprocally, the patrons commanded a following through their mediation.

While James tried to balance Scottish appointments with English, he did not initially recognize the hostility, amounting to hatred, nourished by most Englishmen against all Scots. Scotland was a land of which the English sneered: 'They have not suffered two Kings to die in their Beds these two hundred years.' Looking for peace and unanimity, he found himself surrounded by envy and nationalist prejudice. James was, as thoroughly as if he had come from France, a foreigner, and the retinue he brought with him was composed of immigrants. This was to cause intense rivalry and intrigue.

An example of the anti-Scots mania that characterized the English is found in Anthony Weldon's *A Perfect Description of the People and Country of Scotland*, written in the wake of a visit to his master's native land in 1617: 'The air might be wholesome but for the stinking people that inhabit it… There is a great store of fowl too, as foul houses, foul sheets, foul linen, foul dishes, and pots, foul trenchers and napkins… I do wonder that so brave a prince as King James should be born in so stinking a town as Edenburg in lousy Scotland.' Lady Ann Clifford lamented in her diary the smelly degeneration that had replaced the couth and cleanly time of Elizabeth, and claimed that a visit to Sir Thomas Erskine Jones of James's Scottish entourage had left the visitors louse-ridden.

But James saw himself as incorporating in his own person a fusion of races. In his speech to the 1604 Parliament, he presented himself as sent by God to institute 'outward peace' with foreign nations and 'peace within', an heir in whose blood the 'two princely roses of Lancaster and York' mingled indissolubly with 'two ancient and famous kingdoms'. James was the first monarch to use the phrase 'Great Britain'. The union was close to his heart and he ventured a jest based on the Coronation Oath (in which the king is '*sponsus regni*', husband of the realm), to emphasize his marriage to the whole country: 'I hope no man will be so unreasonable as to think that I, that a Christian king under the Gospel, should be a polygamist and husband to two wives.' Any laughter from his hearers would have been hollow.

Anti-Scots prejudice was the result of Scotland's 'Auld Alliance' with England's traditional enemy, France, along with the raids of Lowlanders across the border, Presbyterianism, and incompatible political and social structures. James aggravated this immemorial grudge by breaking his promise to adopt a principle of 'equal partition' between Scots and English courtiers. He distributed the forty-eight positions in his Privy Chamber equally, but these courtiers had nothing like the access to his person enjoyed by the 'Bedchamber' circle – sixteen Scots, intimately encircling the king. James had come among strangers. The unwise Scots monopoly was perhaps linked with his constitutional terror of assassination and the need for the comfort of familiars. Nothing could have been better calculated to alienate the English from union with a nation which, as Parliament felt, had all but overrun them.

The staff of the Bedchamber literally controlled access to the king at the Palace of Whitehall. Therefore access to these staff, who became power-brokers at court, and shared the king's most intimate life, was the foundation of the patronage system. The Bedchamber Lords monopolized entrance to the Privy Lodgings, helping to dress the king and to supply his wants, sleeping on a pallet at the foot of the bed. Day-to-day intimacy brought them sweet profits in the form of bribes or retainers paid by courtiers to obtain the king's approval for a project or his signature. Factions in court struggled to cultivate these influential people and, if possible, to insinuate one of their own number into the Bedchamber.

One of the difficulties for the English court was the opacity of the Scots language, which was a different though parallel tongue to English. James's speech remained guttural and salted with Scots idiom. Before his accession, his letters reveal a command of a range of styles. There is the rich, earthy Scottish of day-to-day communication: 'therefore be freindlie plaine uith him & in the mene tyme kepe all oure folkis on starting ouir meikill at yone man quihill ye heir mair of me. faireueill, James R.' From these letters we have a near-phonetic transcript of how the king (and probably Prince Henry) spoke. But James was also a considerable linguist, who had mastered Latin, Greek and French, with some Italian and a little Spanish. Long before he crossed the border, James VI commanded a sophisticated courtly English, in which he sparred and negotiated with Queen Elizabeth. In England, he partially anglicized his spelling, writing 'thoght' for the Scots 'thocht' and 'knowe' for 'knaw'. But he kept the usage 'quh' for 'wh' ('quho, quhen, quhat' for 'who, when, what', probably representing a pronunciation, for he also wrote 'quhitehall' for 'Whitehall'). His idiom could be crude, as when, irked by the English populace's longing to come close and see him, he snarled, 'God's wounds, I will pull down my breeches and they shall also see my arse.' The cultural shock of the arrival of the Scots-speaking court in the sanctum of the ex-Elizabethan elite cannot be overestimated.

James's sacking of the almost incredibly tactless Anthony Weldon from his entourage led to the one really colourful image of James to have descended to us, the notorious 'codpiece' portrait of the king:

He was naturally of timorous disposition, which was the reason of his quilted doublet; his eyes large, ever rolling... His beard was very thin, his tongue too large for his mouth, which... made him drink very uncomely, as if eating his drink, which came out of his cup each side of his mouth… His walk was ever circular, his fingers ever in that walk fiddling with that codpiece… he would never change his clothes until worn to very rags.

This description imprinted itself on future generations, but its gross caricature is the product of personal animosity. Unlike Elizabeth, James was careless of appearances. His court was informal, offering less ceremonious spectacle and dignity, but more accessibility. For a generation, exquisite table manners and court etiquette were out of the window, until reinstated by James's fastidious and narcissistic son, Charles, with disastrous effect. Weldon's description of James as 'of timorous disposition' is confirmed by most accounts and was not calculated to impress an English court, saturated with the Italian Renaissance vogue for the virility of the noble man. In an age of manly swordsmanship, James had a phobia about naked weapons, flinched from knives, feared plots and wore body-armour, while he occasionally blockaded his bedroom door during panic attacks. A complex and tortured personal dynamic impelled his pacifying statesmanship and, unlike his son, he was able to change his mind, understanding the uses of pliancy and compromise.

RELIGIOUS BALANCE

Plots and the rumour of plots – especially 'popish plots' – dominated the early years of James's reign. The Gunpowder Plot of 1605, which so gripped contemporaries and remains embedded in English annual rituals, was the third directed against James's person after coming to power. In June 1603 came the Bye Plot to dethrone him: hatched by a Catholic priest to capture James and force him to issue a general toleration, it fizzled out and gave way to the Main Plot. Here, Spaniards were accused of plotting with English Catholics to replace James with Arbella Stuart, his cousin. It is remarkable that, considering the extent of the king's burden of understandable terror about his safety, he took these threats in his stride, refusing to exorcize them by large-scale persecutions. James sought an inclusive 'middle path' between Roman Catholics and Puritans, a settlement that would purge archaic animosities by meeting 'in the midst, which is the centre and perfection of all things', as he told the Commons in 1604. He began as he hoped to go on, by dancing with both sides: leaning toward the Catholics by suspending (not abolishing) the recusancy fines; taking a step or two with Puritan divines by listening to their grudges. In his Protestant subjects however, his benign attitude aroused suspicions.

A group of Puritans had presented the new king with a 'Millenary Petition', which requested church reforms. They requested the abolition of such 'papist' forms of service as signing the cross at baptism, and use of the marriage ring. They wanted the clergy to be free not to wear vestments, and the reform of abuses such as pluralism, absentee ministers and church courts. Overall, their emphasis was on preaching rather than ritual. Their raft of proposals was not in itself extreme, and the king promised to consider them. He kept his word, reacting at the Hampton Court Conference of January 1604 with some graciousness to a set of men whom he privately considered his natural adversaries. He

The intellectual King James I and VI survived a loveless childhood in Scotland, the victim of plots and a kidnapping. Paul van Somer's portrait shows him wearing the Order of the Garter.

acceded to some Puritan requests, but his sympathetic broad-mindedness was momentarily obscured when he lost his temper at Dr Reynolds' injudicious use of the riling word 'Synod': 'A Scottish Presbytery... agreeth as well with a monarchy as God with the Devil. The Jack and Tom and Will and Dick shall meet, and at their pleasures censure me and my Council... Stay, I pray you, for one seven years, before you demand that of me; and if then you find me pursy and fat, and my windpipe stuffed, I will perhaps hearken unto you.'

This outburst delighted the bishops present and gives a memorable voiceprint of James descending into the edgy slang that characterized his rough style of private speech. In retrospect, his 'No bishop, no king' looks forward uncannily to the Civil Wars, when 'Jack and Tom and Will and Dick' would claim spiritual liberty and authority. His vituperation took proxy revenge for his hectoring by Scots Presbyterians, of whose canting insolence he could never speak without hostility. The following day he wrote with glee, 'We have kept such a revel with the Puritans here these two days as we never heard the like, where I have peppered them soundly.' He compared them with rude schoolboys whose buttocks were in need of the rod.

The concessions made by James, who was in favour of a preaching ministry, were quietly dumped by his bishops. The Archbishop of Canterbury, Richard Bancroft, ejected clergy from their livings for refusing to subscribe to the Prayer Book. The great achievement of the Hampton Court Conference was the new translation James ordered to be made of the Bible. In the age of Shakespeare and Donne, Ben Jonson, Beaumont and Fletcher, Webster and Bacon, English literary language had reached a richness, beauty and inventiveness that made Renaissance English the most supple poetic medium, endlessly reinventing itself by neologisms, reviving ancient and archaic words, coining new words from Latin, French and Italian, embracing the vitality of spoken language. The Authorized Version of the Bible, completed in 1611, was and remains a glorious work of English prose, or rather a poem whose sustained sublimity still speaks inspiringly. James put this Bible into the hands of a generation to whom Bible-reading in its own tongue (a crime two generations earlier) was a daily observance, both read aloud and in private. Many knew by heart great portions. To Puritans in particular, the vernacular Bible was a subversive handbook for living, a political guidebook, and a direct personal message – almost, a letter – from God. They acknowledged no higher authority than its revelations, and no judge of those revelations but the individual soul.

James's known distaste for Puritans was shared by many ordinary people and especially by dramatists, against whom they inveighed. The Catholic Ben Jonson created magnificent Puritan caricatures in the characters of Tribulation Wholesome in *The Alchemist* and Zeal-of-the-Land Busy in *Bartholomew Fair*. The latter play, which was performed for King James in 1614, mercilessly parodies the Puritan suspicion of harmless pleasure. James himself sought to please the ordinary people by licensing their 'allowable recreations' on Sundays, attacking the Puritan sabbatarianism that held it a sin to play games on the Lord's Day. In 1618 James would publish a *Declaration of Sports*, asserting the lawfulness of men's and women's dance on Sundays; men might leap, vault and play games, including the May games, Whitsun ales and morris-dances that were seasonal pastimes of the English working people. He asserted the legitimacy of the maypole, which Puritans regarded as the mast of Satan. His grounds for liberalism were the common people's right to enjoyment; their need to stay fit and the innocence of such games (better than 'filthy tipplings and drunkenness' which breed 'idle and discontented speeches in their ale-houses'). And besides, he asked unanswerably, what other times do working folk have to enjoy themselves? In a society where lads were not unknown to violate the Sabbath by playing football in the churchyard, this permissiveness was fiercely resented by the 'godly'.

England's population of known Roman Catholic recusants in 1603 numbered around 1 per cent of the total population, perhaps 35,000. The queen was Catholic and James was inclined to turn a blind eye to their proscribed religious observances, since most Catholics, at least of the older generation, practised a quietist endurance, leaving it to God to restore the Old Religion in his own time. They either took the Oath of Allegiance in a spirit of casuistry, or refrained, accepting the curtailment of rights that this entailed. Or they renounced their beliefs, like the poet John Donne, whose Jesuit uncle Jasper Heywood was executed and whose brother died in Newgate having sheltered a priest. John Donne, from a family of martyrs, chose Catholic damnation by espousing Anglican safety and preferment. Donne grovelled to James's favourite, Buckingham, to get the Deanship of St Paul's in 1621. Throughout his adult life, in suicidal impulses, in the reckless, restless defiance and passionate immediacy of his love poetry and in the violent chiaroscuro of his Divine Poems, Donne shows the sense of having transgressed a taboo, tainted with 'the spider love, which transubstantiates all/And can convert manna into gall.'

Among Donne's papers, Izaak Walton found quotations from 1,400 authors, through whose works he had trawled seeking justification for the choice his ambition had made. This choice, 'the dreadful moment upon which dependeth a whole eternity', as Robert Southwell, the Catholic martyr, had written, was a terrible one for Catholics. Their great families were closely bonded through complex dynastic ties and common suffering. Their network was run by women, whose heroic piety sheltered Jesuit priests in safe-houses, especially in the north and Midlands. The 'Bye' and 'Main' Catholic plots filled the majority of recusants with foreboding and the Privy Council was tipped off by prudent Catholic priests. But the Catholic community itself was strained by profound splits.

THE GUNPOWDER TREASON

The Gunpowder Plot was the brainchild of the charismatic Robert Catesby and not of Guy Fawkes, who was merely the 'very tall and desperate fellow' discovered by the Lord Chamberlain lurking in a cellar beneath the House of Lords, beside an immense stack of timber and coal concealing thirty-six barrels of gunpowder. Fawkes, with his red-brown beard, cloaked, booted and spurred as if for flight, was caught in the dusky bowels of the Parliament building, with a watch (for timing the ignition of the gunpowder), slow matches and touchwood (kindling) on his person. His discovery was illuminated and perpetuated by the official account in The King's Book: the midnight moment of providential revelation, just in the nick of time before King, Queen, Princes Henry and

Charles, the assembled peers, bishops, judges, MPs of the land, and the whole administration of government were blown to kingdom come. The image has a lurid theatricality, like the climax of a play; and the 'Gunpowder Treason' as it was known was in several senses staged.

The invention of the plot by Catesby, Wintour and a small interrelated band of headstrong, violent Catholics was viewed by an unseen audience, in the form of Sir Robert Cecil (now Earl of Salisbury) and his agents. The sensational drama of the aftermath involved show-trials and executions, and set in motion a ritual of commemoration, in bonfires of vengeful joy, to celebrate the deliverance of Protestant England and its king from the devil, the Pope and their agents. If Fawkes has become a folkloric figure, this is a tribute not only to the conspirators' incendiary extravaganza, but to the Jacobean government's ability to turn it into theatrical propaganda.

What distinguished the Gunpowder Treason from other plots was its terroristic magnitude of conception. Historian Ronald Hutton has said that, 'It's the first real attempt to use gunpowder technology for widespread terrorism ... it's the gunpowder equivalent of the atomic bomb in Hiroshima.' Assassination was a commonplace danger to royalty. The gunpowder conspirators used the most modern technology to attempt the annihilation of the entire Protestant elite – that is, the state itself. Fawkes, though not the plot's originator, had military expertise and fanatical commitment. He was a Catholic veteran of the Spanish armies fighting the Protestant Dutch in the Low Countries, a taciturn Yorkshire soldier of monastic piety who brought an understanding of the use of explosives in siege warfare back to England. He had no scruples about making war on his own country: to Fawkes, as to the other plotters, England was under occupation by heretics. He had been educated at St Peter's School in York, nicknamed 'little Rome'; his contemporaries were Jack and Kit Wright and boys who would become Catholic priests, including Edmund Oldcorne. Apart from Fawkes, all the conspirators were interrelated by marriage and two-thirds had been involved in the Essex Rebellion of 1601. They had hoped much from James and they got nothing. The end of the war with Spain had not brought toleration for English Catholics. Recusancy fines had been reinstated after a year and an edict passed ordering all Catholic priests out of the country.

The conspirators' Catholic–internationalist cast of mind is signalled in Fawkes's assumption of an unEnglish name. When fighting for the Spanish, he took to calling himself 'Guido', a romantic affectation that affirmed his roots not in his native land but in his nation of spiritual allegiance. He fought for nearly a decade, holding a post of command when the Spaniards took Calais in 1596. In 1603 he went to Spain to solicit support for an invasion on Elizabeth's death, an adventure that epitomizes the anachronistic mind-set of the conspirators, for the age of financially draining warfare between English Reformation and Spanish Counter-Reformation was giving way to the subtleties of diplomacy.

In May 1604, Guy Fawkes met Robert Catesby, Thomas Percy, Jack Wright and Tom Wintour at an inn called The Duck and Drake in London's fashionable Strand. Here Catesby proposed the plan to blow up king and parliament 'in that place where they have done us all the mischief', as Tom Wintour stated in his confession, published in 1605 as government propaganda. Confessions had been extracted under torture and Wintour's

The Oath

You shall swear by the blessed Trinity, and by the Sacrament you now propose to receive, never to disclose, directly or indirectly, by word or circumstance, the matter that shall be proposed to you to keep secret, nor desist from the execution thereof, untill the rest shall give you leave

Concilivm Septem Nobilivm Anglorvm Conivrantivm in Necem Jacobi I.
Magnæ Britanniæ Regis, Totivsq Anglici Convocati Parliementi.

1. Bates – 2. Robert Winter – 3. Christopher Wright – 4. John Wright – 5. Thomas Percy – 6. Guide Fawkes – 7. Robert Catesby – 8. Thomas Winter.

This engraving of eight of the thirteen plotters taking the oath represents Robert Catesby as number seven and Guy Fawkes as number six.

signature appears to have been forged; however, the snatches of remembered talk have a ring of authenticity. Catesby was a dashing, wild, magnetic man in his thirties, the moving spirit of the plot. A zealot, he was fired by faith and disappointment. Co-opted in 1603, Wintour had not been happy about the logic and logistics of the plot and said so. He had pointed out, with a realism severely lacking among the plotters, that mass assassination might well lead to anarchy, rather than an outright coup. Indeed there would probably have been pogroms of innocent and loyal Catholics throughout England. Wintour pointed out that if the plot failed, 'The scandal would be so great which the Catholic religion might hereby sustain, as not only our enemies, but our friends also would with good reason condemn us.' In other words, the plot would blow up in their own faces: ostracized by their own community, they would have achieved nothing but odium among their own people. Wintour was right.

The rash Catesby cut in on these tempered observations – 'the nature of the disease requires so sharp a remedy' – and demanded to know whether Wintour was with him or not. 'I told him, "Yes, in this or whatever else, if he resolved upon it, I would venture my life."' Catesby's charisma prompted Wintour to surrender his judgement to an overriding will. Yet he continued to enumerate practical difficulties: where would they store the ammunition? How could a mine be brought in? What about the noise of digging? Catesby brushed aside these objections: 'Let us give an attempt, and where it faileth, pass no further.' When the oath was taken on the Catholic Prayer Book, and sealed by the communion and sacrament, it was in this spirit of zealous pragmatism.

Percy, having been appointed a 'Gentleman Pensioner' (ironically, a bodyguard of the King), now rented lodgings in the heart of Westminster. In a city that was a warren of alleys, timbered shops and businesses, the Palace of Westminster comprised a sprawl of medieval buildings, with court offices, shops and storage buildings, and swarms of people coming and going indiscriminately. Parliamentary security was non-existent. Fawkes, installed in the tenement, acquired enough gunpowder to blow up Parliament several times over. Since there was a glut of gunpowder on the market, after the peace treaty with Spain, Fawkes was able to purchase thirty-six barrels – or 10,000 pounds weight – and transport it up to Westminster on the Thames, a thoroughfare busy with river traffic of all kinds.

Plague intervened. The postponement of the State Opening of Parliament till winter 1605 changed the strategy from a single to a two-part action in which Catesby proposed to raise a cavalry uprising in the Midlands, masquerading as a hunting party. This cavalry would ride to Coventry and capture James's daughter, Princess Elizabeth, who would be set up as a puppet queen. Percy secured a lease on a cellar directly beneath Parliament, into which, in the summer of 1605, powder was smuggled, and concealed beneath stacked timber and coal.

When Catesby recruited Francis Tresham into the plot, he initiated a wealthy and well-connected Catholic, who could help with stables, money and houses, but whose rancorous, unstable character was potentially destabilizing. He was concerned for the safety of the Catholic peers who would be blown up with the others, including his two brothers-in-law, William Parker, Lord Monteagle, and Lord Stourton. Tresham has been credited as 'the principal double agent', who broke the secrecy of the plotters by warning Monteagle, himself a dubious character rehabilitated after the Essex Rebellion, who had gained favour with James. He was, like many others, a 'church papist', that is, a Catholic who feigned conversion, conforming outwardly in the rituals of the English church while practising his religion in private. Certainly he played both sides of the fence. Monteagle's part in the unravelling of the plot was lavishly rewarded by the government, which hailed him as a national hero.

The origin of the anonymous letter delivered to Lord Monteagle ten days before the opening of Parliament remains a mystery. *The King's Book* describes the letter's arrival in vivid but questionable detail. Codes and cryptography, puns, riddles and word-games were important in Elizabethan and Jacobean culture, both as the elegant verbal fencing of gentlemen and as the means of transmission of covert information. Pun and paradox, allegory, euphemism and circumlocution, irony and private allusion characterized both published literature and written messages between friends and kin. Cecil's intelligencers were past masters at decrypting every sort of double meaning. *The King's Book* is propaganda, a carefully worded documentary fiction centred on 'The Monteagle Letter'.

Lord Monteagle, the document tells us, was preparing for supper at his house at Hoxton, which he rarely used. It was seven o'clock when his footman, having encountered a 'reasonable tall personage', came in with a letter. Monteagle, puzzled at the 'unknown and somewhat unlegible hand… without either date or superscription', called for help to decipher it. Wondering if it was a practical joke or notice of treason, Monteagle honourably rushed to Whitehall, despite the late hour and the winter dark, to show it to Salisbury. This is the text of the letter:

My Lord, out of the love I bear to some of your friends, I have a care of your preservation. Therefore I would advise you, as you tender your life, to devise some excuse to shift of your attendance at this Parliament; for God and man hath concurred to punish the wickedness of this time. And think not slightly of this advertisement, but retire yourself into your country where you may expect the event in safety. For though there be no appearance of any stir, yet I say they shall receive a terrible blow this Parliament; and yet they shall not see who hurts them. This counsel is not to be condemned because it may do you good and can do you no harm; for the danger is passed as soon as you have burnt the letter. And I hope God will give you the grace to make good use of it, to whose holy protection I commend you.

The manuscript of the mysterious letter warning of the impending Gunpowder Treason, written and delivered anonymously to Lord Monteagle on 26 October 1605.

Salisbury tied it in with rumours of sedition and called in the Privy Council, which agreed to consult James, past master at 'clearing and solving obscure riddles and doubtful mysteries'. Meanwhile, they elected to sit back and do nothing, allowing any project to 'ripen'.

On Friday, King James was relaxing in his gallery after hunting when Salisbury, showing him the letter, solicited his view. Pausing to reread (out of his customary carefulness), James was inclined to take the letter seriously, its style being 'quick and pithy'. Salisbury encouraged the king to exercise his cryptographic skills to further advantage by drawing attention to the apparent nonsense of the clause: 'for the danger is past, as soon as you have burnt the letter', perhaps emphasizing the word 'burnt'. James referred back to the previous allusion to Parliament's taking 'a terrible blow', perhaps emphasizing 'blow', and deduced that 'the danger mentioned should be some sudden danger by blowing up of powder'. He construed 'as soon' to mean 'as quickly', implying that an incendiary assault would shortly be made on Parliament.

Salisbury, 'boiling' with assiduous concern for his royal master's safety, alerted the Privy Council, and a search was instituted the afternoon before Parliament was due to sit. It was now that they spied Percy's knavish-looking man, calling himself John Johnson, skulking near the heap of faggots and coal. They reported back to James, whose royal astuteness overcame his natural reluctance to cast doubt upon his subjects (especially his counsellor, Lord Northumberland, kinsman to Percy). At midnight on 5 November, Guy Fawkes was apprehended and searched, arrogantly confessed his guilt and was taken into custody. At 4 a.m., James was awoken and informed of the narrow escape by a Lord Chamberlain so overwhelmed with nervous relief as to be incapable of coherent speech.

To the 'Monteagle Letter' therefore was accorded official credit for saving Protestant England from annihilation by Catholic treason. But who wrote the letter and why? The original manuscript, still extant, is written in tall, carefully formed and legible handwriting. There are various possibilities. It may have been an authentic warning by one of the conspirators, perhaps his relation Francis Tresham, or Monteagle's sister. But there is a tang of artifice over the episode. The letter reads like a fabrication. It is not even particularly mysterious in its contents: a Jacobean child of ten could have dug out the buried metaphors. Perhaps Monteagle sent it to himself, to evade suspicion. Or Salisbury, welcoming detectable plots as devices that strengthened the king's position as Protestant head of state, caused it to be sent. Detecting the plot at some juncture, he may have arranged its

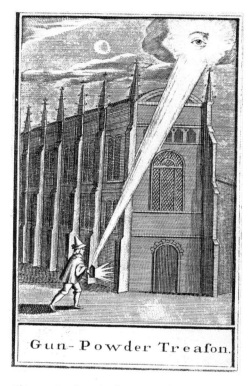

Gun-Powder Treafon.

This engraving shows the all-seeing eye of God detecting the plotters as they advance on Parliament.

discovery on 5 November, which James regarded as his lucky day, and may indeed have arranged to make the convenient vault available to Percy. It is unlikely that one of the conspirators would have alerted Monteagle by a maladroit anonymous letter. A whispered word would have been safer. There is little doubt that Salisbury observed and, to some degree, engineered events.

The King's Book represents the plot as an imminent danger theatrically averted in the nick of time. Fawkes's demeanour is depicted as one of 'Roman resolution', for (the author observes), 'he often smiled in scornful manner' under interrogation, claiming that 'the devil, and not God, was the discoverer… scoffing at any idle questions'. Fawkes gave nothing away all day, allowing his accomplices time to escape. Later, however, he was shown the rack, and talked. James was fascinated enough to interview Fawkes personally in his bedchamber. This unheard-of proceeding, in which the royal victim comes face-to-face with the assassin, is deeply in character for the viscerally curious James. He signed the warrant for Fawkes to be subjected to 'the gentler tortures' (hanging from a wall in manacles), moving by gradations to the rack. Courageous men did sometimes hold out against the manacles, but never the rack. Whether Fawkes was racked is unknown, but he suffered obscenely. Physically and mentally, the tough soldier was so broken that his signature, 'Guido', trembles on the page and he had to be helped up the ladder for his hanging.

Meanwhile the conspirators galloped to their Midlands base, attempting to raise a Catholic revolt. The Catholic families turned them away. As historian Roger Lockyer points out, 'When Catesby arrives and tells them that the king is dead, I feel sure their immediate reaction must have been one of horror because they were loyal subjects… He was *their* king. Secondly, if the king is dead, what sort of horrors does *that* open up?' At Holbeach in Staffordshire, the exhausted, drenched plotters gave the government a final propaganda victory by madly attempting to dry out gunpowder in front of a fire:

> it pleased God that in the mending of the fire, in their chamber, one small spark should fly out, and light among less than two-pound weight of powder, which was drying a little from the chimney in which, being thereby blown up, so maimed the faces of some of the principal rebels and the hands and sides of others of them, blowing up with it also a great bag of powder, which, notwithstanding, never took fire… God had justly punished them with the same instrument.

The document relishes God's retort to the stupefied, black-faced, tottering scoundrels routed by their own gunpowder folly, and justice in the form of a mere sheriff and his

The Gunpowder plotters suffered the barbarous punishment for treason of hanging, drawing and quartering, to public rapture.

men. Readers would have recognized the intervention of that invincible plotter, the predestining Protestant God, who, as the Psalmist says, justly 'has his enemies in derision'. In the battle, Percy and the Wright brothers were killed, while the fatally wounded Catesby crawled into a chapel in the house and died clasping a picture of the Virgin Mary.

A Jesuit priest, Father Garnet, had been implicated against his will, horrified to learn of the plot through the confessional. He was eventually flushed out of a hiding hole in Hindlip House near Worcester, purpose-built as a labyrinth of refuges by the recusant Thomas Habington in the mid-sixteenth century. Each room had a recess, passage, trap door or secret staircase, many walls being false and chimneys having double flues. On 20 January 1606 the local justice began a search, piercing the walls with gimlets, knocking for hollow spaces, combing every inch of panelling. Room after room was disclosed, full of 'popish trumpery'. After eight days Garnet and Oldcorne tottered from their hole, unable to stand the stench of faeces; Nicolas Owen and Ralph Ashley came out starving.

The show-trial on 27 January of the eight surviving conspirators emphasized the uniquely horrific nature of their treachery, for regicide incorporates parricide (the king is 'father of his people') and deicide (as God's anointed).

> How much more than too too monstrous shall all Christian hearts judge the Horror
> of this Treason; to murder and subvert
> Such a King
> Such a Queen
> Such a Prince
> Such a Progeny
> Such a State
> Such a Government…

Sir Edward Coke, the Attorney General, maintained that this was a treason so heinous as to have 'no name' in law. He was careful to implicate the Jesuits, with their perfidious network of 'equivocations', the forked tongue of Rome that undermined the integrity of Reformation England. The conspirators were dragged on wicker hurdles at horses' tails face-down to execution. Their wives and children forced forward in the crowd to reach them, one little boy being heard to call to his father, 'Tata, tata!' They were hanged, cut down still alive, disembowelled, castrated, their hearts ripped out, and the bodies decapitated and placed at various points of the city until they rotted. Garnet too was tortured and his supposed whore, Anne Vaux (actually his protector and spiritual companion for twenty years), was sent to the Tower. At the gentle and courageous Garnet's hanging the crowd expressed no rapture at the death of a detested Jesuit but rushed forward to pull on his legs to speed death.

James probably attended the state trial of the conspirators at Whitehall, hidden behind a curtain: it would have been in character for this complex, reclusive, prurient man to have watched the theatre of vengeance on those who had sought his death by gunpowder. He must have reflected, in the nervous exhilaration of his deliverance, that his own father had been blown up by gunpowder at Kirk o' Field.

Bells pealed through England and bonfires beaconed from parish to parish, resulting, as the cultural historian David Cressy has said, in a 'sudden explosion of light... a kind of wake-up call to the senses' as it blazed across London and out into the countryside. The Gunpowder Treason bonfires found a place in the festive seasonal calendar. From 1606 church commemorations added a solemn element to the revelry. Parishes were sent booklets explaining the 'gunpowder' service and sermon to congregations. In official mythology, the Plot was enrolled as one in a series of great 'Deliverances' of the English, God's 'Chosen People', from Catholic tyranny, in a series from Henry VIII's break from Rome, the reign of Elizabeth and God's storm that wrecked the Spanish Armada in 1588. This providentialism was a belief entrenched in the contemporary view of history, involving the belief in an interventionist God, whose judgements might be 'read' in every detail of private and political life. But the rhyme 'Remember, remember, the Fifth of November,/Gunpowder, treason and plot' conveyed a warning call to vigilance: it could happen again. The Catholics were still there, mingling with the English crowd or haunting the court, or massed in hostile Ireland, entrenched in rural Wales, gathered in areas of Scotland and massed on the mainland of Europe. In May 1641, Parliament, alarmed by the cracking and giving way of a bench, as a portly MP shifted his bulk to retrieve a paper, erupted in mass panic, apprehension 'of some plot (the House at this time also having appointed a committee to take secret examinations concerning divers secret plots) that some ran directly out and cried treason'. Some, noted Sir Thomas Peyton, 'said they smelt powder'.

In 1606 penal legislation against recusants tightened up restrictions and penalties; the Oath of Allegiance was more severely enforced and restrictions on Catholic movements were imposed. They were debarred from practising as lawyers, doctors, judges, army or naval officers, and from bearing arms. In 1610 legislation attempted to penalize recusant women, the soul of the Catholic underground. In 1613 a bill was introduced to force Catholics to wear red hats (like Jews in Rome) or parti-coloured hose like court fools. It never reached the statute books. Yet the end result was a relapse into a more or less merciful tolerance, as it was realized that the Gunpowder Plot was the action of a lunatic fringe, who had been supported neither by a foreign power nor by the quiescent mass of English Catholics. James had more to fear from his own Parliament, his at once chronic and acute want of cash, and wrangling factions within the English church.

THE KING'S PLEASURES

'He is never still in one place,' a representative of Mary Queen of Scots had reported, 'but walks constantly up and down, his gait is erratic and wandering.' In his late teens James had displayed many of the qualities that would characterize his rule: intelligence, 'a high opinion of himself' and the highly strung inability to keep still. Mary's emissary noted defects that might impair his rule: an overweening sense of his own worth and powers, a 'love for favourites... indiscreet and wilful', without regard to the sensibilities of his people, a tendency to idleness and pleasure-seeking, allowing all business to be conducted by others'. In 1607, the Venetian ambassador noted James's absolute passion for 'the chase. For this he throws off all business'. Hunting was a furious addiction to a man who had been hunted and who lacked in other respects the masculinity prized by Renaissance culture. He banteringly called Salisbury his 'little beagle', and was happy to leave business in the overworked Secretary's hands, while he pursued hawks, deer and hogs, reporting back from his truancy, replete with the pleasure of 'the death of six hares, a pair of fowls and a heron'. Contemporary observers were much amazed at James's 'circling walk', which became a jest he accepted with chagrin, nicknamed as his 'deambulatory councils', with which he admitted he 'ofttimes walk[ed] so fast roundabout and about with [Salisbury] that he will be like to fall down dead upon the floor'. James enjoyed a comradely but often prickly raillery with his ministers, which he later reserved for his favourites.

Whereas Elizabeth had had the common touch, presenting a royal image which slightly bent to the common people and inclined to Members of Parliament, shedding something of its courtly lustre upon them, James's court took no trouble to hide its corruption and profligacy. His own major obsessions were his young men and his purse. The two were linked. From the troubled child nurtured by hard-faced men and abandoned by his mother, James had moved to a supplicating and erotically charged bond with the favourite of the moment. Into the laps of these beautiful young men he emptied honours, money and estates. James Hay, who became Viscount Doncaster and finally Earl of Carlisle, ate, drank, gambled, wore and pocketed £400,000 of the Crown's money, according to an estimate by the politician Edward Hyde. James, whose annual revenue in Scotland had been a sober £50,000 a year, called his first years as King of England a 'Christmas time' and gave presents without stint. In 1604 he spent £47,000 on jewels. It was a court that bragged conspicuous consumption.

Jacobean drama passed to the people images of excess, abounding in imagery of cupidity, lust, gourmandizing and perversity, portraying a court devoted to its own insatiable pursuit of novelties, on a scale rivalling the Roman emperors. The theatre presented a blackly comic world of court waste and depravity, whose god was lucre; consumption and lust its sacraments. Jacobean comedy and tragedy commented eloquently on the system of clientage which operated through those who either had great wealth, might come to have it, or were reputed to have it. A philosophy of excess and consumption, the more wasteful the better, was echoed in James Hay's motto: 'Spend and God will send'. The 'ante-supper' was a ritual at the Jacobean court which involved the laying out of a sumptuous banquet, which was then removed and thrown away untasted, to be replaced by a second yet more opulent. On Twelfth Night 1621, one hundred cooks spent the twelve days of Christmas preparing 1,600 dishes. This cost Hay £3,300, the equivalent of the annual income of a wealthy landowner. Sir Francis Osborne in his *Traditional Memoirs* recalled a court attendant smuggling out a pie from the first, discarded, course, 'composed of ambergris, magisterial of pearl, musk etc', value £10, which gave his family food poisoning. While the court feasted, the diet of the average husbandman was dark bread, cheese, cider or small beer (because water was polluted) and milk, with occasional cheese and meat. Bread was adulterated with peas, beans, oats and acorns.

This gross expenditure and consumption drew on a purse that was never remotely adequate to the court's demands. James had to call Parliament for supply: Parliament always retaliated by demanding redress of its grievances in return for any grants, which were never sufficient. James frequently reminded his Parliaments of kings' godlike status. In 1616, in a speech to the judges in Star Chamber, he flexed his prerogative ('encroach not upon the prerogative of the Crown') but saw fit to compromise, while privately considering Parliaments to be brawling hooligans at whose meetings 'nothing was heard but cries, shouting and confusion'. In James's reign, Parliament was in session for only thirty-six months in twenty-two years. The 'Addled Parliament' of 1614, attacking James's abuse of his prerogative, passed no legislation at all, refusing James financial supply until he gave up impositions. He demanded money of the 1621 Parliament for a war to recover the Palatinate, from which the Catholic Habsburgs had driven the Protestant Elector; but he was rewarded with an assault on monopolies as illegal and a rancorous quarrel about relations with Spain, parliamentary privilege and a 'Protestation' demanding 'freedom of speech' as Parliament's inalienable right. In a bitter clash, James ripped the Protestation from the Commons journals and imprisoned prominent MPs.

Rubens' sketch shows the handsome, athletic George Villiers, Duke of Buckingham, who was James's last favourite, his beloved 'Steenie', and Charles I's close friend.

As the MP Thomas Wentworth piquantly put it, to vote the king large sums would be as sane as 'to draw a silver stream out of the country into the royal cistern, if it shall daily run out thence by private cocks'. As the king, ruling virtually without parliament from 1610 to 1621, invented more ways of extorting money, through the sale of crown estates, monopolies, wardships and levying of forced loans, he stumbled upon a lucrative source of revenue in the wholesale creation of new titles of honour. He sold these at a high price, even allowing courtiers to get windfalls by themselves selling knighthoods. In 1611 he established baronetcies, purchasable by anyone with £1,095 at his disposal. In this way, James generated immediate income at the cost of devaluing the foundations of the social hierarchy in 'rank' and 'degree'. In 1615 he began to sell peerages – an earldom costing £10,000 – insulting and alienating the ancient aristocracy. With the death of Salisbury, the Howard family moved into the ascendant, and James made it possible for Lady Frances Howard to obtain a divorce in order to marry his favourite, Robert Carr, now Earl of Somerset, in 1613. However, Frances was implicated in the murder of Sir Thomas Overbury, who had opposed the divorce, and the fall of Carr and his wife revealed to the country the extent of court venality: adultery, incest, peculation, simony and lust, hand in hand with violence.

These themes, mingling imagery of venereal disease with cosmetic art disguising a death's head, became central themes of Jacobean tragedy. By setting their plays in an imaginary Italy, playwrights evaded the censor. Webster, Tourneur and Middleton share a hectic modernity of idiom and represent compulsive and psychopathic transgressions of norms and taboos in a midnight world caught in flares of artificial light; whose revels and feasts are paid for by the sale of farmlands and the beggaring of the poor.

James's favourites were a major reason for the failure of the genuine fiscal reforms and court economies which his treasurers attempted to introduce. By 1620 the royal debt stood at £900,000, and at the end of James's reign at £1,000,000. When Lionel Cranfield, appointed Lord Treasurer in 1621, attempted to make economies by identifying corruptions, he uncovered endemic abuse but could make minimal economies because his researches had enraged those with vested interests.

James chose his favourites for 'no other reason' than personal beauty, as Sir Francis Osborne observed: 'The love the king showed was as amorously conveyed, as if he had mistaken their sex and thought them ladies; which I have seen Buckingham and Somerset labour to resemble, in the effeminateness of their dressings; though in whoreson looks and wanton gestures they exceeded any part of womankind... The setting up of these golden calves cost England more than Queen Elizabeth had spent in all her wars.'

Their means of arousing and maintaining his favour in preposterous shows of camp behaviour exemplifies the king's taste. As with Esmé Stuart in Edinburgh, James would drape himself round his favourites, with a love as demonstrative as it was possessive and beseeching. Robert Carr (originally Ker) had brought himself to James's attention by falling from his horse at the tiltyard in 1607. Anthony Weldon noted that, until then, the Countess of Suffolk had taken it upon herself to select 'choice young men' as bait, daily curling their hair and perfuming their breaths, but that with the

Athletic and cultured, Henry Prince of Wales was the hope of militant Protestants in England. He died tragically in 1612 at the age of eighteen.

ascendancy of the Scottish Carr, English courtiers were forced to leave off their scheming and she her prinking, while all flocked to ingratiate themselves with the new beloved. The new favourite became the conduit of royal favour and benefactions. A favourite influenced not only the flow of bounty but, to a greater or lesser degree, political policy. Carr, made Earl of Somerset in 1613, linked with the Howards, nudged James toward a pro-Spanish foreign policy. But his successor, George Villiers, was to wield immense and, in many eyes, pernicious, influence, not only on James but on his son, Charles I, who became closely bonded to Villiers before his father's death.

The precise nature of the relationship between Villiers and James rests on surmise, but it was widely held that he was the king's 'catamite'. James liked the queen to legitimize the current favourite by recommending him. Somerset had been detested by the court for his arrogance and greed: the queen was therefore urged to endorse Villiers, who appeared to Archbishop Abbot and others 'a modest and courteous youth'. Tiring of Somerset, James had taken a fancy to Villiers, watching him with other young men 'leap and exercise their bodies' after supper. Villiers is described as having 'a very lovely complexion' and a beautiful body, with a capacity for charming conversation and an agile mind. His rise was meteoric. In 1614, Villiers was James's Cupbearer; in 1615 Master of the Bedchamber (a key position in controlling access to the king); in 1616 he was Master of the Horse and Viscount Buckingham; in 1617 Earl, in 1618 Marquis and in 1623 Duke of Buckingham. 'Christ had his John, and I have my George,' James said, expressing through his parallel something of the avid tenderness and blind trust he reposed in his new (and final) favourite.

When Villiers came into favour, James was fifty years old and a lonely man. His elder son, Henry, the Protestant hope of the kingdom, around whom a neo-Arthurian miniature court and cult had gathered, had died at the age of eighteen. Henry, who had been groomed for kingship, seemed to ardent Protestants to be a reincarnation of Henry VIII's short-lived son, Edward VII, a passionate reformer. James's love for his son had been tainted by jealousy of the young man's popularity, his auburn hair, bright blue eyes and expressive face, seeming a pattern of Renaissance princeliness. There are pettily human moments in James's letters in which he resents and covets honours paid to his son. Henry, in return, had resented the hold of favourites on his father's heart, resolving to behave otherwise when his turn came. In the winter of 1612 he died. James also lost his daughter, Elizabeth, when she married Frederick, the Elector Palatine, in 1613. The opening of the Thirty Years War in Europe was to see his son-in-law Frederick accept the elective crown of Bohemia and, with Elizabeth, the tragic 'Winter Queen', be driven into exile after his defeat at the Battle of the White Mountain in 1620. Queen Anne died in 1619.

James saw his pacifist policy and mediatorial role collapse, and he was forced to contemplate invasion of the Palatinate on Frederick's behalf. In the midst of these losses and disappointments his strength was failing. The love he found with Buckingham combined the thrill of Eros with familial tenderness. Buckingham's exactions placed further pressure on a budget that Lord Treasurer Cranfield was at last bringing under come control. James wrote to him ashamedly the following year that he absolutely must have £20,000 for Buckingham's lands and £10,000 for Buckingham's wife's lying-in, plus £3,000 for the favourite's new house: would Cranfield oblige by furnishing this immediately? 'God bless your labours.' Cranfield exposed bribery, theft and waste on a colossal scale in the Household. However, whereas his right hand was setting James's finances to rights, making enemies by his purges, his left was salting money away into his own purse. In 1624 he was himself impeached, for bribery, extortion and deceit.

Ironically, the misogynist king's court came to be overrun by Buckingham's womenfolk, children and relatives, all of whom would share the bounty. While Buckingham addressed James as 'Dear Dad', James's tenderness overflowed: 'for God so love me, as I desire only to live in this world for your sake, and that I had rather live banished in any part of the earth with you than live a sorrowful widow's life without you. And God so bless you, my sweet child and wife, and grant that you may ever be a comfort to your dear dad and husband.' In this outpouring of needy passion, all distinctions of male and female, kin and friend, collapse as James expresses an emotion yearning in its totality. Villiers, who referred to the king as his 'mistress', was James's 'Steenie', for his composed beauty reminded James of the face of St Stephen. James wore 'Steenie's' miniature 'in a blue ribbon' beneath his waistcoat over his heart. 'Blessing, blessing, blessing on thy heartroots and all thine,' he sends to Villiers in an illness.

THE DEATH OF SOLOMON

James in his final years allowed his judgement to become tainted by partiality and left to Charles a troubled legacy. Political and social crisis surged below the surface of the first five years of the 1620s. James promoted 'Arminian' divines such as William Laud (anti-Calvinists, rejecting the doctrine of predestination), banned sermons on controversial matters so as to gag the Puritans, and, soliciting Parliament for money to fund an armed excursion to restore Frederick and Elizabeth to the Palatinate, found himself – and especially Buckingham – attacked on every side on monopolies. He arrested the Earl of Southampton and Sir Edwin Sandys in retaliation. Attacking parliamentary liberties, he refused to allow the Commons to debate foreign policy (which was indeed his right) but without due tact. During a period of severe economic crisis and revival of anti-Catholic feeling as a result of the Palatinate crisis, James inflamed Parliament's feelings beyond endurance, while demanding vast sums in order to negotiate with Spain 'with a sword in my hand'. The estimated cost of sending an army of 30,000 to the Palatinate would be £1,000,000 a year. Instead, Parliament voted inadequate subsidies, asserting the pithy reality that 'we were sent by others' (that is, the propertied gentry of the localities). 'What we give they must pay.' MPs were aware of the effects of the slump in trade in their constituencies; the king was not. He and Buckingham did not care where money came from as long as it came. In December of 1622, MPs passed a Protestation that their privileges were 'the ancient and undoubted birthright of the subjects of England'. Dissolution soon followed, with the arrest of Coke and other 'ill-tempered spirits', who were sent to Ireland or placed under house-arrest. These included John Pym, a JP who was to emerge as a brilliant parliamentarian leader in the 1640s.

After the 'Spanish marriage' fiasco, in which Charles and Buckingham made a hare-brained visit to Madrid to woo the Infanta in person, returning hungry for war against Spain to English Protestant jubilation, the Parliament called to vote money for war against Spain echoed with rumours of a second Gunpowder Plot. The reign of James ended as it began, in a painful ecstasy of anti-Catholic feeling, but with the reins out of James's ageing grip and grasped by those of his favourite and his son, who succeeded him in 1625. James's funeral sermon honoured him as 'Great Britain's Solomon'.

CHAPTER 2

KING
CHARLES
I

When Prince Charles and Buckingham set out on their expedition to woo the Spanish Infanta as the prince's bride, Buckingham wrote to 'Dear Dad' of Charles's mastery of the awkward horses through France: he 'cries still on! on!! on!!! This day we went to a periwig-maker, where we disguised ourselves so artificially that we adventured to see the king.' Under the aliases of plain brothers Thomas and John Smith, they galloped across Europe to astonish the court of Spain, with its grandeur of etiquette, by displays of impetuosity, arrogance and political idiocy. Firework displays, torchlight processions, special events in the bullring and the giving and receiving of resplendent gifts could not disguise the immaturity of their romantic exploit. Buckingham, who was easy about making spur-of-the-moment promises to get what he wanted, was ready to incorporate into the marriage treaty a clause by which James would 'acknowledge the Pope chief head under Christ'. On hearing this, James replied in acid terms: 'I am not a monsieur who can shift his religion as easily as he can shift his shirt when he cometh from tennis.' He seems to have regretted the escapade almost as soon as the two had left court. 'I must command you, my Baby,' he wrote to Charles, 'to hasten Steenie home.'

Not until Charles had clambered over the high wall of the orchard where the Infanta was walking, shocking her into appalled flight; not until the King of Spain had manoeuvred the two impudent young men into a negotiating corner; and not until the courtier Sir Edmund Verney had slapped a priest's face, causing pandemonium, did 'Baby' and 'Steenie' elect to turn for home. Their turn involved a volte-face of revulsion against Spain. They received an ecstatic welcome from England, with church bells, drums and organs, feasts and bonfires, all the way from Portsmouth to Guildford and through London. Their spirits soared at being translated overnight into Protestant heroes: they had suddenly discovered in themselves an aversion to Spain, the Infanta, and all things Spanish, including the weighty golden bowl ceremoniously presented to Charles by the Queen of Spain. He dumped this on a servant to show how little he valued it, and united with the anti-Spanish party in Parliament, proceeding to ruin Cranfield (whom Parliament impeached), and to reverse the nation's foreign policy. 'My God, Steenie, you are a fool and will shortly regret this folly,' said James to Buckingham, predicting that impeachment would be a rod to beat his own back. 'You will live to have your bellyful of Parliaments,' he told Charles.

THE UNEXPECTED KING

The Spanish marriage episode suggests the ineptitude of Charles for kingship. Lacking a sense of the complex realities of European customs, religion and politics, his notion that to gain a dynastic marriage was a matter of climbing walls and making false promises, under the sway of a glamorous companion, was a measure of Charles's tendency to fantasize, to equivocate and, disastrously to push 'on! on!! on!!!' in whatever cause he espoused. The nickname 'Baby' in the prime of manhood (he was now twenty-three) reflected not only Charles's small stature (he was 5 foot 4 inches) and delicate frame, but also the fact that he was a younger son who had never been expected to occupy the throne. By nature fragile, he lacked the education and grooming that had gone to his elder brother, Henry, to fit him for the burden of rule. Charles was and remained the 'baby' of the family.

Born in November 1600 at Dunfermline Palace outside Edinburgh, he had not seemed likely to outlive his infancy and could neither walk nor talk at the age of three. When Queen Anne, with Prince Henry and Princess Elizabeth, followed his father south over the border on James's accession, Charles was left behind in Scotland, too weak to make the journey. He followed in July of the following year by gentle stages in a curtained litter. He was placed in the care of Sir Robert Carey's wife. Carey describes Charles when he came to them as 'not able to go, nor scant stand alone, he was so weak in his joints, and especially his ankles, insomuch as many feared they were out of joint'. His strong-minded and sensible wife spared Charles the remedies for his difficulty in walking (leg-irons) and talking (the severing of a ligament at the base of his tongue):

> Many a battle my wife had with the King, but she still prevailed. The King was desirous that the string under his tongue should be cut, for he was so long beginning to speak as he thought he would never have spoke. Then he would have him put in iron boots, to strengthen his sinews and joints; but my wife protested so much against them both, as she got the victory... he daily grew more and more in health and strength both of body and mind, to the amazement of many that knew his weakness when she first took charge of him.

Living this quiet, country life, Charles was raised outside the hurly-burly of the court, and gradually throve, working on his speech impediment, learning to joust and play tennis and golf. At the age of eleven he left the petticoat regime of childhood for the male world. Beside the tall, confident figure of Henry, initiated so young into the dynamics of power-politics and religious issues, Charles must have seemed to himself an overshadowed, vulnerable figure. His fear of humiliation, lack of humour and ready blush were disadvantages that militated against the dignity appropriate to his station, and perhaps Charles's speech difficulty was the most humiliating factor of all, in an age where the spoken word in oratory, rhetoric and the art of conversation displayed status. From throne, Parliamentary bench, pulpit and judicial bench, verbal mastery in Stuart England was a measure of dominance.

After Henry's death, focus passed to the new heir. Charles was created Prince of Wales in 1616, just before his sixteenth birthday, incorporating him more fully into court life. Exposure to the coarse court customs must have offended his sensibilities, for he was as fastidious in his personal habits as his father was uncouth. Inflexible and incapable of compromise, Charles was disposed to magnify any criticism as a threat to his dignity or, later, as a seditious slight. He spoke little and with diffidence but the tenor of his words could seem autocratic, partly because he hazarded so much to frame them at all. He frequently broke his word and would use dishonest or illicit tactics without compunction, considering that no other person or institution had the right to dispute with a king. He therefore did not hold himself bound by his word. This duplicity, along with a reluctance to communicate and explain himself, would in due course make

Charles's position untenable since, as Parliament in the 1640s was to discover, there was no binding way to negotiate with him.

The Venetian ambassador noted immediately that the Caroline court had acquired new dignity and decorum. 'The nobles do not enter his apartments in confusion as heretofore, but each rank has its appointed place... [Charles] will set apart a day for public audience and he does not wish anyone to be introduced to him unless sent for.' In isolating himself, he controlled and narrowed access to his person, causing the structure of the court day to exemplify and dramatize the young king's belief in rigid hierarchy, minimizing the court's function as an effective point of contact between himself and his subjects. If in this way he sequestered himself from view except at those times when he chose to be observed, he also blinkered his own vision, because that access traditionally worked both ways. Lucy Hutchinson, the Puritan historian, gave a trenchant sense of the young Charles's cleansing of the court:

> For King Charles was temperate, chaste and serious, so that the fools and bawds, mimics and catamites, of the former court, grew out of fashion... Men of learning and ingenuity in all the arts were in esteem and received encouragement from the king, who was an excellent judge and a great lover of paintings, carvings, gravings and many other ingenuities, less offensive than the bawdry and profane abusive wit which was the only exercise of the other court.

This testimony is the more persuasive in coming from the pen of one of Charles's enemies: Lucy Hutchinson was the wife of Colonel Hutchinson, who would sign the king's death-warrant in 1649.

It is ironic that Charles's personal life, temperate and sober, was indistinguishable from the rigours practised by the most Puritan of his subjects. This ethic of continence belonged to a personal need for control and was more comparable with the traditions of Catholic asceticism than with Puritan self-denial. Charles adopted an elaborate protocol modelled on glimpses of the absolutist courts of Catholic Europe, but he went further. Alone among European kings, he required his retainers to serve his meals on their knees. The etiquette with which Charles surrounded himself acted like a carapace, barring intimate contact. His building programmes, according to the latest neoclassical and Counter-Reformation models, his patronage of the visual arts and artists as connoisseur and collector, and the court's self-glorification in expensive masques in which the royal family participated were all part of an attempt to raise England from its more homely vernacular and makeshift traditions into a dynamic European power, with a cultured monarch at the apex.

KING VERSUS PARLIAMENT

With Charles's accession came war. His first Parliaments, concerned about his absolutist tendency, refrained from granting adequate money for the war against Spain, which then extended against Spain and France, causing him to fall back on the Crown's money-raising prerogative. And, with war and the king's perceived assault on the liberty of Parliament and subject, came a disastrous shift in the Church, towards the High Church

'Arminian' doctrines of Laud. Fear of Catholic treason and treachery again tainted the air like a haunting by gunpowder.

Charles's marriage to Henrietta Maria of France, Louis XIII's sister, was intended to cement an Anglo-French alliance: in exchange for secret concessions in relation to the English recusants, Louis would commit himself to aid the Protestant cause in the Palatinate. This agreement was unrealistic on both sides, since neither party could afford to be seen to aid a cause that was anathema to his own nation's religion. Fiasco followed fiasco, as Ernst Mansfeld's expedition to recover the Palatinate foundered, with soldiers dying of cold, disease and malnutrition, or taking the common-sense path of speedy desertion. Buckingham changed tack and planned to strike at the heart of Spain itself, with a fanciful notion of reviving the get-rich-quick Elizabethan spirit of international piracy. Charles's fleet set out with salt-beef, biscuit and beer already rotting in the barrels, because of lack of funds. His inglorious army, having been set down on the coast of Spain, did not drive a purposeful path into Cadiz; instead it paused for refreshments at local farms stocked with vats of wine. Roaring drunk, the army was herded ignominiously back to the ships, the laughing stock of Europe. In the voyage, men sickened on the rotten rations and arrived home in pitiful condition: 'They stink as they go, and the poor rags they have are rotten and ready to fall off if they are touched.'

The parliamentarian Sir John Eliot denounced the shambles of these foreign escapades: 'Our honour is ruined, our ships are sunk, our men perished not by the sword, not by an enemy, but... by those we trust.' The Parliament of 1626 was dissolved by Charles when it moved to impeach Buckingham. In a speech acid with displeasure, he reminded them of their dependence on the Crown:

Now that you have all things according to your wishes... now you begin to set the dice, and make your own game; but I pray you be not deceived, it is not a parliamentary way, nor is it a way to deal with a King.

Mr Coke [Edward Coke, lawyer and parliamentarian] told you, it was better to be eaten up by a foreign enemy, than to be destroyed at home; indeed, I think it more honour for a King to be invaded, and almost destroyed by a foreign enemy, than to be despised by his own subjects.

Remember that parliaments are altogether in my power for their calling, setting and dissolution; therefore as I find the fruits of them good or evil, they are to continue or not to be.

The authoritarian words belied his financial position. He was reduced to funding the war by forced loans, and the imposition of ship money, militia payments and uncompensated billeting of troops. An attempt by Buckingham to intervene on behalf of the Protestant Huguenots in rebellion against the French at the Ile de Ré at La Rochelle failed for want of supply. When the shaky alliance with France broke down, Charles had to recall Parliament for money to fund the escalating war against both Spain and France. Parliament agreed to provide subsidies in exchange for the amendment of their grievances, articulated in the Petition of Right.

CHARLES'S 'PERSONAL RULE'

In September 1628 Buckingham was murdered, knifed by John Felton, a disaffected soldier. Charles's enormous grief was compounded by the tumult of relief and joy that greeted his favourite's death, and the popular acclamation of the assassin as a hero (as indeed Felton saw himself) and the country's saviour. As an anonymous poem of 1628 acclaimed him:

> Live ever, Felton: thou hast turned to dust
> Treason, ambition, murder, pride and lust.

Felton had purged the body politic, and was therefore an agent of justice. He had wiped away the 'slime' from the sovereign's eyes, as another ballad put it. Handbills distributed before Buckingham's death had asked: 'Who rules the Kingdom? The King. Who rules the King? The Duke. Who rules the Duke? The devil.' Charles never forgot the bitterness of the blow. Whereas Buckingham had been for King James an idolized love-object, he had become for Charles friend, companion, brother and counsellor, so necessary to his existence as to be a second self. His loss left a void over which Charles's enemies (his own people) jeered and mocked.

Charles's loss was political as well as personal since Buckingham, for all his arrogance and cupidity, was a pragmatist with the power to keep Charles's feet somewhere near the ground. Buckingham was demonized by Parliament and people and held responsible not only for England's military humiliations, its wrong-footing by Richelieu and a marriage with an odious Catholic queen surrounded by priests singing Latin masses at her court, but for everything that had afflicted the country: from economic crisis to the Arminianism that Charles encouraged in the Church. He had been accused of poisoning King James and committing treason in Spain. The Commons, which in 1629 launched constitutional attacks on Charles's arbitrariness, was essentially the same which had prepared to impeach his friend, in retaliation for which Charles had summarily arrested one of the more vocal of Buckingham's enemies, Sir John Eliot, and committed him to the Tower.

The political system was now in a state of collapse. As the parliamentarian Dudley Digges said, 'We are now upon this question whether the King may be above the law or the law above the King. It is our unhappiness but it is put upon us.' The king and his councillors deepened this feeling by going out of their way to issue veiled threats, to the effect that on the continent, hostility to the royal prerogative by 'the turbulent spirits of their parliaments' had been met by the abolition of parliaments, 'except here only with us'. In effect Charles was tactlessly reminding Parliament that Catholic countries were tending throughout Europe to absolutism. The Petition of Right had been an attempt to stem the tide of Charles's illegal encroachments on the right of citizens and Parliament to the protection of the law.

The key word in both the political and religious sphere was 'innovation'. In levying 'illegal' taxes like ship money and extorting forced loans, Charles was seen as transgressing the limits of his authority. The Petition of Right intended to set a boundary to the Crown's expansion of its powers, but Charles's devious response resulted in a scene of pandemonium. The House refused to confirm the king's right to customs duties until it had discussed the resolution that 'the affairs of the King of Earth must give way to the affairs of the King of Heaven'. Sir John Eliot accused the Arminian bishops of being crypto-Jesuits. The House was ordered to adjourn. Puritan members shouted, 'No! No!' in the Speaker's face but, as he got to his feet to carry out the king's order, he was grabbed and held down by two MPs, with Denzil Holles yelling, 'God's wounds! You shall sit till we please to rise.' The Speaker, bursting into tears, refused to put the resolutions to a vote. Eliot, losing his temper, threw the text into the fire, leaving Holles to recite it from memory, while Black Rod thundered at the locked door and the king threatened to lay siege with the royal guards. The Commons passed resolutions against 'tonnage and poundage' (the king's right to customs duties) without Parliamentary sanction and Church policy. Eliot was again imprisoned in the Tower, where he died in 1632, apparently of tuberculosis, and his name became synonymous with heroic martyrdom in the cause of Parliament's rights. Charles now elected to rule without Parliament, inaugurating a period of 'Personal Rule' which lasted from 1629 to 1640.

Felton had confessed that the Petition of Right had triggered the assassination, suggesting to his fevered mind that by 'killing the Duke he should do his country great service'. For Charles, that made Parliament accessory to murder. In a speech to Parliament, he said that 'the Duke was not alone the mark these men shot at' but the Crown itself, 'to abate the powers of our crown and to bring our government into obloquy, that in the end all things may be overwhelmed with anarchy and confusion'. That the king should recoil from Parliament towards his Privy Council was not in itself an innovation, and it can be argued that Charles's 'Personal Rule' simply continued the custom of his predecessors; but that he turned his wife into a chief counsellor, exploited his prerogative to the full, and rode roughshod over gentry interests was viewed as a violent lapse from royal responsibility.

At the centre of the turbulence stood Henrietta Maria, Charles's French queen, almost as vilified as Buckingham for turning the Caroline court into what was seen and feared as a little Rome, with confessors and priests with their masses, missals, Madonnas, beads and Latin 'spells', whose presence in England was flaunted in the faces of English 'heretics'. When Henrietta Maria came to England as Charles's bride, she was a child of fourteen, knowing no English and exhibiting no intention to learn it. She found herself suddenly thrust into an alien environment and the arms of an emotionally crippled and inexperienced husband whose affections she saw as monopolized by Charles's 'sweetheart', Buckingham. Her French retinue created a miniature Fontainebleau around her, spending lavishly, mocking English customs and endorsing Henrietta's sulks and flounces, until the relationship between Charles and his queen was a scene of tumultuous quarrels, punctuated by her fits of studied neglect and avoidance of her husband. The climax was alleged to be a pilgrimage she made to Tyburn to pray for the souls of Catholic martyrs. After Charles's refusal to appoint Frenchmen to key positions in her household, 'she fell into a passionate discourse, how miserable she was... she would not so much as hear me,' Charles confided to Buckingham. Eventually, in a scene of wild anger in which the queen smashed her fist through a window, Charles sent her

French retinue packing, the Yeomen of the Guard being instructed to 'thrust them and all their countryfolk out of the queen's lodgings'. The next day, Charles ordered that her entire French court be driven away, 'like so many wild beasts, until you have shipped them; and so the devil go with them!'

Henrietta Maria was a tiny, child-like person, quick and vivacious in movements, temperamental and the possessor of a formidable will. She was immediately perceived as unEnglish. Her dark hair was arranged in a row of curls along her forehead. She dressed with the elegant, opulent taste that can be seen in the idealizing portraits by Van Dyck, whom Charles I brought to England in 1632. The stiff, bulbous styles of the Elizabethan and early Jacobean period, with ruff and padded breeches, farthingales and embroidery, had given way to the more natural and sensuous flow of garments over the body's contours, in silk and lace. This modernity reflected continental taste, which stood against the old-fashioned sober black and white of the king's Puritan subjects. The court image was shown to itself and to history through the eyes of European painters such as Rubens, Van Dyck, Honthorst and Mytens. Charles made his court a centre of culture equal to any on the continent, by luring European painters in the Italian and Dutch traditions to set up studios in London.

Van Dyck became the controller of the court's image of itself: Charles knighted him, endowed him with a pension of £200 a year, a fine house at Blackfriars and a summer residence in the country during the plague-stricken summer months. The painter had a private stairway built from the bank of the Thames near his studio, to allow access to the court. The favour Charles showed Van Dyck kept him in England for ten years and he became known as *il pittore cavalieresco*. His numerous portraits of Charles and Henrietta Maria displayed the royal patrons in a language of lustrous colour and serene grace, reflecting the court's taste and self-image.

The equestrian portraits of Charles, one of 1635 showing the king entering through a stagy triumphal arch (*Charles I with M. de St Antoine*), and another painted four years later entitled *Charles I on Horseback*, raise the small-statured, delicate-featured king to an icon of empire, riding high and irreproachable above his subjects and the viewer. In the former, he is in full armour, accompanied by his riding master who gazes upward in awe as he holds Charles's helmet, his ordinariness reinforcing the ethereal remoteness of the royal face. The latter portrait is in partial silhouette: the pale mount with its outrageously coiffured curly mane is almost too massive for its rider. Modelled on Titian's imperial *Charles V*, the portrait shows Charles as a figure of black-armoured authority. In both, the king's gloved hand grasps the royal baton, symbol of his power. Van Dyck painted Henrietta Maria in 1639 as an opulent cornucopia of pearls, from the double string at her ears to her necklace, the pearl-encrusted silk dress with billowing sleeves and a belt of pearls. A jewel- and pearl-encrusted ribbon is draped slantwise, and centrally on her breast is fixed a rich crucifix, from which the largest pearl of all falls like a tear. The effect is of a woman set in jewels, her expressionless face subdued to a symbolism of purity, which is at the same time a badge of status. Earlier portraits, such as that with her dwarf and a monkey, a luxuriant

Van Dyck's magnificent equestrian portrait of Charles I in full armour
represents the king as an icon of imperial authority.

duet of deep blue and rust-red, were more relaxedly elegant. The queen was not in any conventional sense a beautiful woman, but her elegance presided over a new aesthetic of taste, both of dress and of the arts, which Charles patronized as a connoisseur of distinction, whose collection of Renaissance art was unique, and costly.

The imagery with which the Caroline court displayed its idealized image radiated from a core in the intimate and fruitful union of king and queen. After Buckingham's death, Charles, who all his life needed intimate partnership with one cherished individual, whom he was prepared to place above himself, ultimately turned to his wife, and she to him. It was noted in 1629 that the royal couple had, after the disastrous opening of their marriage, fallen in love; that the king was 'a wooer again'; kissing and caressing his wife, uneasy and anxious in her absence. The court was now the centre of government: MPs who had formerly resisted Charles sought to angle their way into the court sphere, including Thomas Wentworth, appointed President of the Council of the North and later Lord Deputy of Ireland, whose authoritarian and intelligent character was to bring him close to Charles as adviser. Wentworth, who held principles in common with Archbishop Laud, promoted jointly with Laud the policy they named 'Thorough', the reform and ordering of the political and religious spheres with the aim of promoting Charles to a more absolute position. Charles's personal rule would be seen by Puritans and radicals as controlled by an infernal trinity of counsellors and agents in the form of Henrietta Maria, Wentworth and Laud.

PURITANS VERSUS CATHOLICS

To a generation of extreme Protestants, Henrietta Maria was a manifestation of the Whore of Babylon, whose rise and destruction was predicted in the Book of Revelation. Lady Eleanor Davies, the millennarian prophetess, denounced the queen and counselled against the toleration of her religion, for 'blind heresy' was 'Her Majesty's Darling'; she played Delilah to Charles's Samson. Charles provided his queen with chapels of baroque splendour, notably the chapel at Somerset House that was designed between 1632 and 1636 by Inigo Jones. It was, as one of her Capuchin monks wrote, 'a paradise of glory, about forty feet in height', with pillared arches, six steps up to the altar, and baroque *trompe l'oeil* paintings of a cascade of angels, suggesting, through ingenious use of perspective and concealed lighting, an infinite series multiplying out into infinity. Around a central dove, cherubim and seraphim circled, raying out light.

This baroque art characterized the Catholic Counter-Reformation; it was modelled on the theatrical grandeur of papal Rome, and spoke a language of propaganda profoundly at variance with English vernacular culture and Reformation distrust of images and icons. The baroque style, whose greatest exponents were Bernini, Borromin and Pietro da Cortona, celebrated spatial dynamism and sumptuousness, resplendent frescoes, ceilings and apses expressive of limitless power – the Ascension of the Virgin, the Trinity in Glory, the apotheosis of a saint, using illusionist techniques such as *quadratura*, whereby walls or columns are extended up into painted ceilings, so that they appear to lose themselves in distant skies. If the buildings commissioned by Charles were less ambitious than this, they were none the less conspicuously unEnglish. Charles sometimes joined his wife for Catholic worship, as did other members of the royal household, including upon occasion their children. This exposed the heir to the throne to contamination by Catholic influences.

The sight of Capuchin monks in the heart of London brought the deepest horror into Protestant hearts. For over a century, since the closing of the monasteries, monks and friars had been anathema and outlawed. The aggressive presence of an apparent Roman core to the Caroline court, flamboyantly declaring its presence through triumphalist architecture, was compounded by the king's taste for foreign artworks, such as those of Reni and Caravaggio. Charles received many gifts of artworks from the Catholic continent. Pope Urban VIII presented the king with a portrait bust of Charles by Bernini, created with the aid of the beautiful and revealing triple-portrait of Charles I by Van Dyck. Traffic with the Vatican, the relaxation of recusancy laws, and projects such as Inigo Jones's rebuilding of St Paul's as an Italianate monument to rival St Peter's in Rome, were to English Protestants unbearably offensive. This was especially so in tandem with the Laudian High Church 'innovations' in Church liturgy and interior layout.

At the centre of this movement toward Rome, Henrietta Maria was seen as the moving spirit. Puritans viewed Charles as an effeminate, under petticoat government: 'governed and overswayed at home under a feminine usurpation... most men suspect she had quite perverted him', Milton was to sneer. Charles's uxorious reliance on his wife, at a period when a woman had no legal being in the law, would be laid bare to the public when Parliament captured and published at Naseby a cache of letters between the king and queen, showing him 'governed by a woman'. As the Personal Rule continued, Henrietta Maria's association with a pro-Spanish faction at court was common knowledge. Around the queen grew the old cloud of suspicion of a Popish Plot.

Radical Puritanism was thriving. Its churches had plain bare walls and no stained glass to intervene between the believer and the light. Its democratizing message of the equality of souls under Christ, its anticlerical animus and its search for simplicity and sincerity in worship grew in strength. Meanwhile, the external glory of High Church liturgy, architecture, episcopal wealth and power, and the hated church courts flourished. Oppression of dissident consciences had the effect either of intensifying the flight of Puritans to the colonies in America or to Protestant countries in Europe, especially Holland (for Puritanism had an international dimension), or of causing Protestants to split off from the mother Church. In the 1630s and 1640s communities of Puritan lay people separated themselves into autonomous 'gathered churches' with self-selected ministers. The violent attacks made by the Laudian Church on the reformers of the 1630s were understood by Puritans using Foxe's martyrs as a template. The Star Chamber Court punished Alexander Leighton's *An Appeal to Parliament*, which outraged Charles and his court by claiming biblical authority for a subject's (loyal) judging of rulers against biblical models. On 16 November 1630, Leighton was whipped, had one of his ears amputated, his nose slit and one side of his face branded; the following week, the other side of his face was symmetrically branded.

But it was not simply extreme Protestants who were shocked by the catholization of worship. Hatred of the overbearing 'Romish' Laud was a galvanizing and consolidating emotion. Laud's central concept was what he called 'decency' or 'Beauty of Holiness': he

Charles allowed Parliament to execute Thomas Wentworth, who had been his right-hand man, in May 1641.

complained to Charles of 'the want of uniform and decent order in many churches of the kingdom', and it was true that many were little better than pigsties, fallen into a state of decay and used for purposes other than worship. Some ministers were lackadaisical, perfunctory, ignorant or drunken, and failed to carry out their tasks. Laud made obligatory ceremonial, priestly vestments, the sign of the cross when approaching the altar, bowing at the name of Jesus and many other rites savouring of Catholicism.

The relocation of the altar to the east end of the church, where it must be railed in, was anathema to Puritans and moderates. The centrality and accessibility of the communion table was important in a church architecture that was a language of Protestant faith, equalizing participants in the eucharist and defining the minister as servant rather than master of the congregation. Like Christ the Good Shepherd, the priest was intended to be the shepherd of the flock. Christ, who commanded 'Feed my sheep', had left the Word as their nourishment. Milton and his Puritan generation were to see the priests under Laud as 'hireling wolves whose gospel is their maw'. In an apocalyptic passage of *Lycidas*, his elegy of 1638, he attacks these wolves who

> for their bellies' sake
> Creep and intrude and climb into the fold!…
> The hungry sheep look up and are not fed,
> But swollen with wind, and the rank mist they draw,
> Rot inwardly, and foul contagion spread;
> Besides what the grim wolf with privy paw
> Daily devours apace, and nothing said;
> But that two-handed engine at the door
> Stands ready to strike once, and strike no more.

The last two lines are full of menace: the grim 'two-handed engine at the door' is the 'Day of Judgement', represented as threateningly imminent. The word 'bishop' was equated by satirists with 'bite-sheep'. The Church fed off its flock by tithes (a tax on every household) and, by operating financial rackets, turned over great profits from the poor. Katharine Chidley was a noted Independent and Leveller (Independents were Puritans believing in total freedom of conscience, and Levellers put forward a political programme of reforms, based on the liberty of the individual). She wrote in her *Justification of the Independent Churches* (1641) of how the Laudian Church was a tyrannous instrument of law and government but also of taxation:

> [Priests] oppress the people, by their cruel forcing of them to pay… they will force poor people even to pawn their clothes for I am able to prove that they do demand of poor people before they can have a child (that is but fourteen, or fifteen years of age) buried in one of the out-Church-yards of the great parishes (which land is the free gift of the dead, for the help of the poor)… it will cost the poorest parents seven or eight shillings.

Congregations were taxed for baptism, which was compulsory; for marriage; for the funeral service and a patch of consecrated ground. Women were taxed for the indignity

On afore
On afore

Hold up your torches for dropping.

Salue festa dies

John Foxe's Book of Martyrs was a vivid report of the Catholic Queen Mary's burning at Smithfield of over 300 Protestant martyrs. It became household reading for generations of English Protestants.

of being 'churched', the ritual cleansing from the impurity of giving birth, derived from the Hebrew purification laws in Leviticus, which many women in the 1630s began to refuse as an insulting hangover from Catholicism. Refusers risked fining and excommunication. Church riots were not uncommon in the early Stuart period, where hostility between priest and flock might issue in the mobbing of an unpopular minister or the slicing up of his surplice by women's scissors. Puritans attacked the 'pomp, grandeur and magnificence' of Laud strutting into the Star Chamber with his retinue, 'some of them carrying up his tail, for the better breaking and venting of his wind'. 'The Church is now as full of ceremonies as a dog is full of fleas,' commented a polemicist.

In a speech to Star Chamber in 1637, Laud attacked undue 'zeal' which, he warned, 'is very dangerous company, where it goes on in the dark'. Excess of zeal was, he said, the quick way to 'sedition'. The Catholic Ben Jonson, in his play *Bartholomew Fair*, had named his caricature Puritan Zeal-of-the-Land Busy, after the Puritan custom of allegorical naming, from Patience and Temperance to Praise-God. Every time the name was spoken, the appropriate virtue would be invoked. Puritans in Caroline England stood out against the French-influenced elegance of royalist styles by their assertively plain and vernacular style of dress, generally black and white, as well as their relative shortness of hair, abstention from swearing, and the manner of their speech and carriage. Sober dress, however, might well be contradicted by passionate behaviour. Just as the word 'Puritan' began as a term of mockery, and was converted to a proud self-denomination, so the words 'zeal' or 'enthusiasm' became the honourable banners of the godly. Zealots were hounded out of their home towns in the late 1620s and early 1630s by the Church. Katharine Chidley and her equally radical son, Samuel, were forced out of Shrewsbury and settled in London. Here Samuel pursued a campaign against the death penalty for small-time thieves ('To take away their lives is A SIN, A CRYING SIN'), and both campaigned for the demolition of all churches: 'Forward,' wrote Katharine, 'in this good work of pulling down the Idols' temples.'

Laud perpetuated the close bonds of association between king and Church, which James had memorably stated in his 'no bishop, no king' outburst at Hampton Court, but without seeing any need for conciliation. The archbishop was at pains to distinguish his rigidly prescribed forms of worship from popish idolatry. He was a devout man himself, prayerful, pious and learned, but with a paroxsymic need to interfere, fussy, irascible and given to bellowing down his adversaries. Sir Simonds D'Ewes, the Puritan diarist, described Laud as a 'little low red-faced man of mean parentage', referred to as 'that little meddling hocus-pocus' or 'The Shrimp'. In the 1637 Star Chamber speech that made martyrs of Henry Burton, John Bastwick and William Prynne, Laud defended his ecclesiastical reform as a cleaning-up operation and a restoration of the Church to its pristine purity rather than a system of 'innovations':

> But this is the misery; tis superstition nowadays for any man to come with more reverence into a church than a tinker & his bitch come into an ale-house; the comparison is too homely, but my just indignation at the profaneness of the times, makes me to speak it... And Idolatry it is not, to worship God towards his Holy Table... May the Holy Table stand this way in the King's Chapel or Cathedrals, or Bishops' Chapels, and not elsewhere?

The allusion to the king's exemplary stationing of his altar shows lack of tact, unconsciously drawing attention to the queen's less than exemplary Catholic chapel at St James. Laud's defence of 'bowing, or doing reverence to the Holy Table' evoked popish genuflection. He was never able to comprehend how foreign these rituals were to English Protestants. A vigorous tradition of Puritan satirical preaching, books, pamphlets and verbal abuse identified 'Romish' practices not only with tyranny but with vanity. This tradition flows from the late Elizabethan 'Marprelate' tracts to Milton's attacks on the bishops' outfits making 'us burst our midriffs' trying not to laugh as they sweep about in silks and satins, 'with geometrical rhomboids on their heads'. He would lambast the bishops as reeking 'scum' on a pot, belching 'beasts', 'gangrene', whose 'devotion', as he put it in *Of Reformation in England* (1641), 'gives a vomit to God himself'.

In 1637 the Puritans Bastwick, Burton and Prynne, convicted by Star Chamber of seditious libel, were fined and sentenced to perpetual imprisonment without access to pen and paper, and to the loss of their ears. Prynne was branded on the cheeks with the letters 'S' and 'L', 'Seditious Libeller'. Great crowds cheered the Puritan martyrs, beside whom, witnessing their ecstatic bravery, stood, white with shock, the young John Lilburne, who was to lead the Leveller movement of the 1640s. As his blood flowed and flesh hissed, Prynne cried out, 'Come sear me, sear. Burn me, cut me, I fear not!' In an age of ferocious punishments, this cruelty was not a punishment dealt out to 'gentlemen'. The Caroline state failed to realize that the stigmas they intended as Cain's marks would be seen as signs of special heroism. Three years later the martyrs would be welcomed back into revolutionary London in triumphal processions, escorted by a cortège of coaches, 2,000 horsemen and an exultant crowd. The gratuitous creation of Puritan martyrs was one result of Charles's abdication of his father's broad church 'middle way'. *The Parliaments Kalender of Black Saints*, a pamphlet of 1644, is a rabble-rousing arraignment of the villains of Charles's reign, including Laud:

> thou traitorously, and against the Laws of God and thy country, didst seek politicly to alter religion, alter the laws of the land, alter the judges… thou didst instruct his Majesty to impose strange taxations, and monopolies, knighthoods, ship-money, new corporation… thy wolvish stomach so sharp that tips of ears must be cooked for thee, Protestants fried, others strangled, and some… soused and pickled in the High Commission.

This fiercely relished satire features the red-faced, stout archbishop as a gourmand partial to the juicy ears of godly men, succulent morsels on the fork of 'His Little Grace'. Henry Parkes wrote in *A Discourse Concerning Puritans* (1641) that the enemies of the godly were 'papists, hierarchists, ambidexters and neuters in religion' as well as 'court-flatterers, time-serving projectors and the rancorous caterpillars of the realm'.

This union between the priests and courtiers was damaging to both parties. Puritanism associated itself with earnest toil, thrift and honest dealing, and set itself against the expensive luxuries of both Church and court. During the eleven years' Personal Rule, the lavish court was perceived as milking and exploiting gentry and populace without scruple. The Privy Council dreamed up schemes for raising direct revenue. Fines for refusal of knighthoods brought in £170,000; 'Forest Fines' were levied by redrawing the boundaries of royal forests at their twelfth-century boundaries and fining those who had enclosed or encroached upon portions for farming, settling and mines; £800,000 was raised through Ship Money; the Court of Wards, in which the king's feudal rights over minors who inherited estates allowed him to extract money from them, was made more profitable; certain monopolies were restored, including the so-called 'popish soap' monopoly, the beneficiary of which was a company containing sundry Catholics.

In 1635 Ship Money was required not only from coastal counties but from inland counties; in 1637 John Hampden was taken to court for refusal to pay the tax, which he denounced as illegal. Given that the judges were Crown appointees, and that five of the twelve declared for Hampden, his defeat was a moral blow against Charles's government. The king's policy, forcing local government to work against its own interests, was bound to operate according to a law of diminishing returns. Despite the fact that the Privy Council made a genuine attempt to reform administrative corruption, through the policy of 'Thorough', what was seen and experienced in the regions was a predatory court of profiteers, enriching themselves at the expense of local livelihoods, with no redress.

In times of economic and agricultural crisis, the majority of the population found itself living near the level of bare subsistence. Bad harvests, rocketing grain prices and depression broke out in the late 1630s, and 1636 was a plague year in which London reported 12,102 deaths; the following year there were 2,875. Corn riots and fenland riots were crucial signs of the distress experienced in impoverished areas during Charles's reign. Fenland communities had lived immemorially on the common land with customary rights to fish and wild fowl, reeds for thatch, turf and wood for fuel. Large-scale enclosure of common fens by Crown and courtiers under the technical guidance of the Dutch engineer, Cornelius Vermuyden, was a profitable investment for the Crown and a threat to the existence of the fen-dwellers. The Star Chamber exacted huge fines on rioters, who were often boys and women. The major female role in riots was in part a result of their husbands' (fallacious) belief that women activists would preserve families from prosecution, since, having no rights under law, they were considered free of legal

Puritans like the Chorleys, affluent Preston haberdashers, were conspicuous for their sober dress, preferring black and white garments without embellishments.

obligation, but also a result of the absolute desperation into which people were pushed. They were threatened with total loss of livelihood. In the fenlands women stoned commissioners and attacked drainers, throwing them into the dykes and holding them under with pitchforks until they choked. They smashed up wheelbarrows and planks. At Holme Fen in 1637, 'a great many women and men' rushed the drainers with scythes and pitchforks to 'let out the guts of anyone that should drain their fens', as they explained. They were covertly encouraged in this by a Huntingdon JP.

Fen and corn riots were conservative and defensive of customary rights rather than revolutionary in intent. Just as in the Church the 'reforms' were perceived by the mass of people as 'innovations', so socially threatened groups directed their violence at violations of customary and legal rights. However, when civil war came, these eastern areas, such as Axholme and Ely, were strong in parliamentary militancy and receptive to the radical social doctrine of the Levellers and the Fifth Monarchist movement, becoming a stronghold of nonconformity. A notorious 'woman of Ely' was vilified by the heresiographers (those who wrote books exposing current heresies) for her Christian ministry. The Star Chamber was used by both Crown and Church to punish fine-refusers and reform-resisters.

The crisis came with Charles's policy in Ireland and Scotland. James I had 'planted' Ireland with new Scots (chiefly Presbyterians) and English settlers, confiscating the lands of indigenous 'savages'; in doing so, he had altered the already complex balance of Catholics, Old Protestants and New Protestants in Ireland. The new colonists reduced the native Irish to serfdom. In July 1633 Charles sent Sir Thomas Wentworth as Lord Deputy. Wentworth was 'severe abroad and in business and sweet in private conversation', wrote the diplomat Sir Thomas Roe: 'retired in his friendships, but very firm; a terrible judge and a strong enemy; a servant violently zealous in his master's ends and not negligent in his own; one that will have what he will, and though of great reason, he can make his will greater when it will serve him, effecting glory by a seeming contempt.'

He imposed his authority ruthlessly on the Dublin Council, standing pointedly outside factional hostilities and expertly playing off sides against one another in the Irish Parliament of 1634. He extracted three subsidies without granting anything in return and pressed ahead with the colonization of Ireland, from which he doubled the revenue, imposing Laudian uniformity. His ruthlessly effective actions formed a pattern that Charles would dearly have loved to emulate in England.

SCOTTISH REBELLION

In Scotland, Charles's attempt to impose the Book of Common Prayer was a masterpiece of incompetence. He required ministers to sign up to the use of the Prayer Book before they had even had a chance to see one. The way Charles's arrogance wrong-footed and alienated even moderates loyal to him can be seen in the case of the Glasgow minister Robert Baillie, who disliked the vitriolic Presbyterian extremism gathering around him but was estranged by the high-handed intervention of England in Scottish affairs: 'Bishops I love; but pride, greed, luxury, oppression, immersion in secular affairs, was the bane of the Romish Prelates, and cannot have long good success in the Reformed.' He is a prime example of a conscience that Charles's fatuous bunglings practically forced into opposition.

In 1637 Baillie was relieved that he had turned down an invitation to preach in favour of the Book of Common Prayer at the synod of Glasgow, since the minister who did was roughed up in the street afterwards by the pious Presbyterian women who made their views bruisingly felt throughout the crisis. Baillie was soon involved in organizing a campaign against the Prayer Book, despite his apprehension at the hectic mood: 'The whole people thinks Popery at the doors… no man may speak anything in public for the King's party, except he would have himself marked for a sacrifice to be killed one day.' He prognosticated 'bloody civil war'. When the National Covenant (the manifesto uniting Scottish resistance to the imposition of the English Prayer Book) was drafted, Baillie objected to a clause – but signed. He overcame his scruples about rebelling against a king. On his way south with the Covenanters in 1640, he wrote to his wife, 'It is laid on me to give his little Grace [Laud] the last stroke, to make, as we hope, his funeral.'

Charles and Laud precipitated a rebellion that marked the breakdown of the Personal Rule. Whereas James had demonstrated acuity and elasticity by allowing Scotland a synthesis of episcopacy and Presbyterian Church rule, Charles fatally forced uniformity on the Scots in 1637. The 'kail wife' Jenny Geddes, a pavement cabbage-seller, entered Scottish history and legend when, on 23 July 1637, she flung her low, three-legged creepie-stool at the Bishop of Edinburgh in St Giles Church, bawling (as he intoned the collect), 'Deil colic and waame of thee: out, thou false thief. Dost thou say mass at my lug?' Her fellow women followed this militant example by mobbing the dean, whom they roughed up, shouting, 'False anti-Christian! Beastly belly-god! Crafty fox! Ill-hanged thief! Judas!'

This demonstration was followed by the election of a Presbyterian group, which in February 1638 drew up the National Covenant, signed by everyone from moderates to radicals, nobles to butchers. Illiterate apprentice-lads, making their mark instead of a signature on the rolls, used their own blood as ink. A Covenanting army marched south against Charles's feeble force, commanded by Henry Rich, Lord Holland. His infantry were hungry, thirsty and overheated in the sweltering sun as they toiled northwards. His cavalry maintained an awe-struck stand-off with a Scots army of 8,000 infantry, who so intimidated Holland that his entire force bolted without exchanging a blow.

The king received a letter from Wentworth, advising him to conclude a provisional peace rather than submit to the humiliation of being routed by his subjects. Charles watched the array of the Covenanting army through a perspective glass, seeing their excellent order and morale, under the good-humoured, homely but disciplined command of Alexander Leslie. Impassioned young ministers bore arms alongside the men and helped dig fortifications and trenches. The Scots carried standards with the motto in gold letters: 'For Christ's Crown and Covenant'. Baillie boasted of the toughness and fortitude of their seasoned soldiers, used to 'lying weeks together in their cloak and boots on the ground, or standing all night in arms in the greatest storm'. They sang psalms and prayed vehemently. The king's camp was split, disillusioned, weary and demoralized. Charles felt obliged to postpone his rout of the Scots and concluded the Pacification of Berwick in June 1639, with a grace whose disingenuousness did not really fool the Scots. Charles promised another Assembly and Parliament to discuss the Kirk's settlement. Support for Scotland was growing in England and Holland. But even as Charles received the freedom of

Aberdeen, suspicions mounted that he intended to renege. The peace fell apart and he sent for Wentworth to return from Ireland and sort out Scotland.

Wentworth believed he could use his Irish solution on the Scots, enforcing conformity on their 'narrow and shrivelled-up hearts'. Unable to conceive of the religious passion that informed the Scottish revolt, he considered the problem as merely political. He advised a recall of Parliament, which would be manipulated into raising money to fund a second 'Bishops' War' on the Scots. Under the spell of this delusion, a Council of War worked out armament plans, to manufacture muskets, cannon, powder, shot and a thousand swords a month. Wentworth's thirst for grandeur was slaked by the belated conferring of a title as Earl of Strafford. A spirit of sanguinity buoyed the court as it celebrated the queen's pregnancy, airy hopes for Scotland and the prospect of a future imaged in a glittering masque by Inigo Jones and Davenant entitled *Salmacida Spolia*. In this spectacle, Charles, dressed in a silver-blue outfit to indicate his celestial status, and Henrietta Maria, auspiciously garbed as an Amazon, were lowered from the clouds in the latest stage machinery, to conquer the powers of rebellion.

The 'Short Parliament' met on 13 April 1640. Speaker Finch, who had been pinned by force in his chair in the last session, demanded on the King's behalf that Parliament punish the vile Scots, repair the insolencies of their predecessors by passing a retroactive bill to grant tonnage and poundage due for the last ten years. He undertook that, if time permitted, Commons grievances might be aired. Pym insisted on the priority of those grievances. He outmanoeuvred Strafford's attempt to play the Lords off against the Commons. After three weeks the outraged and baffled king dissolved Parliament. He had now to scrape together money and men to fight the Scots. Strafford assured the king, 'You have an army in Ireland you may employ here to reduce this kingdom.' Of all measures calculated to inflame the Scots and the English, this, along with Charles's attempt to coax four million ducats out of the hand of the King of Spain, was it.

THE END OF ABSOLUTE POWER

In May London exploded in riots of sailors and apprentices, who converged on Laud's palace in Lambeth, led by a lad beating a drum. When the ringleaders were arrested, the mob released them. The drummer was tortured and the seaman who had axed the archbishop's door was hanged, drawn and quartered as an example to the people. With his rich capacity for making exactly the opposite to the politic point, Charles was showing his nation the violence of his contempt.

Smoky rumours of gunpowder plots seeped up throughout the kingdom: in Colchester, Irishmen were detected sloping round with intent to light fires. Laud's new canons required members of learned professions to swear never to subvert 'the government of this Church by Archbishops, Bishops, deans and archdeacons, &c'. This came to be known as the opprobrious 'Etcetera Oath' enjoining men to hazard their immortal souls for whatever the Church might choose to slip in the bag labelled 'Etcetera' – Beelzebub, for all they knew. New anticlerical riots broke out: a bishop's chancellor, bearing with all due importance his massive mace, was barred the way by a verger bawling, 'I care nothing for you, nor for your artichoke!' at which the congregation rang with cries of 'Artichoke!' The

HENRIETTE MARIE DE FRANCE,
Épouse de Charles I

*Henrietta Maria, Charles I's strong-willed queen, was widely resented for her Catholic intrigues.
Charles called her his 'She-Generalissima'.*

king pressed ahead, allowing Henrietta Maria to put out feelers to the Vatican on the possibilities of a loan. Meanwhile, he called upon the gentry to levy a huge army, which they did with all possible inertia and truculence, apart from the recusants, whose sons were often seasoned soldiers who had fought for Spain and the Grand Duke on the continent and who felt loyalty and gratitude to Charles for protecting them. This in turn horrified the Protestant conscripts: mutineers tore down enclosures and altar rails and went on the rampage in many areas.

Charles would not give up. He travelled to York, followed by Strafford as commander of the rabble-army, 'all the arch-knaves of this Kingdom', as one of their officers remarked. In August a Scots offensive of 25,000 disciplined men swept south, smashed an English force and occupied Newcastle, Northumberland and Durham. In the midst of all this, a remonstrance was sent to the King from Parliament requesting him not to raise troops from Ireland, and Strafford in a ceremony as unreal as a court masque was dubbed Knight of the Garter. Strafford however no longer nourished illusions about the royal plight: 'Never came man to so lost a business.' Anti-Laudian peers were in secret correspondence with the Scots: when Edinburgh Castle fell, Charles summoned a Council of Peers, in which he deployed a move he had used before and would use again, ultimately to suicidal effect: of making oily and insincere concessions to gain time, in the hope of splitting the opposition. He also laid the recently elevated Strafford open to attack. The earl, seeing his danger, might have quit the country but elected to remain and put his shoulder behind the king, who signed an armistice promising to pay the Scots £860 a day while the Covenanting army sat tight on the Newcastle coal field, London's fuel lifeline.

Charles now had to call a new Parliament. The so-called 'Long Parliament' met on 3 November 1640, in an atmosphere of turbulent popular optimism. The constitutional changes that it would institute in the next year and a half were masterminded by John Pym, one of the most astute parliamentarians England has ever known. His profound Protestant affiliations were underpinned by a subtle intelligence which, like a chess-player's, could calculate in advance permutations of moves and their outcomes. He was patient and forceful and could work for sixteen hours a day. The Parliament met with a shared determination that Strafford, Laud and 'all delinquents, all projectors and monopolizers, such as levied ship money, and such judges as gave it law' should be eliminated, as the MP Sir Henry Slingsby wrote in his diary; that parliamentary privilege and the liberty of the subject be reaffirmed and especially that never again would a king be able to dispense with a Parliament. The arrival of the Scots Commissioners, and the inspiring talk of their ministers, brought a new amity between the nations.

Strafford, rightly believing that he had committed no treason, may have permitted himself to stand scapegoat for the king, falsely trusted Charles never to surrender him to their enemies and sought to draw fire away from the Crown. He was committed to the Tower and preparations made to impeach him, as well as Laud, who, broken in heart and body, was taken by water from Lambeth. The king undertook one of his belated side-shuffles by ridding the court of Catholics: too little, too late, and Puritan leaders from the City of London brought a petition for the extirpation of bishops 'root and branch'. The Scots army remained crouched in the north of England, a card in Parliament's hand, which ensured that Pym had a stranglehold over the Parliament for as long as it remained.

'Alas, poor soul,' murmured some of the witnesses at seeing Strafford, stooped and grey with infirmity, stress and excruciating arthritic pain, brought to trial at Westminster Hall. His speech on the king's prerogative, which he compared with a lute, which must be used in harmony with the whole consort rather than 'too high or too low wound up', was masterly. When the impeachment charge could not be made to stick, Parliament resorted to a Bill of Attainder, a legally dubious and archaic measure, whereby a man could simply be decreed a traitor by Parliament, without trial. Charles, having vowed to Strafford to save his life, honour and fortune, stood by him throughout the relentless proceedings by which Parliament and people got what they wanted: the execution of 'Black Tom' on Tower Hill, surrounded by the roaring cheers of the multitude. The king had offered concessions, then plotted Strafford's escape by garrisoning the Tower with his own men; conspired with the northern army to free him; begged the Lords for clemency; held back signing his consent to the execution, until, persuaded that the sacrifice of Strafford would save much innocent blood, he clutched this excuse and, with tears, signed. In the Tower, Laud wrote in his diary that the king they had both strenuously served 'knew not how to be or to be made great'.

The Triennial Act had been passed to set a maximum three-year gap between Parliaments. Now the Court of High Commission, Star Chamber and other prerogative courts were abolished; ship money was decreed illegal; the royal forest boundaries were restored. The Protestation of loyalty to the Protestant Church of England was drawn up. Mobs petitioned, rioted and demonstrated. In 1640–1 England convulsed as the machinery of absolutism was demolished. The whole London community participated

Sir Phelim O'Neill commanded the Irish rebels (or 'Confederation') in Ulster in the Irish Rebellion of 1641.
Twelve years later, he was executed as a traitor.

and became, in the vacuum created by revolutionary times, politicized. As Samuel Butler recalled in his satire, *Hudibras*:

> The oyster women locked their fish up
> Then marched away to cry 'No bishop!'

Pym had liberated forces he would not find it easy to suppress. As the censorship of the press collapsed, floods of printed matter – news-sheets, pamphlets, ballads, broadsheets and books – flowed off the presses. Between 1640 and 1660 more publications came out than in the preceding century and a half. Propaganda on a mass scale bombarded Londoners. Flyposters operated by night, nailing broadsheets to posts and church doors, even to the House of Commons. Newspapers costing a penny each were established by each side of the divide and the profession of journalism took off: there was even a 'she-intelligencer' working for a news-sheet. Radical sects grew and multiplied on an exponential basis, creating more literature and polemics. The 'schismatic' sects Laud had so feared (and hence encouraged) – Brownists, Baptists, Independents, and many too young to have fledged themselves with a name – became spiritual resorts but also centres of radical social thinking.

As Pym worked on the Grand Remonstrance, splits within the parliamentary consensus were beginning to show. Charles and his counsellors, discerning the rift forming between moderate and radical wings, took heart and decided to go in person to Scotland to seek support. He injudiciously left Henrietta Maria at Oatlands as his deputy, with authority to organize and intrigue on his behalf. London was hot and plague-stricken but Pym remained, working to weld Parliament and Covenanters together. In Scotland the king made some canny concessions to the Kirk. At Newcastle, swallowing all his distaste for encountering foreigners on English territory, he graciously reviewed the Scottish army and was charming to Alexander Leslie, their commander, over dinner, mentioning the possibility of an earldom for this honourable soldier. He ratified the previous year's treaty and in every way proved affable – but not, most Scots considered, trustworthy. Pym's efforts in England might well have backfired, had not the Irish Rebellion broken out.

Charles I's spectacular invasion of Parliament with a military escort to arrest five leading MPs violated Parliamentary privilege, a bungled intervention that sealed his fate.

News of Roman Catholic massacres of Protestants and of Charles's complicity in the rebellion reached London in November 1641. Parliament heard with shock details of atrocities against women and children: 'cutting off the privy members, ears, fingers, and hands, plucking out their eyes, boiling the heads of little children before their mothers' faces, and then ripping up their mothers' bowels, stripping women naked…' Protestants all over England were terrified of imminent Irish invasion, and belief in the king's implication in the slaughter (which was estimated at 200,000 victims, but was certainly a fraction of this number) unified all sections of the community. Sir Phelim O'Neill, who had risen with the McGuires, the O'Reillies and the O'Byrnes, torching Protestant homesteads, was showing off a genuine (he said) commission under the King's Great Seal, calling on loyal Irishmen to seize the castles and property of English settlers. Sailors landing in Devon, Bristol, Chester, Wales and Liverpool spread reports of atrocities inland, along with the warning that the king's Irish army was on its way.

Joseph Lister, an adolescent living in a Puritan household in the West Riding of Yorkshire, remembered in his autobiography the (false) news that the Irish rebels had landed and were virtually over the next hill. He recalled that, 'though I was afraid to be killed, yet I was weary of so much fasting and praying' and how Mr Sugden suddenly materialized in the chapel door, wailing, 'Friends… we are all as good as dead men, for the Irish rebels are coming; they are come as far as Rochdale, and Littleborough… and will be at Halifax and Bradford shortly.' The rumour went round like wildfire that the massacre was 'at the king's commission', and how bloodthirsty the 'Papists' were. Ironically, these supposed 'Irish rebels' were probably Protestant refugees from the rising. Irish murderers were fantasized as present throughout England. Thomas Beale, a London tailor, informed Parliament that he had overheard a gang murmuring together about a Catholic plot they had on hand, to 'murder diverse persons eminent in the house of parliament' in return for a rich reward, and that the Catholics in Wales were on the point of rising; the City of London must expect attack at any moment. Recusants were arrested and night watches instituted.

Charles's credibility was destroyed but the moderates' revulsion against the Grand Remonstrance in Parliament tempted him, on his return from Scotland, to deepen the schism in the Commons and, crucially, between Commons and Lords. In the controversial Militia Bill, Pym sought to ensure that all military and naval appointments be placed directly in the hands of Parliament, so that, should the king be granted men to quash the Irish, they could not be turned upon his own people. Riots, violence, saturnalian mob violence in churches and on the streets culminated in both Parliament and the king demanding that the Trained Bands (or militia – citizens who received military training at weekends) mobilize against the other side.

At New Year 1642, the king heard the rumour that Parliament intended to impeach Henrietta Maria for treason. He attempted to impeach Lord Mandeville, Pym, Hampden, Haslerig, Holles and Strode. The queen was now perceived as Charles's major counsellor. She was believed to have precipitated Charles's attempt to arrest the five MPs by invading Parliament with several hundred soldiers, goading him, 'Go, you coward and pull these rogues out by the ears, or never see my face more.' As he left, in her elation she cried out that at last the king was master in his own state. On 4 January 1642, at about 3 o'clock,

Charles arrived to arrest the five who, however, had been forewarned and removed themselves. They probably remained, in full knowledge of Charles's intention, till the last prudent moment before the arrival of the armed column, in order to make the king's violent intention crystal clear. D'Ewes describes the scene with vivid immediacy in his journal:

> His majesty as he came up along the House came for the most part of the way uncovered... bowing to either side of the House and we all bowed again towards him and so he went to the Speaker's chair... close by the place where I sat between the south end of the clerk's table and me; he first spake to the Speaker saying, 'Mr Speaker I must for a time make bold with your chair.'

Through the door, propped ajar by the king's lolling nephew, Prince Rupert, could be seen the soldiers insolently cocking their weapons pretending to take aim. When Charles asked if Pym were present, and then Holles, and was greeted with silence, he demanded that the Speaker, William Lenthall, inform him. The Speaker knelt, regretting that he could 'neither see nor speak but by command of the House'. The king replied, 'Well, well, 'tis no matter. I think my eyes are as good as another's,' and cast his gaze round the sea of faces on the benches. 'Well,' he concluded, 'since I see my birds are all flown, I do expect that you will send them unto me as soon as they return hither.' This anticlimactic breach of parliamentary privilege was the culminating 'innovation' of Charles's reign. No king had ever entered Parliament without invitation or due form.

D'Ewes goes on to construe the failure of the king's plot as 'God's wonderful providence', believing that, had the five members been present, the MPs were to have been massacred by the 'ruffians' conspicuously charging their pistols in the lobby. The Commons Journal calls the soldiers 'Papists and others', whose acknowledged intent was to have slit the throats of all present. Whether this is true or not, it marked a turning point. Hostile mobs seethed round the king's coach, threatening the queen. The five MPs enjoyed a triumphal return to Westminster. The city rang with cries of 'Privilege!' As the Trained Bands came out and were drilled, along with multitudes of sailors from the docks, the king and queen and their three children fled to Hampton Court and huddled together in one bed for warmth and comfort.

Huge demonstrations, mass petitions demanding the fall of 'bishops and Popish Lords' caused the House of Lords to allow through the Militia Ordinance and the bill excluding bishops from Parliament. The capital slid and staggered inexorably into a civil war it had never directly chosen to wage. Royalist MPs withdrew either to their counties or to join the king at York, the queen having left England for Holland, to trade the crown jewels for arms and munitions, while Charles attempted to commandeer the arsenal at Hull. To the Nineteen Propositions of June 1642, demanding the king's submission to Parliament, Charles replied with the sage and pregnant observation that Parliament, in violating the mixed constitution, erroneously claiming to represent the nation, would inspire the common people 'to set up for themselves, call parity and independence liberty... destroy all rights and properties... and... end in a dark, equal chaos of confusion, and the long line of our many noble ancestors in a Jack Cade or Wat Tyler.'

CHAPTER 3

THE
CIVIL
WARS

Few Parliamentarians imagined and no one proposed in 1640 civil war against Charles, let alone his execution. In 1642, appalled at its outbreak, many tried to evade conscription on either side, genuinely not knowing for whom they ought to fight. The MP Sir Thomas Knyvett wrote in alarm to his wife, 'Oh sweetheart, I am now in a great straits what to do.' He had been called up with a commission from Parliament, which he reluctantly accepted, and a few hours later, 'I met with a Declaration point blank against it from the King.' He confided that he meant to 'stay out of the way' until the first muster was over.

Many heartily disapproved of the king's arbitrary and stubborn conduct, yet could not bring themselves to take up arms against him. Sir Edmund Verney wrote, 'I have eaten his bread and served him near thirty years, and I will not do so base a thing as to forsake him.' This would mean, as he recognized, that he would be hazarding his life 'to preserve and defend those things which are against my conscience to preserve and defend'. Many who supported Parliament's aims and claims yet believed it heinous to rise against their sovereign, went over to the Royalists ('Cavaliers', from the Spanish *cabbaleros*, meaning originally 'mounted bandit'). These included, as the Presbyterian minister and autobiographer Richard Baxter noted, a 'great part of the Lords and many of the Commons'. Unease at the outbreak of hostilities went to the heart of every citizen, miniature civil wars being fought out in the hearts of individuals and groups as the internal structure of local and kinship loyalties was wrenched apart. Family fought family, neighbour against neighbour.

Civil wars are fratricidal bloodbaths and only through the distorting lenses of retrospect can they be romanticized. Whole areas (in, for instance, Cheshire and Staffordshire) declared themselves neutral in 1642 and made pacts to defend themselves against invasion from either side. Women frantically held on to their menfolk, begging them not to get involved. Jonathan Priestley, son of a Yorkshire clothier, remembered his mother stumbling along clinging to his brother Samuel as he left to join up with the army of parliamentary leader Sir Thomas Fairfax. Samuel told her he would rather venture his life 'in a good cause' than 'be forced to hide myself in one hole or another'.

The Civil War was not a 'class war' in the modern sense, for there were gentry and nobility heading both sides, though more, as Baxter said, on the Royalist side. It has been aptly called 'the last of the wars of religion': Puritans were solidly pro-Parliament, associating the king's army with Laudianism and Catholicism, subversive of the Reformation in England, which had already been sealed with so much blood. Many Puritans came from the 'middling' ranks of tradesmen and freeholders. Most men did not have the luxury of a choice of sides: they served the side dictated by their local masters. Royalism was strongest in the West Country, Wales and the north of England. London was solidly Parliamentarian, as were East Anglia and large swathes of the Midlands and the south, but, as Lucy Hutchinson acutely observed, 'every county had the civil war, more or less, within itself'.

Each side believed itself to be engaged in a defensive war, to support the ancient laws of England against attack. While Parliament insisted that it was being forced to fight against its king, Charles asserted that his struggle was not 'against Parliament, but against certain men' within the Parliament, 'a faction of malignant, schismatical and ambitious persons'. He was to call a rival Parliament at his headquarters in Oxford, in which the many lords and fewer MPs unwilling to sit at Westminster met – at first as puppets, then nearly as divisively as their sundered brethren in London. Both sides understood themselves to be fighting a conservative war, and Parliament, including Oliver Cromwell, the two Sir Henry Vanes and John Pym, had no notion in August 1642, when the king raised his standard at Nottingham, of republican aims. Their intention was to achieve by force what had been unattainable by negotiation: a just and balanced settlement, whereby the king would govern with the appropriate restraining counsel of his Parliament, with its rights endorsed.

The fictitiousness of this claim to be fighting *for* the king *against* the king, though it has an ancient basis in the legal concept of 'the king's two bodies' (his mortal and fallible 'body natural' and his eternal and spiritual 'body politic'), was easy to expose. Royalist Edmund Verney wrote to his elder parliamentarian brother, to 'consider that Majesty is sacred. I believe ye will all say ye intend not to hurt the King, but can any of ye warrant any one shot to say it shall not endanger his very person?' As legislation proceeded to flow under the stress of daily changing circumstances, Parliament had soon arrogated to itself constitutional powers unknown to precedent. The Militia Bill, which would give Parliament the effective power over the Trained Bands, and which Charles was begged to grant, if only for a while, was a decisive factor. 'By God, not for an hour!' he exploded. The king had already stretched his prerogative into something like divine fiat, so both sides were simultaneously expanding their claims. When far more radical groups emerged, their programmes were also based on fundamentally conservative arguments, looking back to a prior time before 'innovations' had wrested power from the people: in the case of the Levellers, the 'Norman Yoke' – the invasion of 1066 that had allegedly robbed the English of a native democratic and legal birthright. Radical Christian groups splitting off from the church in the 1640s also presented their positions as conservative: they returned to the Word, and to the primitive church.

The death of King Charles I was never intended. It was unpopular. Neither the mass of the people nor those representatives in the Long Parliament who had been purged by 'military cull' gave their consent to it. Not even all the judges at Charles's trial, hand-picked for regicide, assented: many absented themselves from the proceedings. The republic came about by a terrible and exponential unfolding of events, which appears, only with hindsight, inevitable.

TAKING POSITIONS

When the king sent his little son, James Duke of York, into Hull with an elegant retinue, the Governor of Hull, Sir John Hotham, was placed in a dilemma. He received the child and entertained him, thinking all the while of Hull's vast arsenal, which the king attempted to secure by the trick of planting his son and following after. Hotham closed the gates against Charles. The king raised his standard at Nottingham. Forced levies and excise, sequestrations by Parliament of Royalist property and personal donations paid for the war, and there was a chronic shortage of money. Soldiers on both sides were raw and untrained conscripts, inclined to pillage and loot, to go on the rampage, to dissolve away after a cavalry charge, and to be disinclined to fight outside their local area. The king had the advantage of more veterans, and especially young veterans, from the continent, in particular his nephew, Prince Rupert, younger son of the Elector Palatine and the tragic 'Winter Queen' of Bohemia. Elizabeth, now a widow, was Protestant to the bone, and looked on aghast at her brother's conduct.

Charles I raised his standard at Nottingham on 22 August 1642, declaring war on Parliament.
Inauspiciously, the wind blew the standard over.

The young Elector Palatine, after some shilly-shallying, soon allied himself with Parliament. Rupert was twenty-three, a cavalry commander of genius, whose picture by Honthorst shows a beautiful, melancholy face, with the long soft hair of the cavalier, a reserved and grave expression on his face, body-armour crossed by a swathe of silk. His aloof beauty accompanied a passionate courage and intricate knowledge of strategy and tactics. He patiently drilled and trained his men to make the storming cavalry charges that, at the first pitched battle of the Civil War, so astounded and unnerved his opponents. At Edge Hill, Rupert's cavalry charged in close formation at the Parliament cavalry and infantry, which fled straight into their own reserve. However, the battle as a whole was a confused maelstrom, in which neither side could be said to have won, but in which Royalists could claim some advantage. They marched on London, but were halted by the parliamentary forces led by the Earl of Essex at Turnham Green and retreated to Oxford. After negotiations with the 'peace party' in Parliament had broken down in 1643, the king enjoyed a string of victories.

In London, anxiety was profound at the prospect of invasion and the entire civilian population went to work, marching parish by parish, trade by trade, to dig and carry earth to the great fortifications, 9 feet thick and 18 high, stretching 18 miles round the city. Twenty-four forts built of earth and timber were constructed on these ramparts, surrounded by ditches and stakes, mounted with cannon. One May morning hundreds of oyster-women advanced from Billingsgate through Cheapside to Crabtree Field 'with drums and flying colours, and in a civil manner', said an observer, to add muscle to the communal effort. Samuel Butler's satire, *Hudibras*, written in the Restoration, shows how city women:

Raised ramparts with their own soft hands
To put the enemy to stands;
From ladies down to oyster-wenches,
Laboured like pioneers in trenches,
Fell to their pick-axes and tools,
And helped the men to dig like moles.

Overall it was morale, not panic, that rose to meet the threat.

The whole population of England was caught up in the war. One in four males served; and one in ten was at any given time in action during the campaigning seasons of 1643–5. The absence of males placed women in positions of extreme stress and activity, not only the 'great ladies' who defended their ancestral homes, such as Lady Brilliana Harley who held Brampton Bryan for Parliament in 1643, and the formidable Countess of Derby who defended Lathom House for the king. Four hundred women worked on the defences of Worcester under bombardment; the women of Lyme put up a heroic defence. Women acted as fire-fighters and guards, and served as surgeons, nurses, couriers and administrators, pursuing the trades of the men who had been conscripted. They were active in the 'gathered churches' and secured a voice in the pamphlet war. Women demonstrated and presented petitions to Parliament, both for and against war. Peace women, with white ribbons in their hats and pinned to their breasts, marched on Westminster crying, 'Peace! Peace!', demanding an end to the hostilities that were ruining livelihoods, destroying lives and opening the way to hunger and sickness. In August

1643, 'two or three hundred oyster wives, and other dirty and tattered sluts', the news-sheet *Certaine Informations* reported, 'filled the stairs so that no man could pass up and down'. Scoffing male hacks had them down as 'whores, bawds, oyster-women, kitchenstuff women, beggar women, and… abundance of Irish women'. Parliament believed they were either egged on or paid by the Royalists. Other deputations of women were initially well received, such as the 'Gentlewomen, and Tradesmen's Wives of the City of London', led by Anne Stagg, a brewer's wife, who gave in a petition in February 1641, asking for the downfall of Popish Lords and the outlawing of the mass. In the 1640s women began to argue for their right of petition in a way that was new in England, and far less welcome.

Women also bore the crippling financial burdens placed by war upon the community. Food was expensive, trade poor, shops often shut and fuel scarce. The massive taxation levied on top of 'assessments' included duties on basic commodities such as beer, meat and salt. Free accommodation for soldiers in civilian households was a massive imposition. As the war was being waged throughout the country, with skirmishes, marches and musters as well as the pitched battles, scarcely anyone was

The Battle at Edge Hill, the first major battle of the Civil War, characterized by Prince Rupert's brilliant cavalry charge, ended in stalemate.

This pamphlet illustration shows a London woman shaming her husband into enlisting.

unaffected. Sieges subjected civilians to horror. Lucy Hutchinson, describing the Siege of Nottingham, recalled a 'cannon bullet… which took off the head of an old woman' and another that came through a house deserted except for 'a girl that rocked a little child in a cradle. The girl was struck dead and killed with the wind of the bullet' which passed through the wall and a bed head into the next house, leaving the baby in the cradle unharmed. Lucy, using 'some excellent balsams and plasters in her closet', dressed wounds with a surgeon, including those of prisoners. When Captain Laurence Palmer, a fellow parliamentarian defender, remonstrated, she replied, with that gentry Puritan hauteur with which her narrative bristles, that she did 'what she thought was her duty in humanity to them, as fellow-creatures, not as enemies'. She catalogued the petty jealousies and rivalries that split the city, even at the height of its danger.

Until the Battle of Marston Moor in 1644, the Royalists appeared to have the upper hand. The apex of the king's success came with Prince Rupert's capture of Bristol, the country's largest port. The Puritan diarist Nehemiah Wallington, a London turner, wrote that this was the only time in her life that his formidable Calvinist wife, Grace, broke

This Royalist engraving satirizes the pugnacious radical army chaplain, Hugh Peter. Spurious divine inspiration blows in at one ear, the devil whispers in the other and a Dutch Calvinist windmill turns on his head. Peter was executed as an accomplice in regicide in 1660.

down. Like many Puritan women and men, her life was wholly invested in God's war. The godly also joined in interminable and intense meetings to pray for their soldiers. This was militant prayer, which it was believed would move God to turn the battle. The totality of effort which was poured into the war included acts of communal self-denial and purification, including days of fasting and penance. Holidays, saints' days and seasonal festivities, including Christmas and Easter Days and Whit, were abolished as heathen. Iconoclasm was seen as germane to the war effort, in purifying the Church, and attempts were made to evict the corrupt clergy from their livings.

The spiritualization of the army was also seen as essential to the driving forward of the Lord's work in 'smiting his enemies'. The failure of the king's siege of Gloucester and the halting of Charles's advance on London by Essex at Newbury were understood as providential. In Cromwell's fostering of a dynamic spirit able to withstand Prince Rupert's reputation and tactics, a new certainty was instilled in the Parliamentary army. Just as those praying in their homes, meeting houses and churches were engaged in a corporate act of militancy, so also Cromwell understood his actions on the field as psalms in action, praises and vindications of God written out in blood. He organized the men of the Eastern Division into a formidable fighting force, with whom he identified himself and the destiny of God's Chosen People. Richard Baxter, invited to act as pastor to Cromwell's troops, was given to understand that they intended to turn themselves into a 'gathered church'. That is, rather than an army on the march, this body of men would have the internal bondings of a family, sealed together by grace, elect 'brethren' united one with another.

In August 1643, Cromwell had said, 'I had rather have a plain russet-coated captain that knows what he fights for, and loves what he knows, than that which you call a gentleman and is nothing else. I honour a gentleman that is so indeed.' This commitment to a 'spiritual elite' manifested itself in the selection of soldiers whose sovereign allegiance was to their God and to one another in God. The parliamentarian diarist Bulstrode Whitelocke described Cromwell's men as being chiefly freeholders and freeholders' sons (that is, of the yeoman class), 'well armed within… and without by strong arms'. Edward Montagu, the Earl of Manchester and a major-general in Parliament's army, said that Cromwell chose his officers from common men whom he would call 'godly, precious men'. The chaplains to these regiments were of central importance: the minister Hugh Peter, who had spent time in New England, went round with a pistol in one hand and a Bible in the other, easily becoming a figure of black caricature to the ungodly, but demonstrating the new concept of the army as a spiritual instrument. At the same time, Cromwell was a pragmatist and man of calculated action, who rigorously disciplined his soldiers.

The sense of building according to as yet unknown patterns gradually being revealed by the historic moment was echoed on every side. Cromwell as an Independent was committed to freedom of conscience and to the allowability of disagreement in spiritual matters, as long as disputants did not tyrannize over the beliefs of others. In the realm of militant ideas, the idea of 'schism' was subjected to very modern analysis. In Milton's magnificent oration on freedom of speech and a free press, *Areopagitica*, printed in November 1644, he redefines 'schism' in a modern and positive sense. It is the inevitable and fruitful differences between men who are all conscientiously seeking to build the same temple of Truth by hewing blocks of different measurements and sizes from the same quarry, which, however artfully they are aligned, 'cannot be united into a continuity, it can but be contiguous in this world'. 'Let [Truth] and Falsehood grapple,' he says, 'who ever knew Truth put to the worse, in a free and open encounter?' This refers to Jacob's wrestle with God in the Book of Genesis, but also gestures, post-Marston Moor, to trial by strength on the battlefield of England, an argument that intellectuals carried out on paper, generals with swords.

SCOTS AND IRISH ALLIANCES

However, it had not been possible for Parliament to win the war against the king without the help of the Scots, and this, while it brought immediate aid, also introduced an alliance whose inner tensions and innate incompatibilities were bound to become evident with time. When Charles turned to the Irish for aid, Parliament signed in September 1643 the Solemn League and Covenant with the Scots. Taking the Covenant stuck in the craws of the English Protestants, for Presbyterianism was much more than a religious dogma: it was a theocracy, which John Knox had modelled closely on Calvin's in Geneva. Church and State were one, and tightly controlled by the elders of the Kirk. The treaty now made between English and Scots was for the English a matter of sheer political necessity; for the Scots a treaty with the binding power of a religious affirmation. But the divided unity it represented, queasy and volatile from the first, was cemented by the Royalist pact with the Irish, those 'idolatrous butchers', whose league threatened Scots and English far more than they at present threatened one another.

Presbyterian and Independent divines would gather at the Westminster Assembly to discuss a joint settlement of the church, with teeth-gritting patience and excoriated goodwill. Cromwell took the Covenant, though he was regarded with suspicion by the Scots. The Independents nit-picked at the Assembly, to Presbyterian ire, in order to hold the meetings back from reaching any conclusion. The brilliant John Selden, jurist and antiquarian, would frequently enrage the Presbyterians by airily pointing out that the original Hebrew of the text, quoted to mean this or that, meant nothing of the sort.

The longer the alliance could be kept in being, the greater the chances of success in the war. Parliament now had the support of a tightly disciplined and experienced army of 20,000 men looming at the king's stronghold in the north. Meanwhile, Charles's truce with the Irish was a propaganda disaster for him, in confirming suspicions of lurking Catholicism at court, as well as by causing Royalist troops to abscond or mutiny when forced to serve with Irishmen, to whom local people refused accommodation.

When in 1644 the Scottish army crossed the border, Sir Thomas Fairfax destroyed the Irish army in Cheshire. At Alresford in Hampshire, Haslerig routed the Royalists with a superb charge, followed by hand-to-hand infantry engagement. The tide was reversed. At Marston Moor, the psalm-singing Parliamentarians lined up with Cromwell and the Eastern Association cavalry on the left wing, Sir Thomas Fairfax and the Northern cavalry on the right, and the Scots divided into two reserves of about 800 men each, David Leslie having elected to fight with Cromwell. His recognition that Cromwell had turned his cavalry into an incomparable military machine ('Europe hath no better cavalry') was a remarkable tribute from a seasoned veteran general to a complete amateur, who had mastered the art of modern warfare with lightning speed.

Through the damp day the two armies faced each other in a tense stand-off, until the sky darkened and rain began to pour. Rupert slackened his guard, and Cromwell's cavalry swept across Rupert's defensive ditches in one of the new-style charges he had perfected, whereby the horses on a short reign and short stirrups were ridden, in tight formation, rapidly into the enemy, followed up by David Leslie's Scots, who smashed Rupert's flank. His soldiers fled in panic toward York. Manchester's infantry thrust forward, capturing Rupert's cannon. Cromwell then, despite a light wound, kept his Eastern Association men 'close and firm together in a body' according to an eyewitness, and brought them round to salvage Fairfax's position by striking back at the Royalists from behind their own lines. By the time the slaughter was over, a broad harvest moon lit the moor. The buriers counted 4,000 Royalist corpses.

Cromwell's elation and sense of God's transfiguring presence with his army is strongly felt in the letter he wrote on the night of the battle to his sister's husband to tell him of the victory but also of the death of his son, Valentine. It is one of the most personal letters still remaining by Cromwell:

> Truly England and the Church of God hath had a great favour from the Lord, in this great victory given to us, such as the like never was since this war began. We never charged but we routed the enemy. The left wing, which I commanded, being our own here, save a few Scots in our rear, beat all the Prince's horse, God made them as stubble to our swords… Sir, God hath taken away your eldest son by a cannonshot. It brake his leg. We were necessitated to have it cut off, whereof he died. Sir, you know my trials this way; but the Lord supported me with this: that the Lord took him into the happiness we all pant after and live for. There is your precious child full of glory, to know sin nor sorrow any more.

This letter reveals Cromwell's military spirituality, alluding to the biblical 'Song of Moses', which praises God as a 'man of war', liberator of the Children of Israel from Egypt, by opening the Red Sea, having 'overthrown them that rose up against thee: thou sentest forth thy wrath, which consumed them as stubble'. Each victory sealed Cromwell's conviction that he was instrumental to the living wrath of God. He played down the Scottish contribution to victory.

However, divisions in the parliamentary leadership prevented it from capitalizing on the great gain of Marston Moor. The Presbyterians understandably coveted the credit heaped on Cromwell for a joint success, and resented the prestige this gave to the Independents. There was also acrimony between Parliament's military leaders, Cromwell being frustrated at the dilatoriness of Manchester and Essex in pursuing the war. Cromwell's suspicion that the general would tiptoe into peace with the king, if he possibly could, caused rancour. Manchester was not only frightened of winning the war, but scared into inertia by the enormity of the position in which he found himself. He told Cromwell, 'If we beat the King 99 times, he would be King still and his posterity, and we subjects still, but if he beat us but once we should be hanged and our posterity undone.' Exasperated,

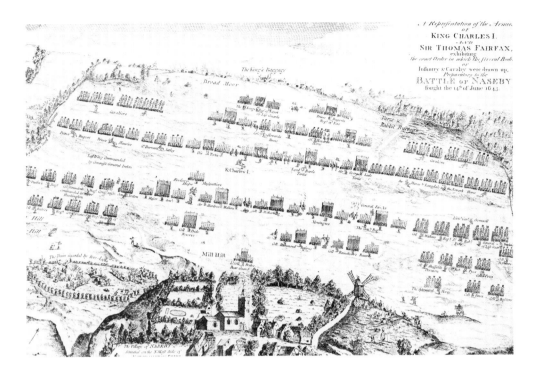

Previous page: *The Battle of Marston Moor on 2 July 1644 marked the Civil War's turning point in Parliament's favour. Amid the carnage, Cromwell displayed his tactical brilliance and the tight discipline of his Ironsides.*
Above: *At Naseby, on 14 June 1645, Fairfax, Cromwell and the New Model Army won a decisive victory.*

Cromwell replied, 'My Lord, if this be so, why did we take up arms at first?' In the Commons on 25 November, Cromwell spoke incisively against Manchester's lackadaisical prosecution of the war, in answer to which Manchester claimed in the Lords that Cromwell hated Lords, vilified the nobility and looked forward to stripping him of his title and making him mere Mr Montagu. He accused Cromwell of high-handedness and vanity.

Cromwell's proposal of the Self-Denying Ordinance banning simultaneous holding of office in Parliament and the army put an end to the dilemma. He further proposed that the army be 'new modelled and governed under a stricter discipline'. The New Model Army was created from the remnant of the armies of Manchester, Essex and Sir William Waller, supplemented by conscripts, London men and Cromwell's Ironsides divided between the companies, under overall control of Fairfax. But in April 1645, just as Cromwell was due to hand over his commission, he was sent north to take on the combined armies of Charles. The Battle of Naseby destroyed the king's last major army. Royalist ranks were swollen by Welsh levies, who, having fought hard, surrendered en masse. One of the most disgraceful atrocities of the whole war occurred in the wake of this battle, when a mass of 'Irish women of cruel countenances', brandishing long knives, were murdered by Parliamentarian troops. In fact, they were probably Welsh women, defending themselves with cooking utensils and crying out in their mother tongue.

THE ROYALISTS BEATEN

Cromwell wrote to Parliament after Naseby and again after the siege of Bristol insisting – and even warning – that the men who had risked their lives for the cause must be granted freedom of conscience in any settlement. London was in a furore of dispute between the Presbyterians and the sects. The correspondence of the king and queen, captured at Naseby among the baggage wagons, revealed the extent of the royal intrigue to enlist help from Denmark, France, Lorraine and the Prince of Orange, and they ended any doubt about the king's intention to launch the Irish Confederate Forces on England. These were published as *The King's Cabinet Opened*, eloquently demonstrating the extent of royal perfidy. The king wandered purposelessly from place to place, his options diminishing by the day. He refused Prince Rupert's advice to negotiate while he had any bargaining counters, and dismissed the prince when he surrendered Bristol, falsely believing himself betrayed: 'You assured me that… you would keep Bristol for four months. Did you keep it for four days?'

The poet Henry Vaughan was serving on the Royalist side at the Battle of Rowton Heath in September 1645, which Charles observed from the walls of Chester. As Charles watched his cavalry hacked to pieces, he voiced the biblical cry, 'O Lord, O Lord, what have I done that should cause my people to deal thus with me?' Vaughan, who lost a close friend at Rowton Heath and never discovered his fate, recalled the terrible moment of loss when, turning round in the battle, 'I missed thy face… here I lost him.' Vaughan was one of the fugitives who 'Left craggy Beeston and the fatal Dee' to limp home into Wales, where the cavalier cause was now finished. Chester held out until starvation and Sir William Brereton, Parliament's commander-in-chief in the region, broke its will in February 1646. Vaughan moved into a retreat from public life characteristic of thoughtful spirits of the Royalist persuasion, and later of Parliamentarians and Puritans who could not stomach the brutalities of the new era, such as Sir Thomas Fairfax and the poet Andrew Marvell. Vaughan's younger brother William died, perhaps fighting for the king, and the experience of travail in the Brecon wilderness drew from him a poetry of profound introspection and a sacramental sense of the natural world. Royalists lived in a reclusive posture of waiting, adapting superficially to the new Puritan administration. The church doors would be nailed shut all over Wales, Vaughan's twin brother, the alchemist Thomas Vaughan, being driven from his living at Llansantffraed, and the only place where Church of England communicants could receive the eucharist in the way they approved was in their own hearts.

PARLIAMENT IN TRIUMPH

In spring of 1646, the New Model Army laid siege to Oxford, from which Charles escaped in disguise, his hair cut short, and wearing a false beard and poor clothes, and staying in inns and alehouses. An innkeeper caught the incognito king and his companions burning documents, and a barber noted that they had been sawing at their hair with knives. Charles eventually gave himself up to the Scots at Southwell, banking on the angry gulf between the Independent-dominated Parliament in London and the

Presbyterian Scots. The king was now held pawn as his father King James had been held pawn as a child, by the Presbyterian Scots, but with the difference that he had chosen his captivity and hoped to manipulate it.

Charles, 'barbarously baited' as he wrote to the queen, was wretched: 'all is I can do is, but delaying of ill'. When Oxford surrendered, three of the king's children, including James Duke of York, were taken into honourable captivity in St James's Palace. Charles refused to take the Covenant and thus ally himself with the Scots, despite the queen's strenuous advice that it did not matter what he promised to whom, since they were all equally heretics. Charles's continuing machinations 'cemented', as Lucy Hutchinson put it, the embroiled Scots and English, into a wish to end the stalemate, the debate in the end being, 'not who should, but who should not, have him'. The English paid the Scots £200,000 to evacuate England and the Scots handed the king over to Parliament in 1647.

Parliament's problems really began with victory. The growth of the sects had caused an explosive dispersal of radical spiritual ideas which the Independents, especially Cromwell, believed should be tolerated. The army he had created, appointing officers who were intelligent men who might, in peaceful times, have remained quietly plying trades, was not only an admirable fighting machine but a body of thinking people, who had given their lives to the dream of a better world and many of whom acknowledged no horizons to their thought. The army acted as their university, encouraging debate and a prayerful wish to interpret the will of God for their generation. Not only did the New Model soldiers believe they should have a part in the formulation of a more just society, but they were owed arrears of pay and felt ill-thanked for the service they had done to Parliament.

During the middle years of the decade, the pamphlet war had taken on an acrimony and daring appropriate to the times. Heresiographers, chiefly Presbyterian ministers, abounded, telling readers how to recognize the 'schismatics and nonconformists' who were bringing religion into disrepute. If they sometimes sound like the Laudians of the 1630s, inveighing against lack of decency and respect in the lower orders for their betters, the ministers, that is because they express a similar anxiety. Robert Baillie, in *Anabaptism, The True Fountain of Independency* (1647), derives the new sects from the Anabaptists, who famously under 'King' John of Leyden turned Münster into the bloody anarchy of a New Jerusalem of polygamy, the abolition of private property and the inversion of the social order. Dr Daniel Featley in *The Dippers Dipped* (1645) complains that the English Anabaptists have introduced unheard-of changes, turning 'stables into temples, stalls into choirs, shopboards into communion tables, tubs into pulpits, aprons into linen ephods, and mechanicals [artisans] of the lowest rank to Priests of the high places'. He is incensed at the leaflets on doors, posts and walls, which advertise, 'On such a day such a brewer's clerk exerciseth, such a tailor expoundeth, such a waterman teacheth…' He and the other heresiographers are much exercised by the lewd practice of converts stripping 'stark naked' and polluting the rivers of England by being baptized by total immersion. Ephraim Pagitt in *Heresiography* (1645) laments that 'every day begets a new opinion' and hence a new sect, and advises readers to hear the madmen at Bedlam rather than listen to the sectarians preach. John Brinsley in *The Arraignment of the Present Schism* (1646) sighs: 'What a multiplicity of divisions is here to be found? Tongues divided: Hearts divided:

Heads divided: Hands divided: State divided: Church divided: Cities divided: Towns divided: Families divided: the nearest Relations divided...'

But the most celebrated heresiographer of all was Thomas Edwards, whose *Gangraena* catalogued heresies gathered with relish and located by a system of epistolary snoopers, who reported faster than his avid pen could transcribe them. The tract's first part, appearing in February 1646, listed a total of 176 heresies promulgated by the 'whirligig spirits' of the times, including the denial of hell, sin, sacraments, the Bible; the belief that all creatures (not just man) shall be resurrected; community of goods and women, the legitimacy of divorce, pacifism, vegetarianism, and (Number 124) the belief that "tis lawful for women to preach, and why not, having gifts as well as men?' He lambasts Mrs Attaway who holds packed meetings in Coleman Street. In May and December of the same year he brought out new parts of *Gangraena*, which listed additional abominations.

He was answered by many Independent writers, including Katharine Chidley and John Goodwin, pastor of St Stephen's Coleman Street, whose congregation had links with the Levellers and especially John Lilburne. Goodwin's *Cretensis* (1646) replied urbanely and witheringly to Edwards, marvelling that Edwards, minting and trading in heresies, stuck to 'so small a number as 180; and did not advance to... 10,000 times 10,000'. Jeremiah Burroughes diagnosed in Edwards 'an odious disease, casting up excrementitious filthiness at the mouth'. John Saltmarsh in *Reasons for Unity, Peace, and Love* (1646) replied that there can and should be unity in diversity of opinion; that to fight over belief is as mad as fighting, 'because we are not like one another in the face'. In *Groans for Liberty* (1646), Saltmarsh drew parallels between the Presbyterians and the Prelates they had ousted in their desire to force the conscience. In a snarling sonnet of the same year, 'On the New Forcers of Conscience Under the Long Parliament', Milton inveighed against 'shallow Edwards and Scotch what-d'ye-call': 'New Presbyter is but old Priest writ large.'

The battle of religious ideas was accompanied by the evolution of political and social programmes. John Lilburne, who initiated the so-called Leveller movement, had as a youth been imprisoned by Star Chamber for distributing seditious literature. Whipped from the Fleet to Westminster with a three-thonged whip, taking about 500 blows, his shoulders 'swelled,' he said, 'almost as big as a penny loaf'. In the Fleet Lilburne had written clandestine tracts which his followers distributed. Cromwell persuaded Parliament to have him released in November 1640. Lilburne had served with Cromwell's Eastern Association until the year of the New Model, when he left to harry the Presbyterian-led government and the Lords on economic, legal and educational, as well as political and religious reform. In and out of prison with his wife and young family, Lilburne was the fiery centre of the Leveller movement, along with Richard Overton, William Walwyn and John Wildman, using the printing press, petitions, demonstrations and a formidable network of contacts (probably that of the radical churches) to press a programme of radical reform from a slavery they dated to the Norman Conquest.

The Levellers derived their democratic model of the state from the 'birthright' of free people, and regarded power as vested by social contract in the chosen representatives of the people. They sought extension of the franchise to all male householders, regardless of property, and insisted on citizens' equal right to law, which should be simplified and purged. In *The Levellers' Large Petition*, they accused Parliament of perpetuating the abuses practised by their predecessors: arbitrary judicial power, a brutal penal system, tithes and trading privileges, pauperdom being the logical outcome of the system.

Parliament's attempts to suppress the Levellers furnished further propaganda. In August 1646, the Lords had Richard and Mary Overton arrested and brought before the Lords. Mary was manhandled when she refused to go, and the baby she was nursing afterwards died. With their menfolk in prison, the Leveller women organized mass petitions and demonstrations and were often a presence in the London streets, wearing green ribbons in their hats and on their breasts, so that the newspapers missed them when they were not active: 'What's become of all my brave viragos, the ladies-errant of the seagreen order?' The Leveller women, led by Katharine Chidley and Elizabeth Lilburne, formulated a claim to have an 'equal interest with the men of this nation, in those liberties and securities contained in the *Petition of Right*'.

It was, however, the politicization of the army that caused the greatest fear, in Parliament, among the grandees in the army and among the elite generally. Cromwell could not control the burning zeal he promoted in his 'russet-coated captains' to fight for a genuinely better world. The fellowship of young men whose allegiance was sealed in blood had hammered out plans for a world that would look more like God's than Mammon's. The army distrusted Parliament's willingness to carry through the work for which they had fought. At the end of the fighting, more conservative MPs began to press for their disbandment. In February and March 1647 Denzil Holles and other Presbyterians gained control of a committee that began to push through a size reduction, without paying the men's huge arrears of pay. Eight militant cavalry regiments elected 'agitators' to represent them. Meanwhile, the king deviously agreed to the Propositions of Newcastle, conceding control of the militia for ten years and a Presbyterian settlement for three. Taking this bait, Parliament voted to disband the army with only eight weeks' arrears of pay.

On 29 May, Fairfax commanded a rendezvous at Newmarket, and on 2 June Cornet Joyce and a party of soldiers captured the king and took him to Army Headquarters, whence he was removed by Cromwell and Fairfax to captivity at Hampton Court. Cromwell seems to have known of the plan, if he did not initiate it. Two days later, the *Humble Remonstrance* announced the army's refusal to disband until its grievances were met. Henry Ireton, a parliamentary commander and Cromwell's son-in-law, drafted *The Heads of the Proposals* reflecting Independent constitutional views. Cromwell negotiated this directly with the king, while the army marched towards London, which it entered on 6 August, to quell counter-revolution. A medley of prophets popped up afterwards to state that they had foreseen this. Anna Trapnel, who was to achieve notoriety in the 1650s as the catatonic rhyming Fifth Monarchist prophetess, claimed to have seen in a trance – as she explains in *The Cry of a Stone* (1654) – the army coming in 'Southwark-way', well before the event. The Fifth Monarchist sect believed in the imminent Second Coming of Christ at the head of an army to inaugurate the thousand-year rule of the saints. To Anna and many budding Fifth Monarchists of that time, Cromwell, who rode in at the head of his regiment, before the 18,000-strong army, was 'Gideon', the Lord's chosen instrument.

To others, such as Mary Pope, a salter's widow, a moderate Puritan to whom zealots were odious and trade the lifeblood of England, the sight of the army advancing into the capital was an outrage. She saw that the army had come to 'nonparliament Parliament, and they intend to nonking the King, and unlaw the laws', as she wrote in *Behold, here is a Word*. Like many other weary Londoners, she had seen enough of the profiteers, squander and plunder, the foundering businesses, the spoiling of crops and especially the cartloads of starving and maimed soldiers with 'their stomachs overgone for want of bread, that they could take little of anything'. But the army was not prepared to go away feeling that they had fought for nothing.

At the Putney Debates in October, a scribe took down the discussion for three days in shorthand. The confrontation is one of the most fascinating in history. Before them, they had the document, *An Agreement of the People*, a series of demands for basic human rights. Cromwell and Ireton prevaricate, attempt to neutralize discussion and direct it into channels in which they, as an elite, are comfortable. But the agitators, especially the magnificently eloquent Colonel Rainsborough, will not allow the central demands to be lost sight of. On the page are the living voice-prints of men determined not to have wasted their struggle for a hollow cause:

> Cowling: 'Since the Conquest the greatest part of the kingdom was in vassalage.'
> Petty: 'We judge that all inhabitants that have not lost their birthright should have an equal voice in elections.'
> Rainsborough: '...for really I think that the poorest he that is in England hath a life to live, as the greatest he; and therefore truly, sir, I think it's clear, that every man that is to live under a government ought first by his own consent to put himself under that government; and I do think that the poorest man in England is not at all bound in a strict sense to that government that he hath not had a voice to put himself under.'

To this Ireton's response turns upon the word 'property': 'I would have an eye to property'. Only the propertied have a 'permanent fixed interest in the kingdom'. Cromwell attempts to mediate, without deviating from the conservative viewpoint. 'No man says that you have a mind to anarchy; but that the consequence of this rule tends to anarchy; must end in anarchy; for where is there any bound or limit if you take away this limit, that men that have no interest but the interest of breathing shall have no voice in elections?' Towards the end of the dispute, as the tone heats, the question is repeated, 'I would fain know what we have fought for.' If it is 'for our laws and liberties', says Rainsborough, that must mean something other than 'the old law of England – which enslaves the people of England'. Hugh Peter suggests a committee. A compromise is mooted: that the poor might have a smaller-proportioned representation – 'a fine gilded pill', sneers Rainsborough. Nathaniel Rich says that many have ruined themselves in giving their utmost to the war, and now will find themselves without a property qualification. Edward Sexby's scornful intervention speaks for all:

> I see though liberty were our end, there is a degeneration from it. We have engaged in this kingdom and ventured our lives, and it was all for this: to recover our birthrights

and privileges as Englishmen; and by the arguments urged there is none. There are many thousands of us soldiers that have ventured our lives: we have had little propriety in the kingdom as to our estates, yet we have had a birthright. But it seems now, except a man hath a fixed estate in this kingdom, he hath no right in this kingdom. I wonder we were so much deceived. If we had not a right in the kingdom, we were mere mercenary soldiers.

These men had moved into a realm of speculation recognizable as modern: alongside Hobbes, Harington, Winstanley and other thinkers whose speculations were freed up by the altered times, the Levellers both of the army and of the civilian world were giving consideration to rights judged by the secular light of reason and the law of nature. Gerard Winstanley and the 'True Levellers' ('Diggers') would take these principles to their logical conclusion in a form of communism, whereby they asserted rights in common to land, food and shelter for all men and women. When the Rump Parliament (the remnant of the Long Parliament, purged by the army in 1648) repressed those voices, the inspirational, turbulent Lilburne (who died a Quaker) said, 'Posterity shall reap the benefit of our endeavours, whatever shall become of us.'

THE END OF THE KING

For the moment, the leadership was able to retain the solidarity of the regiments through the necessity to respond to the emergency of Charles's escape from Hampton Court on 11 November. Cromwell is believed by some to have engineered this escape, as a way of uniting the fracturing army. The king now turned once more to the Scots, with whom he concluded an Engagement to impose Presbyterianism on England, and Parliament passed the Vote of No Addresses in January 1648, to halt all negotiations with the king. The outbreak of what is known as the Second Civil War, but which was really more a series of rebellions by a population that had had enough of wartime taxation, centralization and mayhem, sealed Charles's fate. The New Model Army crushed risings in Wales, Cornwall, Kent and the north, culminating in Cromwell's victory over the Scots at Preston in August. Even so, Parliament pressed on with negotiations with the king on the Isle of Wight, revoking the Vote of No Addresses.

But among the radicals and the 'saints', the mood had hardened. At the opening of the Second Civil War, senior officers and 'agitators' of the army met in Windsor Castle for a three-day session of prayer and debate. William Allen's account of the meeting, written a decade later, gives a vivid insight into the psyche of veterans who had seen their land soaked in blood, only to be faced with renewed violence by the king. Charles was seen as refusing the verdict of providence. Allen remembered their determination to 'call Charles Stuart, that man of blood, to an account, for that blood he had shed, and mischief he had done, to his utmost, against the Lord's cause and people in these poor nations'. He recalled the ease with which the counter-revolution was smashed, 'and the king so

Charles I's dignified and adept behaviour at his trial, surrounded by soldiers, impressed eyewitnesses.
He refused to recognize the court's validity.

infatuated, as he stands disputing punctilios till he loses all, and himself with it, and was fetched away... to execution, which suddenly followed accordingly; and all this done within less than a year'.

The revulsion against Charles as a 'man of blood' who could not be reasoned with or trusted informed the army's *Remonstrance*, demanding that the king 'be swiftly brought to justice, for the treason, blood and mischief he's therein guilty of'. The House prevaricated, refraining from discussing it and continuing to dream up ways round the increasingly threatening situation. The army now took possession of the king, of London and of Parliament, which they purged. On 6 December, Colonel Thomas Pride stood at the door of the Commons with a list of about 110 names, excluding all MPs not sympathetic to the army, so that the House consisted only of hard-line Independents in a 'Rump' Parliament. Two hundred other MPs, unable to stomach the idea of trying and condemning their sovereign, slunk away until the act was accomplished. A hasty apparatus was fabricated to judge the king, in the High Court of Justice held in the Painted Chamber of the Palace of Westminster.

The proceedings in Charles's show trial were swift, brutal, dubiously legal and anxiously muddled. Fifty-nine MPs took part as commissioners in the trial, Vane and (later) Fairfax refusing to serve and others either absconding or attending but refusing to sign the execution order. John Bradshaw, an undistinguished lawyer, served as president, and John Cook prosecuted. Charles refused to plead in front of a court he regarded as illegal: 'I would know by what power I am called hither. I would know by what authority, I mean *lawful*.' Since his judges were making up the law as they went along, there was no authoritative answer to this and Cook's rejoinder that the king was 'elected' was risible. As the historian Mark Kishlansky observes, 'It's impossible to charge a king with treason, since treason is a crime of activity against the king, so what the Parliamentarians were charging him with was activity against himself.' Bradshaw's rough and nervy demeanour was a foil for the exquisite balance and ironic manner preserved by the king, whose speech impediment had disappeared. While the soldiers filled in the embarrassed pauses by shouting, 'Justice! Justice!', cries of 'God save the king!' were also heard from the body of the hall.

On 29 December, the Army Council debating the trial paused to hear the testament of Elizabeth Pool, a young prophetess from Abdingdon. She informed them that, having read the army's *Remonstrance*, she had experienced visionary 'pangs of a travailing woman' to the following effect: she had seen 'a woman crooked, weak, sick', signifying the sick kingdom, to be cured by 'a man who is a member of the army', as directed by Elizabeth. The council thanked her cordially, regarding this as divine sanction for its work. A week later, however, she was back again, with less welcome orders from the Almighty, to the effect that Charles must be tried 'but touch not his person'. She pointed out that, according to the coronation oath, the king was husband to the nation, so that the army was, properly speaking, Charles's wife, and in the last resort must respect him. Elizabeth was packed off unthanked, and published her messages as *An Alarum of War*. The fact that the king's judges would give time to such an intervention suggests the extent to which they were impelled by a painful compound of 'godliness', pragmatism and panic.

After the judgement, the prosecutor John Cook hurried out a pamphlet entitled *King Charles His Case*, in which he accused Charles of violating his coronation oath, the law of reason and the law of nature, in waging war on his own people. He claimed that Parliament was the ultimate and supreme authority under English law and that kings ruled by right of conquest which 'makes a title amongst wolves and bears, but not amongst men'. His arguments struggle on the page with one another, until he arrives at a passage which carries profound conviction, explaining why in the end the regicides had felt they had no choice but to execute the king. Charles, Cook says, was 'politic and subtle', at the mercy of his own compulsive 'meanders in state... serpentine turnings and windings'. When Parliament and the army had tried to fasten on him to negotiate, there had been no holding him for devious slipperiness. Cook ended with conclusions at once vindictive and unctuous, by stating that Charles murdered Christ 'in the saints', comparing him with Richard III, assuring the reader that 'the sun of justice' is shining 'gloriously' in England now, 'but, alas! the poor mole is blind still, and cannot see it...'

Charles's observations on the trial were pithily apt. As the soldiers closed round him to take him away, he said, 'I am not suffered to speak: expect what justice other people will have.' John Lilburne would certainly have agreed with him. The Diggers, ejected from the common lands at St George's Hill and Cobham in Surrey, could not have disagreed. In *A New Year's Gift for the Parliament* (1650), Winstanley pointed out that the estates of the gentry derived solely from the power of the king. 'Search all your laws, and I'll adventure my life, for I have little else to lose, that all lords of manors hold title to the Commons by no stronger hold than the King's will, whose head is cut off; and the King held title as he was a conqueror.' Upon the orchestrated chorus from the roaring soldiers, 'Execution! Justice!' Charles commented, 'Poor creatures, for sixpence they will say as much of their own commanders.' And as Charles was led into his palace, and spotted an old servant weeping, he said, 'You may forbid their attendance, but not their tears.' The regicides would never have any answer to those eloquent tears.

During the trial there had been an intervention from a masked lady in a gallery, thought to be Lady Fairfax, protesting against Bradshaw's claim that the trial was taking place 'in the name of the people of England'. 'Not half, not a quarter of the people of England!' called out a piercing voice. 'Oliver Cromwell is a traitor!' She was hustled away by soldiers.

CHAPTER 4

OLIVER CROMWELL

THE COMMONWEALTH AND PROTECTORATE

The manner of Charles I's confrontation with death would, he was aware, be crucial to the destiny of his heir and a Stuart restoration. On the frosty, sunless morning of 30 January 1649, the king had put on an extra undershirt, in case he shivered and was suspected of cowardice. The scaffold was constructed outside Whitehall, the palace from which he had fled seven years before. He walked out through the Banqueting Hall, beneath Rubens' awe-inspiring painting of the Golden Age of Peace. Now the windows were boarded up and a stale smell tainted the darkened hall.

Charles died so well and with such eloquent resolve that he reinforced (as he had planned) the potency of the mythology that would spring from his 'sacred' blood. Even the parliamentarian Andrew Marvell celebrated the courage and grace of Charles's death, in his 'Horatian Ode upon Cromwell's Return from Ireland':

He nothing common did or mean
Upon that memorable scene:
> But with his keener eye
> The axe's edge did try:
Nor call'd the gods with vulgar spite
To vindicate his helpless right,
> But bowed his comely head
> Down, as upon a bed.

Charles's last words, which were rushed out on a pamphlet, included the forgiveness of his enemies and a majestic articulation of his death as transcendence: 'I go from a corruptible to an incorruptible Crown, where no disturbance can be, no disturbance in the world.' As he prepared to lay his head on the block, silence seized the onlookers. A seventeen-year-old in the crowd saw the axe fall and recalled, 'such a groan as I never heard before, and I desire I may never feel again'. No regicide propaganda could ever counter the waves of strong emotion that passed through the breasts of ordinary people. The Essex minister Ralph Josselin wrote in his diary, 'I was much troubled with the black providence of putting the King to death, my tears were not restrained at the passages about his death, the Lord in mercy lay it not as sin to the charge of the kingdom.' Josselin typified a stunned sense of foreboding: he waited to see whether Providence defined it as a heinous crime or a necessary purgation. The diary makes it clear that he did not really know what to think. But he wept. When Cromwell died in 1658, Josselin did not weep. On 1 September 1658, he indifferently jotted, 'Cromwell died, people not much minding it,' noting it among a medley of domestic events.

Soon after the king's death, a book called *Eikon Basilike* ('The Image of the King') was published, supposedly a collection of meditations and prayers by Charles in the weeks leading up to his death. It was answered by Milton in *Eikonoklastes* ('The Breaking of the Image') with a splenetic smearing of the king: 'He glories much in the forgiveness of his enemies: so did his grandmother at her death. Wise men would sooner have believed him, had he not so often told us so.' Milton sneeringly reminds his readers that Charles belonged to the dynasty of the beheaded Mary Stuart, a Catholic whore. In the same paragraph he rails against the king's attempt 'to catch the worthless approbation of an inconstant, irrational, and image-doting rabble… a credulous and hapless herd, begotten to servility'. Gone is the optimistic belief in the Elect Nation, the openness of every man, woman and child to the dazzling light of gospel truth. The optimist who had pleaded so luminously for freedom of the press, in the hope that through difference of opinion truth would evolve, was to become censor for the Commonwealth government.

CROMWELL'S RISE TO POWER

Marvell, who would in due course work for Milton at the Protectoral Latin secretariat, expressed in the 'Horatian Ode' (which was politically too hot to publish for over a century) a sense of the paradox and ambivalence evoked by Cromwell in his contemporaries and successors. Marvell was sharply aware of Cromwell's violent ambition and his capacity for guile. Cromwell's earlier life, before he entered national politics at the age of forty, is obscure. 'He lived,' says the poet, 'in his private gardens', 'reserved and austere'. This is a euphemistic way of saying that Cromwell came of a gentry family initially from Huntingdon, moving to St Ives and thence to Ely. There are only shreds of information about his life for the first forty years. What filters through is a tale of struggle and nervous affliction in circumstances likely to cause humiliation, rather than hopes for a great vocation.

Just one year older than the king, Cromwell was the sole surviving male child of the younger son of Sir Henry Cromwell, of Hinchingbrooke, built on the site of what had been a convent before the Dissolution of the Monasteries. The family's wealth derived largely from the sequestrated estates of the Reformation, tying the Cromwells in closely with the landed Protestant interest. But whereas his uncle, Sir Oliver, was one of the richer county knights, Sir Henry's ten children had devoured his patrimony, and Cromwell's father, Robert, as a younger son, was comparatively poorly off, with an income of perhaps £300. A JP, he had served as a Member of Parliament under Elizabeth. However, Oliver Cromwell was one of seven children, with sisters for whom dowries must be provided. When his father died, Cromwell was eighteen: he left Sidney Sussex College, Cambridge, after only a year and became the surrogate father of the family, remaining close to his mother into her old age. Cromwell's early history seems to be one of clutching on to gentry status and, for want of means and because of peculiar but obscure difficulties entailed by his temperament in relation to authority, failing to do so. His income can have been no more than about £100 per year.

When Cromwell moved from Huntingdon to St Ives, he was forced to live, not as a gentleman, but as a yeoman farmer, working the land with his own hands. The degradation involved for one of his origins, well-connected and married to the daughter of a London fur trader, was considerable, as he arduously clung on in the face of financial rigours and the problems caused by his own bumptiousness and verbal incontinence, as well as a tendency to what would now be seen as depression, or manic depression. In the mid 1630s his conditions improved when he received a small but significant legacy from his uncle. But some defining years were mortifyingly spent as a member of the 'middling' sort. Cromwell served inconspicuously as a Member of Parliament in Charles's last Parliament in 1628–9, witnessing the tumultuous session in which Holles and Valentine thrust the Speaker back bodily into his seat, with oaths, and mayhem prevailed. Thus Cromwell's formative experience of government as a man just under thirty included coercive violence in the Chamber: over twenty years later he would himself dissolve Parliaments in volcanic indignation. He seems to have been from earliest times impolitic, with a streak of crudity in his speech, ebullient and pugnacious; a man of action constrained to words.

Marvell suggested in his ode that Cromwell made a meteoric rise from nowhere – a force of nature 'burning through the air' like a thunderbolt – but this was not the case. In the 1628 Parliament, eight of his cousins sat on the benches. He was related to a large number of the MPs in the Long Parliament, including Oliver St John and John Hampden, who had been imprisoned for their refusal of the forced loan. He was also associated with Viscount Saye and Sele, Lord Brooke and the Earl of Warwick. In his dealings in Huntingdon, he struggled in a mesh of factions, never demonstrating political sagacity or subtlety, involved in furious rows about the use of a bequest for a lectureship and an attack on the newly dominant family of the town, the Montagus, concerning the town charter, with the result that in 1630 he was required to apologize for 'disgraceful and unseemly speeches' against the mayor and another official. The case, referred to the Lord Privy Seal (the Earl of Manchester, with whom Cromwell would come to wrangle on a national platform), was adjudicated in the mayor's favour, and Cromwell was reported to have acknowledged that his words were 'ill… spoken in heat and passion', and to have retracted them. It is clear that Cromwell ate bitter herbs as a penalty for his compulsive outspokenness. Some of the impatience, unpredictability and verbal aggression displayed in his later public life come into relief here. In the bitter wake of these disputes he moved to St Ives to farm, living a de-gentrified existence by the sweat of his brow.

Cromwell may have experienced bitter rejection. Certainly in the years 1629–31, he underwent a nervous illness that reads today very like a nervous breakdown. In London, as a Member of Parliament, he visited the royal physician, Sir Theodore Mayerne, in September 1628, six months after entering the House. Mayerne's notes specify a stomach disorder, probably of nervous origin, since he comments, *valde melancholicus*, inaccurately translated as 'quite depressed' by most modern historians. The term 'melancholy' had a more specific medical application, denoting an excess of the humour of 'black bile' that produced the effect of saturnine or manic 'melancholy'. The Renaissance view of melancholy associated it with the scholar's disposition, dark and brooding, or expressive of genius and the madness that is neighbour to genius. It was also understood to be suicidal and introverted, subject to imagination. Melancholy was also an aspect of the Puritan temperament and (confusingly) a cult among Royalists, who might be pictured dressed in 'sad' colours and wearing a mournfully stoical expression.

Cromwell's own physician, Dr Simcott, recorded in 1636 an illness certainly of psychological origin, whose symptoms included inertia (Cromwell would lie in bed 'all melancholy'). Cromwell would send for Simcott at midnight or the early hours,

A broadsheet illustration of Charles I's execution records the nation's shock at the death of the 'royal martyr'.

A liuely Representation of the manner how his late Magesty was beheaded uppon the Scaffold Ian:30:1648:

Weep, ENGLAND weep, help all to raise loud cry,
How ENGLANDS Glory, and her shame did lye.
Who like a lamb was to the Scaffold ledd.
And low as death stoop't his Anointed head,
Who did a willing Sacrifice become,
To expiate who procur'd his Finall doome.
And by Rude hands being brought upon the stage,
Lost his owne Life to please theire Cruell rage.

complaining that he felt himself to be dying. He entertained 'strange fancies' about the large cross at the centre of Huntingdon, alternating with delusions of grandeur, believing that he would become 'the greatest man in the kingdom'. Dr Simcott labelled his deluded patient 'splenetic'. Again, this does not mean 'angry' but refers to the current view of the spleen as the seat of morose and morbid feelings. The diagnosis is the same as that of the London physician's. This experience of 'the dark night of the soul' corresponds to an experience reported in detail by most Puritans when experiencing the throes of conversion. The template may be found in John Bunyan's spiritual autobiography, *Grace Abounding to the Chief of Sinners* (1666), which chronicles a crisis spanning the years 1649–55 and involves frantic fluctuations between despair and conviction of salvation, often on the same day. Cromwell's haunting by the Huntingdon cross is comparable with Bunyan's obsession with the bell tower at Elstow Abbey: he nourished terrors that 'how if one of the bells should fall?' In his fits of despair, he 'blessed the condition of the dog and toad… yea, gladly would I have been in the condition of dog or horse' and, in his horror of reprobation, he found oaths and blasphemies tumbling out of his mouth so that he had to hold his chin to shut his mouth.

Cromwell was ridiculed by his enemies as an upstart yokel, whose bulbous features and shabby dress betrayed low origins.

Correspondingly, the Fifth Monarchist prophetess Anna Trapnel described taking knives to bed with her; Nehemiah Wallington, born the year before Cromwell, described ten attempts at suicide at around the age of twenty, including hanging, poison, cutting his own throat and throwing himself in the Thames. He took ratsbane but only vomited, attempted to leap out of the window but was unhurt, and took a sword to bed. He became afraid of his very shoes, and threw them away, believing that since the devil could come in any likeness, 'he can come in the likeness of my shoes'. John Rogers rushed into barns, stables, privies, 'anywhere (pretending I had business) on purpose to pray, sigh, weep, knocking my breast, curse that ever I was born'. He saw devils with flaming eyes, angels in trees and was fearful of bushes and birds, lest they tempt him to suicide. The Baptist minister Henry Jessey took down in shorthand the following conversation between two adolescents undergoing attention-seeking spiritual crises:

> Miss A: 'I must be damned.'
> Miss Sarah Wright: 'I am damned already, from all eternity to all eternity: it's nothing to do, but it's done already.'
> Miss A: '…I was but an hypocrite, and an hypocrite's hopes shall perish.'
> Miss SW: 'I have been an hypocrite, a revolter, a back-slider.'
> Miss A: 'I know it shall be well with you.'
> Miss SW: 'As well as it was with Judas, who repented, and hanged himself…'
> Miss A (getting up to go): 'I think I shall perish before I see you again.'

At the same time, Puritans undergoing this long process would oscillate between despair at having committed the unpardonable sin and ecstatic transcendence. Cromwell's assertion during these crises that he was destined for greatness would also be intrinsic to the conversion process, since, if he could ascertain by listening to God's voice that he was indeed among the saved, this made his vocation instrumental in God's design. A temperament like Cromwell's, highly emotional (so that he wept easily all his life and could work himself up to sobbing as he talked) and subject to fluctuation of mood and outbursts of rage, would make the familiar process all the more intense. Bedridden inertia at this period of crisis was reiterated in later life in spells of dithering and torpor, which would suddenly resolve themselves as he sprang into action as if hearing a prompting voice.

Suicidal urges and the conviction of sin were not only intrinsic to Calvinist pathology, but a qualification, representing the sufferer's release from merely 'formal' religion, into surrender to the living God, experienced as an indwelling presence. An extant letter of 1638 from Cromwell to the wife of his cousin, Oliver St John, shows that he has completed the rite of passage:

> Truly no poor creature hath more cause to put forth himself in the cause of his God than I… He giveth me to see light in His light. One beam in a dark place hath exceeding much refreshment in it. Blessed be His Name for shining upon so dark a heart as mine! You know what my manner of life hath been. Oh, I have lived in and loved darkness and hated the light. I was a chief, the chief of sinners. This is true; I hated godliness, yet God had mercy on me. O the riches of His mercy! Praise Him for me, that He hath begun a good work should perfect it to the day of Christ…

Anna Trapnel was a notorious Fifth Monarchist prophetess, whose subversive messages were delivered in rhyme during trances.

This letter is not really a personal testament. The admission that he had once been a great sinner is obligatory, and the worse the sinner, the greater the glory to God in the token of his saving power. Agnes Beaumont, a Bedfordshire Baptist, told of how there was hardly a corner of the house, or the barn, cowshed, stable, hedge or nearby wood at her home in Edworth, where she did not fall on her knees in 'floods of tears… with admiration of the love of Christ to such a great sinner as I was… my tears have been for joy'. If anything, Cromwell's letter is a little too formulaic, as if the exclamatory rhetoric, composed of a mesh of biblical references favoured by Calvinist converts, were being offered as a token whose exchange value will be instantly recognized by the recipient. It has less personal flavour than most such testimonies.

Cromwell could take refuge in a style that favoured the glib and the prolix, and would develop a rambling, obfuscating manner of speech when Protector, which camouflaged rather than revealed meaning. He could wear the Puritan declamatory style like a bandage or armour. The claim to be 'the chief of sinners' is a conventional boast of humility, which equates the writer with St Paul, 'the chiefest of sinners' and the greatest of Apostles. Wedged in the paradoxes of Puritanism we find the cloven complexity of Cromwell, in naivety and craft, humility and hubris, genuine personal qualities and what his enemies branded as hypocrisy. The warlord who could melt; the machiavellian politician who listened; the authoritarian who believed in freedom of conscience: all find expression in the language of Puritanism.

Cromwell's election in 1640 as Member for Cambridge implies the pulling of strings and perhaps it was his association with the Earl of Warwick that appealed to the constituency of the rich university town. He is supposed to have arrived in Parliament looking every inch the country bumpkin, wearing a 'plain cloth suit', poorly tailored, a hat minus a hatband and shabby linen, his tight neckband flecked with blood. This description sheds as much light on the assumptions of Sir Philip Warwick, the royalist who had time and inclination to inspect the Member for Cambridge's outfit, as it does on Cromwell himself. To men of his persuasion, externals were trivia. In the Long Parliament he showed no tact or finesse and his turn for breast-beating lachrymosity (dropping 'tears down with his words') made his more polished colleagues cringe. It was in his contributions to the Militia Bill and his trenchant action in the summer of 1642, in preventing Cambridge wealth from finding its way into the king's hands, that Cromwell came into his own. He marched his men on King's College, Cambridge, with drums and flags, hectored his aged uncle Oliver and captured most of the college plate for Parliament, to the value of about £20,000.

SOLDIER AND STATESMAN

The rapidity with which Cromwell mastered military strategy has raised the question of whether he had somehow gained experience on the continent in the Thirty Years' War. More probably, he picked up knowledge as he went along, in part from military manuals, but mainly through experience, administrative capability of a high order, analysis and appraisal of the day's 'work' on the battlefield and the intensification of what might be called fraternal discipline in his regiments. The troops Cromwell led were bonded as if in a military kinship group, with high standards imposed from above and encouraged within individual soldiers. Emphasis on refraining from swearing, drinking and womanizing in the Cromwellian troops was intended to curb a laxness equated with military turpitude. Cromwell's ability to provide for their welfare, in ensuring that they had enough food, supplies, uniforms and ammunition – his mastery of logistics – was crucial, although arrears of pay were unavoidable. His troops respected the fact that Cromwell was a front-line commander, who insisted on being seen to expose himself to the same dangers as

Oliver Cromwell's military genius and ruthless idealism took him from the minor Huntingdonshire gentry to supreme power as Lord Protector, feared and respected throughout Europe.

themselves, sometimes having two or more horses butchered under him. His personal bravery was linked with the reliance he placed on God's providential care.

Cromwell's constitutional opportunism, his ability to capitalize on the immediate occasion, was another factor in his military success. In the maelstrom of battle he could focus with fierce coolness on the next move. This capacity, a two-edged sword when it came to settling a form of government in the wake of the wars and regicide (since each was experimental, improvised and liable to collapse), was linked with his Providentialism. The assurance that the Lord would provide for his own served Cromwell well as a military commander. It discharged his habitual tension as legitimized, indeed sanctified, violence.

As leader of the East Anglian counties, Norfolk, Suffolk, Essex, Cambridge, the Isle of Ely and (after May 1643) Huntingdonshire, Cromwell was able to use the network of congregational churches to hand-pick the 'right kind' of soldiers for his troop, a subculture to which he had belonged since his conversion, and which could furnish what he called, 'a lovely company... honest, sober Christians'.

It was noted that 'he loved his soldiers as his children' and would indulge their horseplay and leisure antics. The singing of psalms for which his army was famous was another means of bonding. In battle he is described as ecstatic: 'He did laugh so excessively as if he had been drunk; his eyes sparkled with spirits,' an eyewitness reported. His euphoria before battle was an expression partly of his sheer pleasure in fighting and of that inspiration which had assured him that one day he would be a 'great man': it girded him round with a sense of supernatural safety at the heart of danger. He described his psychological state before Naseby in revealing terms:

> When I saw the enemy draw up and march in gallant order towards us, and we a company of poor ignorant men, to seek how to order our battle – the General having commanded me to order all the horse – I could not (riding alone about my business) but smile out to God in praises, in assurance of victory, because God would, by things that are not, bring to naught things that are. Of which I had great assurance; and God did it. O that men would therefore praise the Lord, and declare the wonders that He doth for the children of men!

The Puritan anti-logic of divine paradox structures Cromwell's emotion here. *Because* 'we' were just 'poor ignorant men', *therefore* 'we' were bound to win. He takes his text from the many revolutionary passages in the Old and New Testaments to the effect that the last shall be first and the Psalmist's confidence that God will avenge the oppressed. When Cromwell describes himself 'smiling out to God in praises' as he readies his army for battle, he is feasting on the pledges of the Psalms:

> The Lord shall laugh at [the wicked]: for he seeth that his day is coming.
> The wicked have drawn out the sword, and have bent their bow, to cast down the poor and needy, and to slay such as be of upright conversation.
> Their sword shall enter into their own heart, and their bows shall be broken.

By this logic, to rank among the 'poor ignorant men' is to start with an advantage. As a pragmatist, Cromwell will also have known, as Prince Rupert did not, that his men outnumbered the Royalist army at Naseby by about 14,000 to 9,000. The conceiver of what Rupert called the 'New Noddle Army' was therefore justified in his optimism. However, these biblical texts promising that the last shall be first and the first last were precisely those that fired the radicals and Fifth Monarchists. Cromwell impregnated his army with a spirit which, when he rose to the summit of political power, would rear against him.

Cromwell was a soldier–statesman, with all the contradiction that implies. If the epic simplicities of the battlefield satisfied his need for transcendence, his experience of the Parliament for which he fought was full of intrigue, compromise and mixed signals, mined with a warren of committees and commissions. He worked in close alliance with a group of Independents, the 'honest party' as they called themselves, who co-ordinated their work in the two houses. In the Lords, Cromwell's collaborators were Viscount Saye and Sele and Lord Wharton, and in the Commons, St John, the younger Vane, Sir John Evelyn and Saye's son, Nathaniel Fiennes; they timed their manoeuvres with deft skill. For long periods of years or months when he was away at war, from August 1642 until November 1648, he left it to this grouping to manage the cause of toleration and the conclusion of a just, honourable agreement with the king.

Cromwell's position was never, of itself, strong in Parliament, and in practice it was only when he was riding on the back of spectacular popular victories, such as Marston Moor, Naseby and Preston, that he could warn Parliament about the super-importance of totalizing the war, in order to drive the hardest possible bargain with the king in securing comprehensive Protestant tolerance. Cromwell's vitriolic attacks on Lords Essex and Manchester in 1644 were choreographed by the 'honest party', without whom his position would have been weak. After Fairfax's urgent request that he join him in the field rescued Cromwell from the terms of the Self-Denying Ordinance, his army command was renewed only provisionally, effectively gagging him politically. However, the trust and understanding between Cromwell and his friends in Parliament was such that their concerted actions achieved a string of what Cromwell regarded as 'Providences' to match those won on the battlefield: the creation of the Committee of Both Kingdoms, the New Model Army, the Self-Denying Ordinance, the adoption of the *Heads of the Proposals* as a basis for a settlement. He was inclined to regard these political achievements as all the more assuredly providential because they had been won in the teeth of powerful opposition. Cromwell reverenced the institution of Parliament: he had never sought to subject the rule of law to the sword. But he was not a natural Parliamentarian and was easily rendered impatiently bemused by its shifting alliances and filibusters.

With increasing precariousness and instability Cromwell straddled his double allegiance to army militants and Parliament. His face-to-face negotiations with the king estranged the army, while Parliament's pusillanimity alienated him. It was not without overwhelming struggle that Cromwell came to a position where he must view his old allies as backsliders who had broken a sacred trust: the sword became in 1648 a 'lawful power'. Cromwell's habit of not appearing in person until significant actions had been taken by the army reinforced his reputation as a devious mover-behind-the-scenes. The theme of 'hypocrisy' is one that trails him like a billowing shadow. His acts of deadly calculation, after characteristic phases of vacillation, seem to betray a hysterical quality not incompatible with a highly wrought nature under intense strain.

Around the signing of Charles's death warrant clustered tales implying Cromwell's maniacal coercion of reluctant judges to set their signatures to the document. This must have seemed a Faustian moment. It would be natural to recoil at the eleventh hour from an act traditionally so heinous and of such finality. Cromwell is supposed to have engaged in loud buffoonery with Henry Marten after they had both signed, inking each other's faces, in the solemn grandeur of the Painted Chamber. He is alleged to have yanked the reluctant Sir Richard Ingoldsby to the table and traced his signature for him. No doubt some of these tales were the product of the scapegoating after Cromwell's death and Charles II's return, when some signatories tried to wriggle out of the guilt sealed by those indelible signatures. Lucy Hutchinson certainly said so, with customary asperity. But Cromwellian displays of violently conflicted behaviour were not out of character. In *The Hunting of the Foxes… by Five Small Beagles,* a Leveller pamphlet of March 1649, the authors vividly describe his condition of exalted agitation, concurrent with a focused pugnacity: 'You shall scarce speak to Cromwell about anything, but he will lay his hand on his breast, elevate his eyes, and call God to record. He will weep, howl, and repent, even while he doth smite you under the first rib.'

Although they present the gestural vocabulary of the 'saint' as a front for an underlying power-drive, which knows exactly where to strike and wills the destruction of those it seeks to deceive, the godly body-language was probably just as real and compulsive as Cromwell's need to immobilize the enemies of his policies. The laying of the hand on the breast to express probity, the raised eyes in witness were valid testaments to a drive that increasingly saw that it must dabble in unwholesome means to gain the desired end: nothing less than the New Jerusalem.

THE COMMONWEALTH

With the king dead, Cromwell was left with the Rump of the Long Parliament, less than half the representative assembly elected in 1640. Further, persons on whose political judgement and skills he had relied refused to serve, and Fairfax, having temporized his way through the (to him) unthinkable execution of the king, was to retreat to his country estate at Nun Appleton, away from the bloodstained theatre of action. England, when it awoke on the morning of 31 January 1649, found itself de facto a republic, without any programme as to how to organize that state, with all its imponderables. Parliament lost little time in printing a new Great Seal, minting coinage stamped 'The Commonwealth of England' and bearing the motto 'God With Us'. In March it formally abolished the monarchy and the House of Lords and arrested the Leveller leaders. Lilburne, eavesdropping in an antechamber to the Council of State, heard Cromwell pounding the table with his fist, hollering, 'I tell you sir, you have no other way to deal with these men but to break them, or they will break you.'

Parliament began to raise urgently needed funds by selling the dead king's priceless art collection, jewels and treasures, and his magnificent antiquarian library. The new rulers kept St James's Palace and Windsor Castle for their own official use. A Council of State of forty-one members was created as the new legislative centre, and based at Whitehall, where John Milton as Secretary for Foreign Tongues was also allocated rooms. Among all this novelty, Cromwell was besieged from many sides by hostile forces: the wave of poignant sentiment that met the king's death was accompanied by suspicion that Cromwell coveted the crown. A ballad of April 1649 shows 'Cromwell on the Throne' proclaiming:

> So, so, the deed is done,
> The royal head is severed,
> As I meant when I first begun,
> And strongly have endeavoured.
> Now Charles the First is tumbled down,
> The Second I do not fear;
> I grasp the sceptre, wear the crown,
> Nor for Jehovah care.

The Levellers protested against what they regarded as Cromwell's usurpation of the kingship, and sections of the army mutinied. The young Leveller officer Robert Lockier was shot. His funeral procession poured through London, ending in the militant Leveller women in their green ribbons who now, in the desperate last years of the movement, took the places of their menfolk in bombarding Parliament with demands for liberty and the release of the Leveller detainees. Cromwell was grabbed by the cloak as he left Westminster by a radical woman, who threatened, 'Sir, if you take away their lives, or the lives of any contrary to law, nothing shall satisfy us but the lives of them that do it, and Sir we will have your life too if you take away theirs.' The anonymous woman had earlier retorted to an MP's observation that it was strange for women to petition, that, 'It was strange that you cut off the King's head, yet I suppose you will justify it.'

This awareness of the Commonwealth's precarious foundations in an unprecedented and illegal act of violence was to jeopardize all Cromwell's actions. The new republic floated out into a sea of uncertainty, having severed its bond to civil law and law of custom: it was founded on homicide (some said parricide and deicide) and was therefore open to attack from within and without. The radical forces released by the maelstrom overflowed into the communist experiment of the Diggers, who established their first community on 1 April 1649 at St George's Hill in Surrey. In August, driven off the common land by local interest groups, they moved to Cobham Heath, where they ploughed and planted, building a second Jerusalem innocent of private property, the earth's 'common treasury' shared and worked in stewardship. Christ had come again, reborn in every awakened man and woman. Gerard Winstanley, leader and spokesman for

This is the second of Parliament's Great Seals of England, validating its authority, issued in 'The Year of Freedom 1651'.

the movement, wrote that Christ is present in anyone who acts in 'love to his fellow creatures; feeding the hungry; clothing the naked; relieving the oppressed; seeking the preservation of others as well as himself', and caring for all other creatures, including the animal species. In these working Edens, the 'spreading power of Righteousness and Wisdom' would create an England without paupers or beggars. Other colonies sprang up in Buckinghamshire and the Midlands, but were also crushed.

Religious groups proliferated too, including the Ranters, not a distinct sect but groups or individuals who combined in different measure antinomianism ('to the pure all things are pure') and pantheism (God in the Creation). Their beliefs were an extreme development of the Puritan regard for the individual spirit's insights and freedom from Church authority. Some held that there was no such thing as sin, hell or the devil, which were myths fabricated by the elite to control the poor, that God was in nature, in a pipe of tobacco, in an ivy leaf, in fornication and polygamy – or indeed any collection of heretical notions the individual wished to espouse. Ranters viewed themselves collectively as 'my one flesh' and addressed one another as 'Fellow creature', annihilating distinctions of rank. They stressed the unity of creation and freedom from the moral law. Some modern historians have questioned whether the Ranters existed except in the fervid imaginations of their contemporaries. But Quakers George Fox and Margaret Fell narrated in detail many encounters with Ranters, from whom they were concerned to distinguish themselves, and Bunyan describes disputing with them.

Ranter writers, such as Abiezer Coppe, were graduates of the army. Coppe had formulated in a visionary, parabolic style a dream of 'parity, equality, community', which saw personal property as theft. He demanded bread for the hungry, here and now. 'Did you not see my hand, this last year, stretched out? You did not see. My hand is stretched out still.' Lawrence Clarkson discerned the divine in all living creatures, as did Jacob Bauthumley, reverencing 'the least flower or herb in the field'. This original and thoughtful man was burned through the tongue for blasphemy. Many of those identifiable as Ranters were also ex-Levellers or had been in the army. They were of low birth and as anarchists they were the target of the Blasphemy Act of August 1650, which effectively snuffed them out. Meanwhile, groups of Seekers gathered throughout the nation, unable to commit themselves to any structure and assuming a posture of listening and prayerful expectation. Cromwell and Milton would probably both have called themselves Seekers. In these groups George Fox would sow the seed of Quakerism that swept the land in the 1650s. Their aggressive refusal of deference and tithes, their belief in spiritual equality for men and women, and servant and master, and their custom of church interruption and the making of civil mayhem, caused intense trouble to Cromwell. This was not least because he respected and was painfully drawn to much that inspired them in their doctrine of the 'Inner Light', that of God in all believers. More dangerous to the Commonwealth throughout the 1650s were the Fifth Monarchist sect.

CROMWELL'S IRISH CAMPAIGN

Cromwell shelved the intricate dilemma of domestic concerns by taking an army to Ireland to smash the threat to the regime by royalist–Catholic forces. Having quelled another Leveller army mutiny at Burford, he took ship at Milford Haven for Dublin in August, as Lord General of the expeditionary force that would enact the massacres of Drogheda in September and Wexford in October. Cromwell despised the Irish, as did most Englishmen, as base, drunken, idolatrous savages, enemies of both civilization and the true faith. When Milton wished to make odious comparisons, he would say, 'worse than the wild Irish'. Cromwell had stated that, 'I had rather be overrun with a Cavalierish interest than a Scotch interest; I had rather be overrun with a Scotch interest, than an Irish interest… all the world knows their barbarism.' The manner in which Cromwell acquainted the Irish people with English 'civilization' has been a byword for barbarity ever since, although it is maintained in Cromwell's favour that he distinctly ordered his troops not to kill civilians.

This was Cromwell's first and last journey overseas and he was violently seasick the whole way. His motives were mixed: to defend England's western flank against royalist threat; vengeance for the 1641–2 massacres; the desire to confiscate land to pay the soldiers in debentures and the investors in the Adventurers' company set up in 1641; and, perhaps, the diversionary tactic of a leader who has made his reputation as a warlord and who seeks to consolidate his grip on power, not by legislating at home but through conquest abroad.

Drogheda was a major fortress 30 miles from Dublin, whose medieval walls (22 feet high and 6 feet thick at the base) were believed by the inhabitants to be impregnable to siege. Sir Arthur Aston, who was holding the town with about 2,000 men, boasted that 'he who could take Drogheda could take Hell' and confidently expected 'Colonel Hunger and Major Sickness', the enemies of besieging armies, to see off the parliamentary troops in an extended stalemate. However, Cromwell had brought the latest technology, of a sort never previously seen in Ireland: he stationed a plethora of siege guns and field pieces at two tactical positions on raised ground to the south, now known as Cromwell's Mount, and blasted two holes in the walls with massive shot, the largest being perhaps 2 stones in weight.

On 10 September Cromwell summoned Aston to surrender the town, under a white flag, promising 'no quarter' as the penalty for refusal. Aston refused and the blood-red flag was raised, refusing clemency to combatants, according to the conventions of contemporary warfare. Drogheda put up strenuous resistance and, although Cromwell's cannon breached the wall at St Mary's Church, the hole was too small to admit his cavalry. The ditch around the walls filled up with corpses. At the second attack, the English still could not make progress through the breach. At about half-past five on 11 September, Cromwell himself, in a cold sweat of rage, spearheaded the charge through the breach. Aston and his men retreated into the palisades at Mill Mount, from which it was said they were enticed down with promises of mercy and killed. Cromwell's army, berserk with bloodlust, murdered two to three thousand people in Drogheda. One street is called Scarlet Street, from being awash with blood. The priests and friars were either murdered or burnt.

Cromwell's reputation for invincibility, and his inner conviction of God's justifying hand, was reinforced by Drogheda. He informed Parliament, 'I am persuaded that this is a righteous judgement of God upon these barbarous wretches, who have imbrued their hands in so much innocent blood.' He went on to state that this slaughter would

The savagery of Cromwell's massacre of 3,000 soldiers, civilians and priests of Drogheda in 1649 was merciless, despite its legitimacy according to prevailing codes of war.

doubtless 'prevent the effusion of blood for the future', 'which otherwise cannot but work remorse and regret'. This tortuous sentence takes the form of faintly squeamish defensive accusation. The letter to Parliament is unusually flat in tone, in contrast to the victory epistles of the Civil War. Historian Michael O'Siochru comments: 'I think Cromwell feels the need to justify what takes place at Drogheda... a number of his commanders and perhaps even the troops as well... are a bit shocked at the extent of the slaughter.' No comparable bloodbath had been perpetrated in the English Civil War, which chiefly observed a 'gentlemen's' code, and the perpetrator seems stunned in its aftermath. Several towns did surrender in the wake of Drogheda.

The carnage at Wexford was arguably yet more atrocious, for Cromwell let his men run amok, and wrote home to Parliament boasting that he had lost twenty men to 2,000 of the enemy. From first to last there appeared in Cromwell's bearing an impatience to get the subjugation of Ireland over with. But the Irish did not oblige. They were still in arms until 1652, when the Act of Settlement brought forfeiture of estates and hundreds of executions. The real effects of the war were diminished tillage and depleted livestock in an already impoverished country. Cromwell's policy to Ireland after the cessation of hostilities was a continuation of James I's 'transplantation', with Catholic landowners driven to the western province of Connaught. Cromwell dreamed up the scheme proposed to his son, Henry, Lord Deputy of Ireland, of shipping a thousand Irish boys and girls to the sugar plantations of Jamaica. Henry, somewhat more enlightened than his father about Ireland's welfare, was troubled about clothing the little colonists and the mass transportation was quietly aborted. The Levellers were unique in their time in expressing common cause with the native Irish, in seeking their 'just freedoms... from the power of oppressors'.

Cromwell's army's peregrinations around Ireland continued remorselessly from victory to victory, with the exception of his outwitting by the brilliant major-general Hugh O'Neill at Clonmel. He was recalled to England at the end of May, 1650, and returned to a hero's reception, but also to threats to the fledgling republic over the border in Scotland.

THE THREAT FROM SCOTLAND

The twenty-year-old King Charles II had been persuaded to accept the Covenant in exchange for the Scottish Crown and the promise of restoration to the Crown of England. Charles was subjected to pulverization by sermon, demands that he denounce his mother and father, graces of dire longevity before meals and spartan living presented with smug expressions denoting that the young man should be thankful for salutary mortifications.

While Cromwell had experienced no compunction in shedding Irish blood, as Lord General he was queasy about invading the territory of his godfearing but misguided and obstinate 'brethren', the Scots. Fairfax had flatly refused to lead the pre-emptive strike. In September Cromwell lured Leslie's Scots army into range at Dunbar, where, with all his old *joie de guerre* and adroit tactical reckoning, he inflicted a crushing defeat. Hemmed in beneath Doon Hill, a steep rise on which the Scottish army had secured itself, Cromwell, after prayer, was observing through perspective glasses, when he made out shimmerings on the ridge which the enemy was stealthily leaving: 'God is delivering them into our hands, they are coming down to us,' he crooned with a rush of his old delight. Leslie, his comrade at Marston Moor, had at first shrewdly hobbled the English with delaying tactics, so that Cromwell's men, lacking tents and haring up and down, perished from exposure, dysentery and fever. Behind Cromwell's shrunken army lay the sea, before him the swollen Broxburn. Leslie assumed that Cromwell planned to do the sensible thing and ship his drenched, cold men out of this dead end. But Cromwell, thrusting forward with Lambert's cavalry and a mass of infantry, swiftly crossed the burn and broke the Scots ranks. At the climax of his victory he was seen to burst into compulsive laughter. Again he could boast of having lost only forty men compared with 3,000 Scots killed and 10,000 taken prisoner, more than his entire army.

Fifth Monarchists at home were beginning to see visions of what, perhaps, Cromwell was also envisioning behind that mask of terrible mirth: the beginning of the end of the world, with the Lord General at its head. The Dunbar victory over the Kirk seemed little short of a miracle. Anna Trapnel claimed to have viewed the battle during a fortnight's fast, from a shamanic perspective on the battlefield. She described the Scottish advance down the ridge under a great canopy of light, which then skimmed across the sky to illuminate Gideon/Cromwell: 'I saw myself in the fields, and beheld our Army, and their General, and hearing this voice, saying, Behold Gideon and the happy ones with him.' Dismayed at the poor condition of Gideon's army, however, Anna quailed. The Scots formed a massive arc around the English, but Anna was relieved to see the Lord General spring his pre-dawn ambush. 'I saw the Scots fall down before them, and a marvellous voice of praise I heard in our Army: then was I taken weak… as soon as this vision was over, I broke forth into the singing of their deliverance in Scotland.' Anna's prophetic credit soared in London, as people flocked to peep at events in Scotland through her divining eye. As Bulstrode Whitelock more succinctly put it, 'The Scots were driven like turkeys.'

Charles, excoriated by the sour-faced rantings of the Presbyters, went out hunting one day and rode for forty-two miles. He was apprehended, harangued and sent to be crowned at Scone. He then marched south with a new army martialled by Leslie, which Cromwell permitted to travel down into England. Charles II, hoping to attract and recruit Royalists along the way, found no support, since he had attached himself to the loathed Scots Presbyterians, and, surrendering his initial plan to march on London, was accepted into Worcester, where Cromwell, putting off the day of Nemesis until 3 September 1651, the day of Dunbar, routed the Scots army with terrible carnage. Charles's escape in disguise – hiding for two days in the 'Royal Oak' near Boscobel, using the system of Catholic safe houses and the help of sixty dauntless individuals, to leave the country from Shoreham – became the stuff of romantic legend.

MANAGING THE PEACE

Cromwell, still uneasily straddling the gulf between army and the Rump Parliament, was now presented with the exigencies of peace. The Rump was in no sense a revolutionary body: its members' instincts were conservative and it attempted little radical legislation. The gentry in the Commons had no answers to the problems caused by the bitter economic hardship in the wake of the wars, the increase of vagrancy, disabled soldiers, orphaned children, together with the increase in enclosures that stiffened the resolve of Diggers and Levellers that England should be a land flowing with adequate milk and honey for the suffering many. In the boroughs, many of the old gentry refused to serve or were considered unfit to continue, so local administration was purged, and places filled with new men. The Act of Oblivion, passed in 1652 to forgive the 'rancour and evil' of the wars, excluded noted royalists, thus allowing for continued confiscations. While the laws against recusants were eased and Sunday church attendance was no longer compulsory, fundamentalist laws were enacted by the Rump to clean up private morality. Adultery and incest were punishable by death, but juries would not convict. Fornicators were punished by three months' imprisonment; prostitutes by whipping, branding with the letter 'B' ('bawd'), imprisonment for the first offence and hanging for subsequent offences; sodomy, rape and bigamy were capital offences, and fines for swearing were rigidly imposed.

Genuine, though not substantial, law reform was inaugurated in a commonsense Act of October 1650 to make the law more comprehensible by instituting English rather than Latin as the official language of public records, and substituting normal handwriting for the obscure 'court hand'. But significant law reform did not happen. There were too many vested interests in the Rump (half of whom were lawyers and had lawyers as clients) and the problem went too deep for a burdened legislature. The law as it stood weighed heavily on the poor and ignorant; the court of Chancery was byzantine, and judges operated a system of bribery; the criminal law benefited the literate, who could escape hanging by reading a 'neck verse' from the Bible, while the illiterate were condemned. Samuel Chidley protested in 1651 that, 'To take away the life of any man only for theft is iniquity... it is inhumane, bloody, barbarous, and tyrannical.' He protested against the law for 'pressing men to death, because they will not hold up their hands at the bar, or say they are guilty or not guilty'. He pointed out the psychological effect the terrifying court procedures had on simple people, making the 'poor creatures... open their mouths to confess their own guiltiness'. Nothing was done, but much talking went on in the Chamber. Cromwell listened to the turgid word-mongering with baffled dismay and mounting inner anger.

The religious settlement was intended as a measure to ensure toleration for those sects that did not threaten sedition. A state Church was envisaged, with ministers vetted for spiritual and intellectual qualities. Cromwell hoped that the settlement would in practice function loosely; he spoke insistently on the side of the widest possible toleration: 'I had rather that Mahometanism were permitted amongst us than that one of God's children should be persecuted.' But he came down on the side of keeping tithes, the 'abomination' that outraged the sects more than any other grievance. Cromwell, like most of his class, had benefited by the lay impropriation of tithes before he had entered the public arena, and saw this as a secular rather than a spiritual issue. The movement to destroy the tithe system, which was such a crushing burden to the poor, was taken up by the Quakers, who produced monster petitions demanding (not requesting) their removal.

The Quakers (originally a term of abuse for the Religious Society of Friends) were the most radical movement of the 1650s. George Fox, a weaver's son, was born in Leicestershire in 1624. Wandering the hills and towns of the Midlands and the north, 'as a stranger in the earth' as he says in his *Journal*, he became convinced of the unique veracity of the 'inner light' of all believers, and began his campaign of heckling the profane paid ministers in 'steeplehouses', attacking social hierarchy, scolding magistrates, speaking for the poor and oppressed, founding groups of Friends, enduring (happily) 'bruising, beating, blooding, stoning, and throwing... down'. Meetings were pure of show or form, Friends gathering in silence to listen to and then deliver and act upon the word of God. As Laud had placed the altar above the pulpit, and the Puritans the pulpit and Bible above the altar, Fox placed the spirit above the Bible. When the charismatic, pale-eyed young man, a tall and burly figure in his leather walking dress, arrived in Lancashire and Westmorland, he found groups of Seekers waiting for the Light, and convinced them that it had come. Each convert became automatically a minister and apostle, whether man or woman, servant or lord, freed from all earthly allegiance, exclusively a citizen of the Kingdom of God. In the footsteps of Jesus he preached gloriously in the open air, from a rock on Firbank Fell , to over a thousand people, to whom he explained that the church was no more holy than the mountains.

In June 1652, the twenty-eight-year-old prophet arrived on the doorstep of the great house of Judge Thomas Fell and his wife Margaret at Swarthmore, near Ulverston. This magnificent woman and all her daughters were convinced; she made her home not only a

The army purged the Long Parliament in 1648, leaving only the 'Rump', which went on to execute Charles I and to govern the republic until 1653.

meeting house but the administrative centre of the Religious Society of Friends, which became a ministry that visited all parts of England, Wales, Scotland and Ireland (and saw the inside of prisons everywhere they went). Friends were called 'Quakers', Fox says, because they 'bid [the magistrates] quail at the word of God' but more probably because when they were 'in the power' they would quake, jerk, cry out and fall around the floor in their ecstasy. This uncontrolled behaviour, together with their abuse of priests, university dons, magistrates, MPs and persons in authority, was in strange contrast to their quietist and austere composure of manner, their manifest piety. Quaker peripatetics went in ones and twos throughout the known world with their message of new liberty: to America, where the first missionaries were women: Mary Fisher (who later made an extraordinary one-woman pilgrimage to Turkey, where she met the Sultan and sought to convince him), Ann Austin and Elizabeth Harris. Mary and Ann were 'stripped stark naked' by the New England authorities and searched as witches. William Robinson, Marmaduke Stephenson and Mary Dyer were hanged by the Massachusetts General Council in 1660. Katharine Evans and Sarah Chevers were held for several years by the Inquisition in Malta. Many Quakers wrote and published testimonies, warnings and condemnations. Their habit of 'going naked for a sign' and other extreme actions appalled contemporaries.

This militant movement was so successful among the lower and middle orders that by 1660 there were between 30,000 and 40,000 ministers in Britain. For Cromwell, it was a source of profound perplexity. George Fox wrote to him in 1654 from the Marshalsea Prison assuring him that he was no threat to the secular system, for 'with a carnal weapon I do not fight, but am from those things dead'. Cromwell understood and respected that language: impressed, he released Fox, saying, wisely, 'you are no fool'. In 1656, Fox rode in Hyde Park alongside Cromwell's coach, complaining to him about persecution of Friends, and followed this up by a visit to Whitehall in which he advised him to 'lay down his crown before Jesus. And I was standing by the table; and he came and sat upon the table's side by me and said he would be as high as I was.' Cromwell's body language here shows Fox's knack of opening people's hearts working well on Cromwell by arousing his sensitivity to the suggestion that worldly power was cutting him off from his spiritual roots. In March, 1657, Fox was back with Cromwell in the park, warning him against accepting a crown, 'and bid him mind the crown that was immortal. And he thanked me.'

When Friends came to Cromwell asking to take the place of others in prison, Cromwell looked round his colleagues and wondered aloud which of them would do the same for him. Fox's last meeting with Cromwell came in 1658 when he 'looked like a dead man'. Cromwell's conflicted attitude to the movement shows the pressure placed on his conscience by a movement whose spiritual integrity made a striking impression on him, but whose social expression was anarchistic. He shifted around in intense discomfort on the artificial boundary he had erected between religious and political issues, in a world where the one implied the other.

In the period of government by the Rump, the Quaker movement was only just beginning to put down its strong root-system. Foreign and domestic policies were pressingly urgent because of a trade depression: this resulted in the passing of the Navigation Act in October 1651, limiting the import of goods into England to carriage by English vessels or ships of the country exporting. This was a reaction to the intense trade rivalry with the Dutch, which overflowed in 1652 in war with Holland, a country with whom the English republic had much in common and whose side Cromwell spontaneously took as integral to the crusade for a Protestant Europe. The Calvinist Dutch had thrown off a Spanish dictator, and offered a model for the embryonic republic. Hugh Peter had reported on how well paved, clean and orderly the Dutch towns were. It was the very success of the sister republic that made it a threatening competitor.

In April 1653 Cromwell dissolved the Rump Parliament. He did so with violent suddenness, rushing through Whitehall in a red-faced fury, dressed in a plain black coat and grey worsted stockings, accompanied by musketeers. The reason for this sudden eruption is difficult to ascertain, and does not seem to have been (as previously thought) his rage at the Rump's insistence on prolonging its own sitting. Raging up and down 'with as much passion and distraction as if he had been distracted', Ludlow noted, he kicked at the floor and emitted a tirade of insults. Some MPs, he said, were whoremasters; some ('looking then towards Henry Marten and Sir Peter Wentworth', as Whitelock observed) were drunkards, others corrupt and unjust, and they had better all go. When the Speaker continued to sit, Major-General Harrison grasped him by the arm and tugged him up. 'Come come, I will put an end to your prating!' Cromwell shouted. 'You are no Parliament. I say you are no Parliament. I will put an end to your sitting.' Calling in the musketeers, he drove the MPs out, with words so violently infantile that even Harrison was embarrassed, When Henry Vane objected, 'Sir, this is not honest,' Cromwell made for him shrieking, 'O Sir Henry Vane, Sir Henry Vane, the Lord deliver us from Sir Henry Vane.' Then he directed his berserk attention to the mace on the table, solemn symbol of Parliament's authority, crying, 'What shall we do with this bauble?' A bauble was a licensed fool's stick with bells: the soldiers carried it off. By midday the House was cleared and the tantrum over. The doors were sealed and some joker pinned up a poster reading, 'This House is to be let: now unfurnished.'

THE 'BAREBONES' PARLIAMENT

Whitelock, concussed, reflected on the injustice and injudiciousness of this arrogation of power and reported that 'all honest and prudent indifferent men were highly distasted at this unworthy action', which, it was felt, played straight into royalist hands. Cromwell was probably reacting to the long stress of his attempt to hold the army back from its hostility to the much-talking, do-nothing Parliament. Wishing, however, to avoid the charge of imposing martial rule, Cromwell now devised a new form of government, whose constitution suggests that there may have been a strong element of millennial zeal as well as pent-up animosity in his dissolution of the Rump. The Nominated Assembly, nicknamed the 'Barebones Parliament' after one of its most notable Puritan members, Praise-God Barebone, a vocal Baptist leather-seller, was an attempt to create a government of the godly. The members were to be mocked by Clarendon as 'inferior persons, of no quality or name, artificers of the meanest trades, known only by their gifts of preaching and praying'.

Cromwell's mind, vertiginously seeking out God's will in a maze of uncertainty, dared to hope, using the most cloudy and preachifying language, that 'Barebones', as he announced at its opening on 4 July 1653, was called, 'with a high call... it is marvellous and it is of God, and it hath been unprojected, unthought of by you and us... Indeed I do think something is at the door. We are at the threshold ...' He spoke in a notably holy manner, 'frequently weeping'. His insistence on the importance of the uncalculated providence that falls into men's laps when they least expect it is a characteristic sleight of Cromwell's. The bout of temper that dissolved the Rump thereby becomes a 'leading' from the Almighty, like those 'rousing motions' that in Milton's *Samson Agonistes* inspire the blind hero to pull down the temple on the Philistines. This trust of intuition as the moving of the divine power fortified Cromwell in his constitutional ventures into the unknown. The governments of the 1650s were, in the deepest sense, experimental. God, he tells Barebones, has all along kept 'things from our eyes, so that in what we have acted we have seen nothing before us'.

Far from being a hopeless bedlam as it was later reputed to be, 'Barebones' achieved much in the few months in which it was allowed to function – arguably too much. It opened with short-lived bursts of rapture among the Fifth Monarchist 'saints' in London: John Rogers hailed Cromwell as 'the great Deliverer'. 'Barebones' was composed of about sixty radicals and eighty-four moderates. But the radicals were themselves divided and there were only twelve Fifth Monarchists among their number, who acted together as a group. Streamlining proceedings with committees, they transacted voluminous business, the radicals forcing a four-day debate on the abolition of tithes and the lay patronage of ministerial livings, drawing up a bill to abolish the Court of Chancery, introducing motions for total freedom of preaching, and many other measures which, had they been passed, as they almost were, would have had far-reaching consequences. The elite outside Parliament was aghast. The 'Barebones' radicals attacked property, alarming the moderates, who crept in and assembled early in the morning of 12 December 1653, while the radicals were at prayer, and, despite fierce criticism from Harrison, resolved to surrender government into Cromwell's hands. The Fifth Monarchy men and women were now implacably opposed to the Cromwellian regime.

THE LORD PROTECTOR

When Cromwell assumed the title of Lord Protector of England on 16 December 1653 by the Instrument of Government, he wielded incomparably greater power than a king. However, the historian Blair Worden has aptly insisted that, 'he accepted the Protectorate almost in desperation, like a drowning man clutching at a raft,' for Cromwell's interest was never in 'the trappings of power', solely in securing godly stability. The problem of how his authority should manifest itself so as to be distinguished from a monarchy while borrowing the gist of monarchy's stabilizing rites was worked out from day to day. Cromwell was to be known as 'His Highness', until now an exclusively royal title, signing himself 'Oliver P' and taking over Whitehall as his residence. The extent to which, in his new position, he dominated a schismatic world can be shown by the collapse of the Protectorate with Cromwell's death. It was essentially the child of his driven, conscientious and awe-inspiring pugnacity. The title 'Lord Protector' had a long history in English tradition, being the title used by regents during an heir's minority, and perhaps intended to signify a desire to renounce power once the young Commonwealth was stabilized.

During the investiture, which took place at Westminster Hall, a solemn procession of civil functionaries and military leaders processed to what had been a royal throne, where Cromwell, led by Major-General Lambert carrying the sword of state, and dressed in a black plush suit with a gold-banded hat, walked to the left of the throne, before taking an oath and being invited to take possession of the throne. He was invested with the sword of state and he gave to the Lord Mayor tokens of delegated power, the seal and the sword of the city. This ceremony has vestiges, in austere form, of the coronation ceremony that consecrated kings as God's anointed, but it was terse and plain by contrast. It was succeeded by a sermon in Whitehall Palace Banqueting House. Under the great Rubens ceiling, with the painting of James I apotheosized as Justice and Peace, beneath which Charles I had walked to his death, Cromwell assumed his new ceremonial role. Royal protocol was also revived for the Protector's function as head of state meeting diplomats and dignitaries: the royal barge and state coach were at his disposal, and the Banqueting House hung with rich tapestries would be taken over to receive ambassadors. Elaborately staged public receptions would imprint upon foreign nations the power and dignity of the new Protectorate, and Oliver often wore sumptuous attire considered appropriate to this role.

At the same time the personal mode of life of the Protectoral family became opulent. The ex-king's possessions, from a red velvet upholstered close stool to silk curtains, precious Raphael cartoons, tapestries, paintings and statuary, were set aside for the Protector. Cromwell began to spend weekends at Hampton Court, where he could hunt and hawk and, strolling in the Long Gallery, admire the Mantegna tapestries of the triumphs of Julius Caesar. Cromwell's court became a centre of culture, where poetry, music and painting were encouraged. The first opera in England was put on in Protectoral England, and the poet Katherine Phillips ('the matchless Orinda', friend to Henry Vaughan and linked by marriage to Cromwell's circle) created an early salon, a 'Society of Friendship' in which a cult and poetry of women's love flourished.

The image of Cromwell as killjoy is entirely false: much Puritanism was not, in essence, puritanical. That the Commonwealth did intrude into the sphere of private morality, attempting to force virtue and suppress vice, was a tragic failure to trust that important strand of Puritanism stressing the God-given joy of existence. Milton had written in *Areopagitica* of the wrong-headedness of attempting to 'regulate all recreations and pastimes, all that is delightful to man'. In his divorce tracts he spoke of the beauty of married love, 'in the mutual enjoyment of that which the wanting soul needfully seeks', and saw virtue as having its roots in happiness. When, in his despair, after the loss of the Revolution, he came to write *Paradise Lost*, the great misogynist paradoxically wrote not just a religious and political epic, but one of the greatest erotic poems in the English language. The language of poetry, he said, should be 'simple, sensuous and passionate'. Lucy Hutchinson, the gentry-Puritan, emphasizes how cultured her husband was, how elegant his hairstyle, having all a gentleman's taste and sensibility, falling to 'the practice of the viol, on which he played excellently well' and teaching both his sons and daughters music, dancing and all things pertaining to the education of gentry. She was spiteful about Cromwell's wife and children, whose splendours she called 'scarlet on the ape', while allowing that Cromwell (whom she loathed) cut a dignified figure in office, for 'he had much natural greatness in him, and well became the place he had usurped'.

The Protectorate's political achievements were necessarily modest, in that Cromwell, like James I, felt called upon to play to the antagonists in the state. He told his first Parliament in 1654 of the paramount need for 'healing and settling', and placing old wounds behind the regime. He coddled the sensibilities of the gentry who dominated local and central interests: 'a nobleman, a gentleman, and a yeoman. (That is a good interest of the nation and a great one)', while initially interfering minimally with local government. The poor laws functioned as well as or somewhat better than they had before, for there was less corruption in the Protectoral government than under the Stuarts. Cromwell turned England into an international and trading power, with great prestige. Having made peace with the Dutch in 1654 on terms favourable to national interests, he would go on to declare war on Spain.

After the abortive Penruddock rebellion of March 1655 in Wiltshire, in which a small royalist force seized the sheriff and judges of Salisbury but was swiftly routed, England was parcelled into eleven administrative areas under major-generals. These officials, to Lucy Hutchinson, 'a company of silly, mean fellows', became hated, and the whole process was a fiasco. In attempting to force morality down the throats of the population, they alienated ordinary people by denying their amusements, and by muscling in on the provenance of local administration they offended the elites. Furthermore, the 'decimation' tax on royalists they were supposed to collect did not bring in enough to pay for the new militia they led.

Cromwell was forced to call yet another Parliament, which was programmed to fail by the Council of State's decision to exclude a hundred MPs, and the disgusted absconding of sixty more. Though they voted the requisite money for the war against Spain, their corporate brutality over the Quakers and especially the James Nayler case appalled the Protector. The tenor of their debate may be gathered from their discussion as to whether wandering harpists, pipers and other minstrels should be banned. They decided not to ban singing, since, 'Singing is a natural, playing an artificial music.'

James Nayler had ridden into Bristol on an ass, greeted by women with palm branches crying, 'Holy, holy, holy, Lord God of Israel', as a way of demonstrating that Christ was in him. Nayler, a beautiful but volatile spirit, was the most extreme of the Quakers, surrounded by women. While many MPs bayed for the death penalty for his 'blasphemy', a prolonged debate in Parliament determined on 'clemency'. The official record of the debate shows the brutal thinking of MPs:

Colonel White proposed that his tongue might be bored through.
Colonel Barclay, that his hair might be cut off.
Major-General Haines, that his tongue might be slit or bored through. and that he might be stigmatized with the letter B.
Colonel Coker, that his hair might be cut off.
Sir Thomas Wroth, Slit his tongue, or bore it, and brand him with the letter B…
Sir Gilbert Pickering, His hard labour and imprisonment will be sufficient. I have, within these two days, talked with a very sober man of that sect, who tells me Nayler is bewitched, really bewitched; and keeping him from that party that bewitched him, your imprisonment will do.

Nayler, brought to the bar, explained that he did not consider himself to be God, as alleged, but that God was in him, and Lord Strickland, listening with care to Nayler's words, realized that there was a bundle of unmediated contradictions in Nayler: 'I do not believe (by what I have heard) that he did say he was Jesus or Christ, though I think the women do believe him to be Christ.' Nayler's life was spared, by 96 votes to 82, and he was whipped by the hangman through London, sustaining 360 lashes, pilloried, bored through the tongue and his forehead branded with the letter 'B' for 'Blasphemer'. He was ridden backwards into Bristol, whipped again and imprisoned in Bridewell with hard labour. His tragedy, the result of a rivalry over leadership with Fox, divided the movement. Heartbroken, Nayler left prison contrite. He died shortly afterwards in 1660, praising the spirit of tender endurance: 'I found it alone, being forsaken. I have fellowship therein with them who lived in dens and desolate places in the earth, who through death obtained the resurrection and eternal life.'

There was something orgiastic about the eagerness of the Parliament to subject Nayler to torture for what was, at worst, an error of judgement.

Cromwell's death mask shows his broad, strong-featured face, with the warts he instructed official painters to include in official portraits.

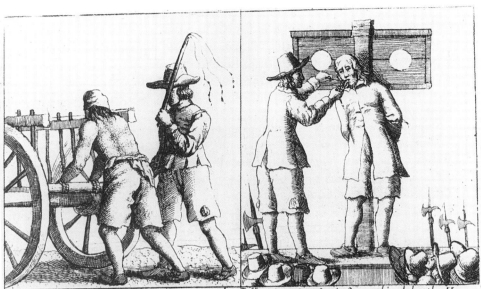

Iames Nailor Quaker, ſet 2 howers on the Pillory at Weſtminſter, whiped by the Hangman to the old Exchainge London, Som dayes after, Stood too howers more on the Pillory
ᴵⁿ at the Exchainge, and there had his Tongue Bored throug with a hot Iron, &
Stigmatized in the Forehead with the Letter:B: Decem: 17: anno Dom:1656: ʼ

*The charismatic Quaker leader, James Nayler, was punished for blasphemy in 1656 by branding, whipping,
the pillory, imprisonment, and boring through the tongue.*

Cromwell was appalled at this unchecked persecution. He sent his secretary to Nayler in
prison, offering to call in a doctor, but was refused. He put it to a meeting of army officers in
February 1657, when proposing a two-chamber Parliament as a check on the Commons, that
Nayler's suffering constituted a test-case: 'Unless you have such a thing as a balance, we
cannot be safe… By the proceedings of this Parliament, you see they stand in need of a check,
or balancing power, for the case of James Nayler might happen to be your case.' The present
law had not allowed him to intervene. In a new constitution, the *Humble Petition and Advice*, a
new instrument of government was hammered out which dispensed with major-generals,
adopted a second House and offered Cromwell the crown.

There was clearly an element of severe temptation, for over a period of weeks in
1657 he hesitated, refused, undertook to search his conscience and pray about it, became
fraught with tension, smoked heavily and became ill, gave it to be understood that he
intended to accept, started jesting about the crown as a 'feather in a man's cap'; then, at
the last minute, on what would have been his accession day, withdrew as if his hand had
been scalded. It seems likely that the army leaders made it clear that they would not
tolerate 'King Oliver I'. But something in Cromwell rose in agreement, with a kind
of self-veto.

It was in character for Cromwell to scan for providences, in order to ascertain the
will of God. In 1655 he had received a severe blow when the 'Western Design' failed. An

English military–naval expeditionary force had been sent to attack Spanish colonies and subvert Caribbean trade: this disaster of mismanagement ended in the deaths of over half the force and the imprisonment of the two commanders. Cromwell shut himself away, in the conviction that he had lost God's favour. This should be interpreted against the background of Cromwell's own millennial aspirations (he was inviting the Jews back into England, in part to prepare the way for the return predicted in the Book of Revelation) and the ferocious attacks of the Fifth Monarchists on him as the enemy of Christ. Anna Trapnel put it into words from, which he would have angrily winced, when she said, 'As to thy name General… where is thy victory, thy righteousness, they zeal, thy love, thy conquest now?' She said he had better have died in his tent on the battlefield than 'to come into this great Palace, which the Lord will rend from thee'.

Cromwell's soldiering had always had a mystical tinge: he had been Christ's General in a way that had been at once literal and mystical, and perhaps in the back of his mind floated the constant sensation of Christ's imminent proximity on the field of war, if only he could read the will of God aright and obey it. At the last minute he drew back from the kingship, in case it might be at once heinous and impractical. In the event, Anglo-French allies were to defeat the Spanish at the Battle of the Dunes off Dover in 1658 and the English would retake Dunkirk, which the Spanish had used as a base for piracy.

This second investiture was a coronation in all but name. The coronation throne, otherwise known as St Edward's Chair, in which English monarchs had been enthroned since 1308, was brought from Westminster Abbey to Westminster Hall and placed on a platform, draped in 'a prince-like canopy of state'. On a table, covered in pink Genoa velvet fringed with gold, were placed a robe of purple velvet, lined with ermine, a gilt-bound Bible, a sword and a sceptre. The ceremony was almost completely secular, and the Speaker of the House took the role traditionally assigned to the Archbishop of Canterbury.

Cromwell enjoyed this regal status for just over a year. On the anniversary of the Battles of Dunbar and Worcester, 3 September 1658, he died. After an autopsy, the corpse was embalmed and placed in a double coffin of wood and lead but his spleen had suppurated to the degree that 'the filth broke through them all' and it was considered prudent to bury him immediately. A wax effigy was now constructed, using his death-mask for the face, to lie in state with magnificent obsequies, a royal tradition. The effigy was dressed in the Protector's finest outfit, topped with a purple robe. An orb and sceptre were placed beside it and the cheeks painted. On a chair behind this idol was placed 'an imperial crown'. Half-way through the lying-in-state the effigy was sat up, the lids were opened over its glass eyes and the crown was placed on its head. This proceeding would have seemed so preposterous to the Cromwell of Marston Moor, of Dunbar, of the 'Barebones' Parliament as to be impossible, a nightmare or a mockery.

John Aubrey attended the funeral, which he described as 'superb'. He noted the 'velvet bed of state drawn by six horses housed with the same… Oliver lying in effigy in royal robes, and crowned with a crown'. He expanded on the richly caparisoned horses and the retinue of soldiers, 'but it was the joyfullest funeral that ever I saw, for there was none that cried, but dogs, which the soldiers hooted away with a barbarous noise; drinking, and taking tobacco in the streets as they went…'

CHAPTER 5

KING CHARLES II

PLAGUE
AND
FIRE

s the fleet of King Charles II crossed the Channel for his Restoration, Lady Ann Fanshawe was with it. She describes the voyage with exultant serenity: the ships ploughing through the waves to music, over a Channel strangely calm and luminous as if seen in a masque or dream.

Who can sufficiently express the joy and gallantry of that voyage? To see so many gallant ships... to hear the trumpets, and all other music; to see near an hundred brave ships sail before the wind with... above all, their glorious majesties of the King and his two brothers, – was so beyond man's expectation and expression. The sea was calm; the moon shone at full; and the sun suffered not a cloud to hinder the prospect of the best sight; by whose light and by the merciful bounty of God he was set safely on shore at Dover in Kent upon the 25th of May, 1660.

Samuel Pepys, 'with child to see any strange thing', was in the boat with the king as it sailed from Holland. He watched as Charles changed the names of the ships from their republican names to royalist ones: the *Naseby* became the *Royal Charles*; the *Speaker*, the *Mary*; the *Dunbar*, the *Henry*. At a breath all Cromwell's providential battles were blown out like candles in the great reversal of 1660. Pepys, who nearly blew his own eye out firing off a gun in the deafening salvo of naval acclamation, was thrilled to sit with the king on the voyage and be told the amazing story of Charles's escape from Worcester. Upon disembarking at Dover, with a little dog Charles was fond of (which had shat in the boat, making them all laugh and Pepys privately to think that 'a King and all that belong to him are but just as others are'), he watched the greeting between Charles and General Monck, who had been instrumental in gaining his recall. 'Infinite the crowd of people and the gallantry of the horsemen, citizens and noblemen of all sorts,' he recalls. Dover Beach was black with people, and the road to London an uninterrupted mass of cheering folk, 'like one street', as Ann Fanshawe said.

CONCILIATION, COMPROMISE AND CONSTANCY

Meanwhile, as republicans and regicides either crossed the Channel in the opposite direction, used all their influence to escape punishment or waited with pale, stoical faces to account for themselves, there was a rustling as thousands of officials turned coat and a frantic scratching of quills on paper as poets who had perhaps eulogized the Protectorate polished their couplets to eulogize the monarchy. John Dryden, who had been Cromwell's chamberlain and had lamented the Protector's death in *Heroic Stanzas* (1658), came out in a rash of anxious poetical sycophancy to welcome Charles in *Astraea Redux* as Justice, 'Long-Suffering, Goodness, Mercy' returned to the abject and chaotic English shores.

Charles, returning at the age of thirty from an exile that had lasted all his young manhood, had the easy cynicism to smile ironically at the sudden new monarchists who mushroomed in the dark soil of his native land. He understood the necessities and intrigues involved in survival, having dodged from country to country on the continent, according as Commonwealth and Protectoral foreign alliances dictated, forced to scrounge his court's living and eat the bitter bread of charity. Dryden was to become one of the most celebrated dramatists and the wittiest satirists of the reign. He would attain the laureateship and be converted to Catholicism, in which faith he would, like Charles himself, die.

Charles had given up expecting to be restored to the throne of England. When the Protectorship had passed to Oliver's son, Richard ('Tumbledown Dick' to the Cavaliers), hope had been at a low ebb, in the absence of any sign of popular will for his return. Even as Richard's fragile reign spiralled towards chaos, there appeared no stirring of active royalist counter-revolution. Penruddock's rising in 1655, and later Sir George Booth's 1659 rebellion (which he initiated in Cheshire, Lancashire and north Wales in favour of a free Parliament), went off like damp squibs, though the latter caused profound terror in the north. Autobiographies and diaries record the population's weariness of instability. In July 1659 Manchester was called to arms, 'upon the score of the Quakers being up', which the moderate Presbyterian minister Henry Newcome took leave to doubt. But 500 men mustered in Warrington under Booth. In August there was an alarm that the Levellers were coming with a regiment from Yorkshire. Then came a 'terrible' alarm, as 'the Earl of Derby came in with a troop of horse; and they shot off their pistols, which did somewhat disturb us'. Throughout August Newcome was too nervous to preach or do anything more than huddle waiting to see if Manchester would be sacked, and after Booth's rebellion, he was stigmatized for trying to mediate between Booth and General John Lambert. The town was full of soldiers, people being hauled out of bed to prison, the taking of horses, seques-

The Restoration of Charles II from exile in Europe in 1660 was greeted by ecstatic crowds.

trations, the plundering of houses. Newcome, with his non-martial, non-ideological, compromising mentality, was typical of those who had felt the earth shifting under their feet for too long, and asked only that the violence and change should end.

In April 1659, Generals Fleetwood and Lambert had forced Richard to dissolve his Parliament and resign. They recalled the Rump, which tottered back, rubbing its eyes, and was in turn dissolved by the army. A euphemistically titled Committee of Safety was then set up, leading to a violent split in the army, so that the country only just avoided civil war. On New Year's Day 1660 General Monck crossed the Scottish border into England, stating his intention to deliver the nation from 'the intolerable slavery of sword government'. In a country frantic for peace, Monck, with Fairfax's co-operation, recalled the Rump, fleshed out with excluded members of the Long Parliament, which agreed to dissolve itself. A new Parliament, known as 'The Convention Parliament', was elected. Monck and Charles, ably advised by Edward Hyde, had been engaged in secret correspondence, and Charles issued the Declaration of Breda in April 1660, a masterly document, which offered a tolerant and soothing message to all sections of the population. It promised to leave the problem of confiscated property to Parliament, pledged 'liberty to tender consciences', thus reassuring Independents and the army, and allayed the fears of Interregnum collaborators by pledging a free and general pardon for all except those named by Parliament.

Oliver Cromwell's elder surviving son, Richard, became Lord Protector in 1658. Nicknamed 'Tumbledown Dick' by the royalists, he was deposed the following year.

Charles was well qualified to take over power harmoniously. All parties in the twenty years of conflict had become sullied and implicated: Charles, through sheer absence, was free of all implication. His reputation (despite his many mistresses) and his loyalty to the Church of England had been preserved intact and he had never allowed himself to become embroiled in foreign entanglements sufficiently to damage his reputation. He also had the capacity for compromise so critically lacked by his father, as well as the common touch, and a warm charm and gentleness of manner immensely to his advantage. A decade of exile had deposited in him a cynical, hard-boiled political realism which, with his urbane wit, permitted him to take men at the lowest common estimate. On the euphoric day of his welcome into London, Charles commented that so many people had assured him that they had always longed for his return that it must have been his own fault that he was out of the country so long.

He was constitutionally idle and dilatory, with an intuitive awareness of when it might be better to do nothing. In person he was impressive, extremely tall (well over six foot), and with engaging manners. He started as he was to remain for twenty years, in chronic debt. The smooth constitutional transition did not include a financial settlement. Nor did Hyde insist on this, for a country bled dry by years of punitive taxation and a new economic downturn might not warm to the idea of being further squeezed. The royalist intellectual Sir Samuel Tuke described the king's appearance in 1660:

An affable cynic, philanderer and amateur scientist, Charles II governed deviously, lived amorously, spent prodigally and died a Catholic.

He is somewhat taller than the middle stature of Englishmen… His face is rather grave than severe, which is very much softened whensoever he speaks; his complexion is somewhat dark, but much enlightened by his eyes, which are quick and sparkling.His hair, which he hath in great plenty, is of a shining black, not frizzled, but so naturally curling into great rings that it is a very comely ornament.

Tuke noted Charles's athleticism, his love of tennis, walking, riding and swimming, and emphasized his 'easiness of access, his patience in attention, and the gentleness both in the tune and style of his speech', reassuring to those meeting him for the first time. The republican Edmund Ludlow, however, sickened by the sight of the Cromwellian army leaders attending 'this cowardly enemy' and the 'giddy multitude' fawning on him, saw only a hideous creature passing along the street: 'his looks were ghastly at the best… full of revenge'. Charles's face was gaunt and lined, and wore an expression of settled melancholy much at variance with the popular image of the 'merry monarch'.

As the Revolution had foundered, there were republicans who notably disdained to turn coat or renounce their most profound beliefs. In 1660 Milton published under his own name, in the teeth of the merely obvious, a virulent attack on monarchy, *The Ready and Easy Way to Establish a Free Commonwealth*, at a time when others had either gone expediently silent or were publishing anonymously. There is no publisher's or bookseller's name on the book. He pointed out that most salient of facts: that a monarchy is expensive:

a king must be adored like a demigod, with a dissolute and haughty court about him, of vast expense and luxury, masques and revels, to the debauching of our prime gentry, both male and female; nor at his own cost, but on the public revenue; and all this to do nothing but bestow the eating and drinking of excessive dainties, to set a pompous face upon the superficial actings of State, to pageant himself up and down in progress among the perpetual bowings and cringings of an abject people.

The second edition came out in April; Charles returned in May. The blind, heroic Milton went into hiding in a room in Bartholomew Close, off West Smithfield. The ten days during which the Commons debated on whose should be the twenty names extra to the regicide signatories, for execution as traitors, must have been the darkest days of Milton's life. Slowly the names came out:

John Milton, poet and revolutionary, narrowly escaped execution at the Restoration and composed the great epic, Paradise Lost, *in his blindness.*

Lenthall, Vane, St John, Haslerig, Lambert… On 16 June, the immediate arrest was ordered of Milton and John Goodwin, and books by each were burned by the public hangman. The nineteenth name was declared as Goodwin's. One name remained. Milton was proposed but found no seconder. The poet was spared, an experience that may have been as painful to Milton as it was to John Hutchinson, who never got over the dishonour of having been spared when so many of his friends suffered death. It is thought that Andrew Marvell, MP for Hull, and possibly also the royalist poet, Sir William Davenant, for whom Milton is believed to have intervened in similar circumstances, spoke for him. Milton emerged from hiding, only to be taken into custody. He received an official pardon in December and was persecuted no further by the regime; only by his own wrestle with despair. He was already composing at dictation *Paradise Lost*, the child of the Revolution and its defeat:

> More safe I sing with mortal voice, unchanged
> To hoarse or mute, though fallen on evil days,
> On evil days thought fallen, and evil tongues;
> In darkness and with dangers compassed round,
> And solitude…

For Milton, fallen on evil days, evil tongues, and for many who had remained faithful to the 'good old cause', Israel had turned about in the wilderness and gone creeping back into Egyptian captivity.

Charles urged the Convention to pass the Act of Indemnity and Oblivion, which pardoned all but a hundred individuals. He balanced the conciliation of his erstwhile enemies against the reward of his long-term friends, rather in the former's favour, embittering his allies but ensuring that he quietened by stroking sensibilities he would have exacerbated by punishing.

RETRIBUTION AND TOLERATION

The body of Cromwell, along with those of Ireton and Bradshaw, was dug up and the putrefied corpses dragged through London on a hurdle, to be hanged in their green-stained grave clothes at Tyburn. The heads were hacked off and impaled on poles at Westminster Hall. The surviving regicides were executed, drawn and quartered in an atmosphere of terrible festival. For the surviving 'saints', the epoch shook their faith to its roots. 'The Lord has blasted us and spit in our face,' said Fleetwood. 'God did seem to be more cruel than men,' recalled Lodowick Muggleton, founder of a mystical radical sect, the Muggletonians.

In October, Pepys was part of a crowd watching Major-General Thomas Harrison hanged, drawn and quartered. As Harrison was pulled through the streets of London, a jeering watcher cried, 'Where is your good old cause now?' to which Harrison nobly replied, 'It is in my heart and I shall seal it with my blood.' Pepys described how 'cheerfully' Harrison met his terrible end, expecting to be sitting on the right hand of Christ that very day, although 'his wife doth expect his coming again'. The diarist meditated for a while on his strange fortune in seeing King Charles I beheaded at Whitehall and now this theatre of retribution: and strolled off with his friends to dine on oysters at the Sun Tavern. The king, who had prevented the execution of the nineteen regicides who had turned themselves in, was sickened with the bloodshed. Only ten died at this time. The shadow of the Revolution lay like a dark pall over the whole reign and every twitch of unrest was looked upon as possible sedition. Plague became an all too real symbol of rebellion: the London mob which (the affluent believed) fomented the plague had also generated fever in the body politic. Charles jested with the embarrassed republican commanders of his spanking new navy that, having had a dose of plague, they would be immune to any new infection. In the king's jokes lay a dark kernel of caution.

Although all his instincts and endeavours lay in the direction of toleration, this was not the view taken by the bitter Cavalier Parliament that sat from 1661 to 1678. The religious settlement enshrined in the Act of Uniformity of 1661, restoring bishops and ejecting Presbyterian and other undesirable ministers, prohibiting religious meetings outside the restored Anglican Church, treated all nonconformists as well as Catholics as if they presented the same degree of threat. But half Charles's family was Catholic and most of the sects simply wanted, as he was aware, to worship in peace. One thousand dissenting clergymen were evicted from their livings. The severe Acts of persecution that followed, known misleadingly as the 'Clarendon Code', included the Conventicle Act of 1664 which banned religious services other than those of the Church of England, with punishments of fine, imprisonment and transportation. In 1665 the Five Mile Act prevented dissenting ministers from living within five miles of a town. The Bishop of London stated as the reason for this severity that, 'Those who will not be governed as men, by reason and persuasion, shall be governed as beasts, by power and force.'

The Manchester moderate, Adam Martindale, was a typical victim of these severities. Tried for rejecting the Prayer Book, he lost his living under the Act of Uniformity and lived poorly by school-mastering and working the earth at Tatton, under the kindly eye of Lord Delamere, patron of Presbyterians. At the Restoration Martindale suffered much abuse from a 'rabble of profane youths' who set up a maypole in front of his church on Bow Hillock, 'a rendezvous of rake-hells' where the lads and lasses traditionally danced and sang on Sundays. He accordingly preached against maypoles as 'a relic of the shameful worship of the strumpet Flora in Rome' and not long afterwards his wife, with three other brawny young women, sawed it down in the night. At this, the magistrate sent the constable to arrest the women, but found it impossible to prosecute them as there was no law on the statute books against mutilating maypoles. The incident finely captures the release of pent-up spirits as ordinary people returned to the traditional amusements which, as James I had seen, constituted all that made their lives worth living, and their spleen against the killjoys who had repressed their need for recreation; as well as the humourless but spirited energy of the 'godly', whose watchword was always 'Up and be doing'. By placing all shades of dissent in one category, the Cavalier Parliament did what the Commonwealth with its schisms had never managed to do: it created a large movement of English nonconformity, which throve under pressure for centuries.

Charles's instinct for toleration is shown in his attitude to the Quakers, whose visits he welcomed with amused curiosity, allowing them to keep their hats on in his company and to address him by the equalizing 'thou'. In 1660 Margaret Fell, the 'nursing mother of Quakerism', swept down on Charles in her black and costly silks, to rebuke him for the persecution of Friends, her gentry status affording her an entrée into the court that she used energetically. She saw the king weekly in the summer months of 1660 and deluged him with letters, interceding not only for Friends but also for the Commonwealthsmen who had persecuted Quakers. Addressing Charles and his brother James as 'Dear Heart' she warned them roundly against their dissipated mode of life, accusing them of spending their short time in England in 'wildness, in wantonness, in vanity, sporting yourselves' and signing herself, 'from one who cannot flatter'. The king, knowing that the Quakers had never been supporters of Cromwell, believed the assertion of the Peace Principle by Margaret Fell and George Fox. He intervened to free 700 Quakers from prison but, since their objection to taking oaths meant that they could not swear the Oath of Allegiance, they were gobbled into prison in greater numbers than Charles could free them. Charles's gentleness to the Quakers caused his government some embarrassment.

Venner's Rebellion in January 1661 put paid to hopes of toleration. Thomas Venner, a die-hard Fifth Monarchist, planned a violent uprising to inaugurate Christ's Second Coming. Most Fifth Monarchists, viewing the Restoration as a merited punishment on England for its sins, had adopted a posture of quietism, but on Sunday 6 January, Venner and fewer than fifty followers marched on St Paul's with a rallying-cry of, 'King Jesus, and the heads upon the gate!' Having worsted an armed party, they retreated into the woods near Highgate. On 9 January they emerged, to fight ferociously against the Life Guards and a whole regiment. Cacophonous panic spread and mass arrests began. Over 4,000 Quakers were imprisoned all over the country, in the most squalid conditions, as well as Baptists and members of other sects.

A period of atrocious persecution began, with local elites using every kind of violence on meetings and individuals. In London, when all the male Quakers had been beaten and imprisoned, the women took their places; when the women were arrested, the children came out; when meeting houses were razed to the ground, Friends came and prayed in silence on the ruins. John Bunyan, the Baptist minister of Bedford, used his years in prison to write the great testament to the Christian journey, *The Pilgrim's Progress*: 'As I walk'd through the wilderness of this world, I lighted on a certain place, where there was a den… And as I slept I dreamed a dream: I dreamed, and behold I saw a man clothed with rags… a book in his hand and a great burden upon his back…' This monument of the Puritan plain style, which brings into literature the colloquial language of the common people, also contains an allegorical account of Bunyan's trial, and gives a taste of the impartial judicial language which condemned dissenters. Faithful's judge at Vanity Fair, asked if the prisoner may speak a few words in his own defence, replies, 'Sirrah, sirrah, thou deservest to live no longer but be slain instantly upon the place…'

In 1662 the Quaker Act inaugurated ten years of religious suffering, which the king was unable to mitigate. Charles's Declaration of Indulgence, issued in December 1662, requesting the right from Parliament to spare persons from the full rigours of the law, was opposed, even by Hyde, as being an undue extension of his prerogative. The Commons refused even to discuss it and Charles was forced to revoke it the following year. For twenty years, the king compounded his own problems by swimming against the tide of Anglican intolerance for the sake of Catholics and Dissenters. His own views concerning religion seem to have been lackadaisical. Sermons he took as a soporific, and a preacher once called to another sleeping statesman, Lord Lauderdale to awaken him, explaining courteously, 'My Lord, I am sorry to interrupt your repose, but I must beg that you will not snore quite so loud, lest you should awaken his majesty.'

The detection of a 'northern conspiracy' provoked summary arrests and new heights of cruelty. Margaret Fell, tried at Lancaster in 1664, told the judge, 'I have the King's word from his own mouth, that he would not hinder me of my religion, God forbid (said he) that I should hinder you of your religion, you may keep it in your house.' Margaret was sentenced to *praemunire*, the medieval penalty of forfeiture of all her property and life imprisonment. Jailed along with George Fox in Lancaster Castle, Margaret remained there until her release by order of the king in 1668, writing four major books in prison, including *Women's Speaking Justified* (1667).

MONEY AND WAR

If Charles was unsuccessful in obtaining religious toleration, a position of relative impotence in relation to Parliament was reinforced by having to go to them with a begging-bowl, as had his father and grandfather. The settlement initially made on him of £1,200,000 per annum was insufficient to the requirements of a monarchy where lavish display was expected as a demonstration of rank. The sum was, in any case, notional, as it failed to materialize in full. The unpopular Hearth Tax was instituted in 1662 by the Cavalier Parliament, to add to the king's revenue. This tax was a levy on each house in relation to the number of hearths it contained. But the Cavalier Parliament failed to grasp the nettle of the king's finances in part because its members had not a secure grasp of public finance, and in part because of the awe-inspiring spectacle of the court's profligate spending. As Milton had prophesied, monarchy cost 'vast expense and luxury'.

Commercial interests and the English wish to recapitulate the foreign greatness it had lost with Cromwell led to the declaration of the Second Dutch War in 1665, which opened to a sensational naval victory off the shore at Lowestoft but issued in abject humiliation when, in 1667, the Dutch admiral, de Ruyter, broke through the boom across the Medway, sailed to the shipyards at Chatham and bombarded the English fleet, which was in dock for lack of funds. They towed away the *Royal Charles*, leaving warships blazing. The humiliating war, which had been opposed by Hyde, now Earl of Clarendon, was blamed on the unpopular earl by the populace, Parliament and Lords. The king, who had never liked the pompous, dictatorial Hyde, only used and needed him, sacrificed him and allowed him to be threatened with impeachment. Clarendon fled to the continent, where he devoted himself to writing his *History of the Great Rebellion*. Cynicism and faction held sway in the court, while the king retired as often as possible from dry public affairs into the company of mistresses, to his yachts (introduced from Holland by James), his home laboratory and the Royal Society, his clocks, astronomical telescope and microscopes, and to labouring to beget an heir on his Portuguese Catholic wife, Catherine of Braganza. That she was the barren party was proved by the many beautiful bastard children Charles sired and genially acknowledged, by serial mistresses, all of whom benefited in lands, jewels and titles. The eldest and favourite of his illegitimate children was born in April 1649, to Lucy Walters: his name was James, Duke of Monmouth, who, by standing as the Protestant alternative to Charles's hated brother, James, would become a personal nemesis.

By 1665, five years after Charles's accession, it was not yet certain that Catherine would never produce an heir. Then the nation was hit by a double catastrophe, seen by many in all parties as a judgement upon sin.

THE GREAT PLAGUE

Pepys, walking through London and seeing faces at a ground-floor window, was rattled to see, or think he saw, plague victims breathing out on passers-by, 'in spite to well people'. He shrank from the contagion with anger at such malevolence. Probably the faces he saw at the window were intimating nothing of the sort. Pepys was inwardly articulating the gentry's unconscious fear of the poor as a breeding-ground of fatal disease and envious insurrection. During the past decades, the sense of threat had been well-nigh constant: every man's hand had seemed to be against his neighbour. The fratricidal hostility simmering just beneath the surface of English social life, even in the relative political calm of the Restoration, was everywhere incipient. The experiences of plot, plague and fire bled their implications into one another, so that the seditious 'overturning' of the Civil Wars was understood in terms of the sickness of the body politic, and mobs were understood both literally and metaphorically to be carriers of plague. Plague might be God's punishment for plots, as might fires, ignited by plotters wishing to overturn the framework of society.

Pepys remained in the City of London during the plague, doing his bit for the navy, as he told Sir William Coventry in August, 1665: 'You, Sir, took your turn at the sword; I must not therefore grudge to take mine at the pestilence.' The Dutch War was still raging: Pepys's work on the Navy Board was to professionalize the administration of the service. He sent his household away to the fresh air of Woolwich, then moved them to Greenwich. He was one of few members of the elite to remain in London. The court decamped to Hampton Court, thence to Salisbury, but, the disease following them there, they retreated to the safety of Oxford, which had been King Charles I's headquarters in the Civil War and was thus commodious for persons used to a high measure of comfort.

The Great Plague that ravaged London and other cities in 1665 was the last wave of the pandemic that, as the Black Death, had cut the population of fourteenth-century Europe by one third. London had suffered devastating outbreaks in the fifteenth and early sixteenth centuries, climaxing in the appalling plagues of 1563, 1593, 1603 and 1625. There had also been outbreaks in the mid-1640s as people were uprooted and enclosed in garrison towns. Bristol lost a quarter of its population in 1644–5 and at Newark in 1646 a thousand lives were lost. As the 1665 plague flared up in London, and sent its hot fingers out in the form of affluent refugees fleeing, country-dwellers were instantly alerted and avoided London traders who might sell an infection with a purchase. The Essex minister Ralph Josselin was appalled in 1665 that the government had issued 'no call to repentance'. He trembled for his young and feckless son Tom, whom he had sent to the capital as an apprentice six years back. Later he heard that the plague had struck Colchester and feared it would reach him at Colne, but comforted himself at Tom's being home, where he would remain until February of 1666. The search for causes of these devastating bouts of plague focused itself on the ethical and theological (for some, the astral) plane, as manifestations of divine anger. The plague thereby became symptomatic of non-medical problems, boils that must be diagnosed by prayer, and lanced by penitence, public penance and the purgation of the body politic, before the curse could be considered diagnosed.

The famous diarist, Samuel Pepys, not only recorded Restoration gossip, intimate experiences and the vivid colour of day-to-day life, but was also an able naval administrator.

Medical remedies owed more to imagination than reason. Aubrey quoted an eminent physician as saying that, if patients knew what quacks their doctors were, 'they would stone 'em in the streets'. Thomas Sydenham, perhaps the greatest of seventeenth-century physicians, maintained that physicians were a health hazard. Without antibiotics there was no treatment for plague: doctors prescribed to the rich exotic remedies or prophylactics, such as dried unicorn's horn or copious quantities of finest wine; to the poor, opiates or innards of toad. Because plague was supposed to be generated by foul vapours emanating from the earth's entrails and hanging on the air in 'miasma' or virulent atoms, herbs with refreshing, tangy odours were thought to protect against infection: nosegays of scented plants such as rosemary, whose price soared in time of epidemic. The London apothecary, William Boghurst, defined miasma as, 'a most subtle, peculiar, insinuating, venomous, deleterious exhalation arising from the maturation of the ferment of the faeces of the earth'. Each epithet expresses the despair of science, a compound of bafflement and repulsion, attached to a conception of earth as a female and cloacal underworld, with an animal compulsion to void her waste products. This image is linked with the recognition that the excrement of Londoners must have something to do with the cycle of plague, for householders were often requested to clear the street of effluent and middens, which, however, often ended up in the backyard.

Natural causes of plague were officially recognized and treatments investigated. The trouble was that the investigations tended to fizzle out into unimplemented reports.

In 1630 the College of Physicians and Sir Theodore Mayerne had been asked for guidance as to preventative measures. The College's analysis stressed public hygiene and population density, sewage and garbage in the streets, standing water, offal and rotting meat and slaughterhouses. Mayerne pointed to vagrants as carriers. He recommended a board of health for the capital and other cities, and the creation of isolation hospitals ('pesthouses'), district administrations and the slaughter of stray animals, including rats and mice, and the quarantining of ships from foreign parts. He drew on the plague-control methods in France and Italy for his proposals, which, because of costs, were not implemented. It was not known until the end of the nineteenth century that the bubonic plague bacillus is spread by the fleas of the black rat, *Rattus rattus*. The flea transmits the disease by injecting an undigested remnant of its last blood-meal into a new victim. Hence vermin extermination would have been an appropriate measure, and some parishes did employ rat-catchers, but the efficacy of this approach was cancelled out by the mass slaughter of dogs and cats, rats' natural predators, which was put into operation as the plague gathered force.

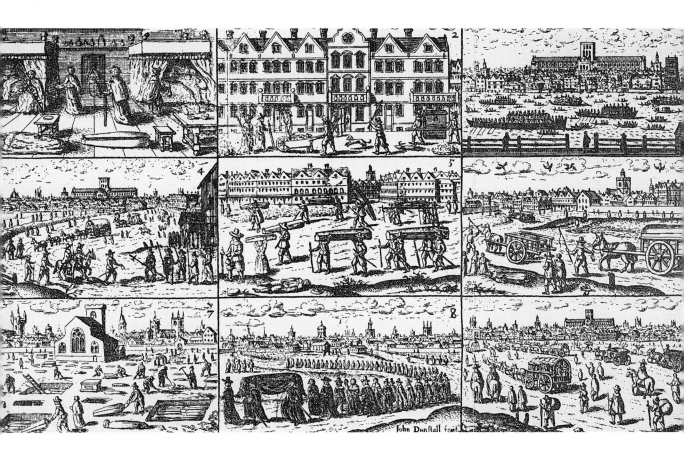

The devastation caused by the Great Plague, leading to mass burials in common pits, is graphically portrayed in a contemporary broadsheet.

The poor, who were the major victims of the Great Plague, left no testaments of how they lived and died. The Pepys-eye view and those of the diarists and letter-writers of the time are always views from above, tending to see the poor as beasts of burden, not quite as human as 'persons of quality'. It is the church wardens' and vestry minutes, the hearth tax accounts, poor law returns and local assessments, as well as the Bills of Mortality which had been initiated in the sixteenth century to indicate the onset of plague epidemics, which give some fragmentary insight into their suffering and the way they coped as individuals and communities. As the historian, Justin Champion, observes, 'One has enormous respect for the churchwardens who actually compile the accounts that we use… These are people who are looking after the community's welfare. They are recording meticulous details… how much a padlock cost and a shilling for the barbed wire, that was keeping the fence together. But that's what life's made of. Those little incremental bits of data.' It is from this scrupulous detail that the experience of the plague can be reconstructed.

In March of 1665, one case of plague appeared in the parish of St Giles. It had been an exceptionally bitter winter, with the Thames frozen over for two months, weather conditions that were known not to favour plague, and this, combined with the fact that plague was endemic to London, running at low levels every summer, raised no immediate concern. But the Great Plague was to kill at least 100,000 people, one in every three of the population of a city that had mushroomed, trebling its size in sixty years. The toll of deaths may well have been significantly higher, since people understandably tended to conceal the cause of death and, towards the peak, individual deaths went unmarked, the plague cart collecting bodies en masse at night, to be deposited in unconsecrated plague pits without memorial. Before the plague, a decent burial had been important to Londoners, and even when parishes were paying for the burial of paupers, a certain sensitivity was preserved, but mass death broke down these taboos.

The initial plague centre was St Giles-in-the-Fields, at the western margin of the city. In late June the Privy Council placed officials of adjacent parishes in the streets as warders to isolate the sick within the area and contain vagrants, but the plague had already got away, or may have had several simultaneous places of origin. A look at Cock and Key Alley, a street in St Dunstan in the west, a cramped courtyard behind a tavern, between Fleet Street and the Thames, reveals the community in miniature, struggling for survival. Parish documents help reconstruct this alley, which housed thirty poor families, in wooden tenements where space was at a premium and a family might have to share a room. The tenements were built outwards from the core buildings, extemporizing as London bulged to accommodate the constant rush of immigrants. At the best of times, these families clung on to the London economy by their fingernails. A widow such as Mrs Andrews eked a living by caring for parish orphans and disabled children; William Gurney ran the alehouse and sold groceries; John Gale doubled as a blacksmith and fireman; Thomas Birdwhistle was a parish scavenger responsible for clearing away the muck from the streets; and John Dudley was collector of alms and parish constable. William Penny was a grave-maker. Penny had until recently been receiving the alms Dudley collected. He lived in a single room with his wife and two younger sons, Edward and John, while his elder son acted as his apprentice. In this community on the edge of

This engraving from 1600 shows the London skyline dominated by medieval St Paul's Cathedral,
surrounded by overcrowded, timber-framed houses and tenements.

survival, the person with the greatest prestige was Henry Dorsett, the senior churchwarden. Yet Dorsett too knew what it was to balance on the precarious threshold between pauperdom and relative stability.

Dorsett was now in an administrative position in Cock and Key Alley. He raised taxes and donations, appointed constables and rakers to cleanse the streets. Literacy qualified him as a man for this position, since the preservation of order and financial administration at local level depended on the detailed recording of every parish transaction. The meticulous minutiae of these parish accounts reveal traces of the ordeal undergone by families such as the Pennys and widows such as Mrs Andrews. At the best of times they lived in conditions of filth and stench inimical to life, doing the ill-paid, unpleasant jobs nobody else wanted to do. But at least they had roofs over their heads. They came under the umbrella of the parish, slipping in and out of a condition of partial dependency.

When the plague was perceived by the city to be taking hold, alehouses, cock- and bear-pits, theatres and all places where people mingled at close quarters were shut down, William Gurney's tavern being among them. Then stray dogs and cats were rounded up and exterminated, at the rate of two pennies per corpse. The Chamberlain disbursed funds for the killing of approximately 40,000 dogs and 80,000 cats. The historian Carol Rawcliffe observes, 'It's ironic that all these animals are being exterminated when they would be able to kill the rats which are spreading the plague.'

In May the Lord Mayor had the Plague Orders issued by every parish priest, with the regulation procedures to be followed. Any affected family was to be locked in its house for a quarantine period of forty days, both the sick and the healthy persons. Some welfare might be provided in the form of food and the attentions of a nurse. A red cross a foot in height and the inscription THE LORD HAVE MERCY UPON US was painted on the door, while watchmen were engaged to ensure that nobody escaped and searchers appointed to examine the dead bodies for the telltale buboes in the groin or armpit, swellings that could be as large as a hen's egg, and the 'tokens' or blotches on the skin. Death was swift but terrible after the onset of symptoms, with intense pain in the tender swellings, high fever and raving delirium. The policy of boarding up the whole family certainly increased the death toll, mortally endangering the entire family group. Within the household it created foulness: houses became boxes of filth that had to be unsealed to allow food to be handed in and the dead to be carried out.

The first victim in Cock and Key Alley was a child, Dorothy Chessington. With the spring, the heat increased. Pepys experienced a pang of agitation on seeing a door in Drury Lane marked with the cross, a novelty that would become a norm: 'It put me into an ill conception of myself and my smell, so that I was forced to buy some roll-tobacco to smell to and chaw – which took away the apprehension.' Pepys provides valuable insights not only into the external sights of London but also into his internal responses: he begins to imagine that he is breathing in the fume of contagion and resorts both to smelling the sweetness and chewing tobacco, believed to be an antidote to the vapours. By and by he observes his nerves calming, no doubt aided by nicotine. Pepys's invincible hedonism made diversion swift and easy. Next day he was too taken up with the naval victory at Lowestoft for morbid preoccupation.

The court lingered in London to greet the victors, the Duke of York and the other naval commanders, before absconding to purer regions. Physicians and clergymen decamped, along with persons of substance, abdicating all responsibility for the thousands with nowhere to go, no means to travel and no certificate to leave. The historian Steven Porter describes the mass exit: 'The wealthy and the well-to-do left first of all – the court and then the gentry, even the people from the middling sections of society, if they'd somewhere to go, they left… And the physicians went because they said they had to go with their clients who of course were the wealthy. And a number of the parish clergy also left and that was really thought to be improper.'

In Cock and Key Alley only John and Elizabeth Davy were permitted grants to leave the stricken city. Londoners' sense of betrayal by the clergy was strongly felt, in a city whose affiliations had been overwhelmingly Puritan before the Anglican clergy were forced on them. Some priests did remain to share the dangers with their flocks, but the Bishop of London, disgusted by the ignoble exodus, felt called upon to warn his self-interested shepherds that they would lose their incumbencies if they did not return. Nonconformist ministers, excluded by the Five Mile Act, came in to comfort the afflicted, bury the dead, and preach against the depravity and vanity of the court. Throughout the crisis, the Quakers maintained their high morale. According to their fastidious records, 1,177 Friends died in London. Many of them were in prison, and, using their sophisticated system of relief donations, Gilbert Latey, a former court-tailor, channelled money from the country meetings for the London victims. Ellis Hookes, a Friend ministering to the sick in London, wrote of the desolation of going to bed unable to sleep 'a wink for the groans of them that lay a-dying'. The Quakers encouraged one another to show compassion 'not only though especially to them of the household faith, but to all that are in distress', as William Caton put it.

With the exodus of the rich came a financial crisis, since the well-to-do were no longer available for local levies: they had not only escaped the disease itself but shrugged off any responsibility for its victims. The plague was appropriately known as 'the Poor's Plague', although the Archbishop of Canterbury, the Bishop of London, and various persons of note remained, such as the Earl of Craven (who later made a report to the Privy Council on the government's handling of the crisis), and high-minded people such as George Monck, Earl of Albemarle. The Lord Mayor carried on his affairs within a specially designed glass chamber, which would prevent infection. The financial shortfall was in part answered by charitable collections from all over the country, commanded by the king, and from the pockets of private individuals. But in London itself trade was at a standstill, and realization dawned of the interdependence of the society that lived on exchange that was no longer to be considered safe. Coins changed hands after having been dipped in vinegar; all comestibles were suspect, since bread and other foodstuffs might well carry contamination. The interface between man and man was covered in a patina of dread.

Because the plague took a pneumonic as well as a bubonic form, spreading through sneezes and coughs, attacking the lungs, people wore masks. Apothecaries who continued to visit households, a lucrative but dangerous profession, often practised a kind of barrier nursing, entering stricken houses wearing waxed leather coats and beak-like face masks containing aromatic herbs. This strange garb may indeed have given protection from the fleas, as might the vinegar daubed on their hands. They were in the front line of what care there was, along with the nurses and searchers, often needy women from the bottom of the social heap. These women picked up a bad reputation, as if malevolently pledged to spread disease: they were believed to rob the dying and dead or to strangle them to hasten their passage. In actuality they often acted with extraordinary probity. Nurse Fletcher in Cock and Key Alley had the integrity to declare one pound, eight shillings, which she had found in Mr Short's trunk, a large sum to her. Female deaths outnumbered male in the plague year, because of their front-line role, and as housekeepers and servants left to safeguard their absentee masters' houses from looting.

In Cock and Key Alley the second person infected was the widow, Rebecca Andrews, who was boarded in with the foundling in her care, Lawrence Dunstan. John Gale, the smith, was paid three shillings and tuppence for fixing hasps, hooks and padlock to her door, and John Dudley was set to keep her house under surveillance. Widow Briggs and Widow Manton became searchers in the alley, and were ordered (as potential carriers of the disease) to live together. Rebecca Andrews died, followed next day by the child. Brokers of the dead would confiscate belongings of those without heirs; these goods would be sold and the proceeds used to pay for apothecaries and nurses for paupers. By late June, Anne Bradshaw, Daniel Jackson, Peter Ray and Roger Charles had died in the alley, and the Pennys were incarcerated when William Penny detected the tokens on himself. As he was the gravedigger, one of the few thriving trades left in London, his son Joseph was deputed to remain outside the house and take over his work. The Penny children died first.

August was scorching hot. Pepys blenched as he met corpses in London's narrow alleys. But a morbid yen seized him to go and view the plague pit at Moorfields, an itch almost libidinous to find out, '(God forgive my presumption) whether I could see any dead corpse going into the grave'. He did not. Within a couple of months the sight of corpses was so normal as scarcely to impinge. In the four weeks of August, numbers of plague deaths leapt from 2,817 to 3,880 to 4,237 to 6,102. Experiments with fumigation appeared hopeful when James Angier burnt a mixture of brimstone, saltpetre and amber in a street off High Holborn, creating a stench so hellish that the very rats ran away. Inhabitants were ordered to burn fires in their streets in early September: the air was thick with smoke for three days until a rainstorm quenched them. The death toll went on remorselessly rising, to reach 6,988 in the first week of the month. Major streets became eerily empty. The passing bell chimed without interruption until it gave up altogether. To John Evelyn, London seemed a phantasmal ghost-city, full of 'coffins exposed in the streets and the street thin of people, the shops shut up, and all in mournful silence, as not knowing whose turn might be next'. On 20 September Pepys observed recrudescence in the streets round Whitehall, where grasses had seeded themselves. The level of the churchyards was rising higher with new burials. The Bible taught that 'in the midst of life we are in death': now the hosts of the dead seemed to turn the city into a necropolis.

Through it all, the urban poor trapped in their atrocious affliction coped and kept some sort of order in the absence of the 'noble' sort. A small number of riots broke out as people fought the death sentence of family incarceration. But in general the system held. However, the rituals that asserted civic and religious values of life began to collapse. A dead child was tossed over the wall into a churchyard. The dead no longer had names. As swollen graveyards could take no more, dead carts went round collecting bodies like so much waste. Joseph Penny's business thrived: he helped to bury 500 parishioners in seven pits, sealing them under planks. The intolerable stench of putrefaction pervaded the city. In October Joseph himself died.

The plague suddenly abated with the first frosts and refugees began to return, too quickly as it turned out, for they had less immunity than those who had lived through the epidemic. There was a new small peak in December, causing transient agitation. In February 1666 the court returned. In Cock and Key Alley thirty-six men, women and children (half the inhabitants) had died. Of the gravedigger's family, only Elizabeth remained alive. The churchwarden bought back the tools of her husband's trade: 'Three shovels and a basket: 4 shillings and 4 pence.'

Recuperation in London, and in the other towns affected, was rapid. The capital was an irresistible magnet to those, especially young people, in search of employment and an environment less constricted and more potentially lucrative than that in the provinces. London was now porous with vacancies, which were quickly filled. As the death rate fell to pre-plague levels, the birth-rate rose, and within a generation the capital had replenished its stock. But it took longer than a generation to shake off the infection of the public imagination, where the plague stuck like a *memento mori*, before which the community had been helpless. Pepys survived, perhaps because he had a blood group not favoured by the fleas of *Rattus rattus*: he noted that when sharing a bed in a dubious Portsmouth lodging-house with his friend Timothy Clarke, 'all the fleas came to him and not to me'. His elasticity of spirits was such as to permit him to rebound from the universal woe into a perverse state of sybaritic contentment: on the last day of 1665, he was able to record, 'I have never lived so merrily (besides that I never got so much) as I have done this plague-time.'

THE GREAT FIRE OF LONDON

In 1667, Milton's great epic, *Paradise Lost*, was licensed for publication, to be sold by three booksellers on the margins of the charred ruins of the City of London. The poem had been completed by the Plague Year. The epic opens in a hell where fire and despair are a single demonic terrain, where all underfoot is molten: 'a fiery deluge, fed/With ever-burning sulphur unconsumed', whose soil under the 'unblest feet' of Lucifer is a surface of solid flame, like a volcanic wasteland, 'a singed bottom all involved/With stench and smoke'. When John Evelyn ventured out into the City of London on 10 September 1666, he entered a territory of apocalyptic catastrophe: 'I went again to the ruins,' he writes, 'for it was now no longer a City.' As he walked through the still-smouldering remains, he frequently lost his bearings, 'the ground under my feet so hot, as made not only sweat, but even burnt the soles of my shoes'.

As Dr Simon Thurley, Director of the Museum of London, points out, 'For the previous ten or fifteen years, people had been worried about what might happen in 1666. It was regarded as the most dangerous year because 666 is the mark of the beast in the Book of Revelation in the Bible.' The year was expected to bring forth wonders or horrors. Hester Biddle, the Quaker prophet, had issued a blast of *The Trumpet of the Lord* in 1662, from Newgate Prison: 'Oh London London!... [God's] notable, terrible, and dreadful Day is coming upon thee as at noon day, and from it thou canst not escape... Oh! Calamity, upon Calamity, Misery upon Misery, Plagues upon Plagues, Sickness upon Sickness, and one Disease upon another... I will bathe my Sword in thy blood, and I will give thee blood to drink.'

The remaining Puritan incendiaries after the Restoration promised plague and it came; they prophesied fire, and that came too. Hester hurled her verbal thunderbolts predicting the 'fire of the Lord' a 'furnace in England'. She pointed to the 'high and lofty ones' who neglected to 'feed the hungry, clothe the naked, but they are ready to perish in the streets; both old and young, lame and blind lyeth in your streets, crying for bread, which even melteth my heart'. It was hardly surprising that the torrid predictions of fire were fulfilled, given the packed, inflammable state of London, with its huddling, interconnected timber tenements, and the absence of a centralized fire-fighting corps. Hester, a firebrand who was in and out of prison fourteen times after the 1650s, and would even take herself off to remonstrate with Louis XIV in 1696, was herself an economic casualty of the Fire. Her husband's cordwaining business never recovered and she ended up living in widowed penury.

In 1661 John Evelyn had deplored the way 'this glorious and ancient City… should wrap her stately head in clouds of smoke and sulphur, so full of stink and darkness'. Fires were commonplace in the timbered buildings that shouldered each other for space in the prestigious, medieval centre. The tight-packed lanes, yards and alleys crammed the areas off the main streets with businesses and families, and the use of lath and plaster infilling for timber-framed buildings (known as 'paper buildings') was a recognized fire hazard. Regulations had been adopted to introduce brick and stone rather than wood in new buildings, to replace thatch roofs with tiles, and to stop the practice of 'jettying', or building projecting upper storeys to eke out space. This encroachment into the street was an open invitation to fire to leap the fire-break. Fires were expected and normal. But when the Great Fire came, it seemed like a visitation from God – or the Pope. A Catholic arsonist conspiracy had been detected in April of 1666 and its protagonists executed. They had by intriguing coincidence timed their projected attempt for 3 September, Cromwell's 'Dunbar' day, for astrological reasons. The astral influences had indicated that this would be an auspicious date on which to destroy the shrine of lucre and Protestantism.

That summer, like its plague-stricken predecessor, had been tinder-try. Just after midnight after his hard day's work on Saturday, 1 September 1666, Thomas Faryner and his household took themselves off to bed as usual. Faryner was the royal baker in Pudding Lane, a profession like brewing, dying, metalwork and laundry, to which fire was endemic, because of the nature of forges, ovens and fuel. (In 1676 an oil shop would cause a fire that devastated Southwark High Street. In 1698 a laundry-woman's negligence would initiate the destruction of Whitehall Palace.) Ivan Day, the food historian, points out that, 'Cook shops where you could buy a pie or piece of roast pork often contained four or five spits with about six joints on, turned by two or three little boys, so what you have is an enormous fire, sometimes going up canopies that were made of wattle and daub.'

In a bakery, quantities of flammable material – faggots of kindling wood or gorse – were stored, to feed the intense bonfire in the large beehive-shaped oven, heating the bricks. When the embers were raked out, the first batch of wholemeal bread (cheet or cockle bread for the commoners, 'gentlemen's loaves' made with refined white flour for the 'quality') went in at a high temperature, succeeded by pies as the oven lost heat and finally, more delicate foods, like custards and biscuits. Take-away 'chewit pies', wrapped perhaps in yesterday's pamphlet or news-sheet, were also baked. The royal baker mass-produced for the guilds' official feasts. In a bolting house separated from the bakery stood vast hutches of flour, which had to be sieved through silk, muslin and rag. Country house bakeries were situated well away from residential accommodation, but in the city the bakery might stand, like Faryner's, in lethal proximity to other businesses. In a cellar adjacent to his bakehouse, a twentieth-century excavation disinterred the remains of carbonized barrels of pitch. This inflammable tarry substance, in common use for waterproofing, would have sent a timber-framed warehouse up like a bomb, when ignited by the bakehouse fire. The whole area, near the Thames, and at the centre of a thriving trade area, was a fuel deposit, with stacked barrels of substances such as wine and oil.

Only the most elementary fire-fighting equipment was available in 1666: buckets of water, grappling hooks – and prayer.

Faryner insisted that he had raked out the embers of his oven and closed all doors in a responsible manner before retiring to bed. But from its first deep sleep, the family was awoken by choking smoke and evacuated the house from the windows. Raising the alarm was initially a slow business of drumming a general alert and assembling a chain of people with buckets of water: hoses did not yet exist. When the fire had consumed Pudding Lane, it burnt the Star Inn on Fish Hill, at the end of London Bridge, and seized on Thames Street, running parallel with the river, where oil, hemp, flax, pitch, tar, cordage, hops, wines and brandies were warehoused: all combustible. What happened in the Great Fire resembles a firestorm rather than the localized fires of, say, the London Blitz. In a firestorm, radiated heat, shooting upwards and branching sideways, creates its own wind by sucking air into the base of the fire to replace the gases it ejects into the atmosphere. Its energy can drag objects into it and flatten a person in its path. The descriptions by Pepys, Evelyn and the two Puritan ministers, Edward Waterhouse and Thomas Vincent, bring out the devouring momentum of the fire as it thrust forward the line of radiated heat, like a creature with its own volition.

When the Lord Mayor, Sir Thomas Bludworth, was first roused, he was famously unimpressed and grumbled that a woman could have pissed it out. The real experts were ignored. When sailors advised the creation of a significant firebreak by using gunpowder to blow up houses around the fire, the mayor could not get his officers to co-operate: short-termism prevailed, since each man had a vested interest in keeping his own property intact, if it were not in immediate proximity. By the end of Sunday, the fire had swallowed about half a mile along the Thames, from Queenhithe to Cannon Street. Guildhalls and churches had been gutted. When Pepys contacted the king and the Duke of York, he was dispatched to the mayor, with orders to demolish houses in the path of the fire. Bludworth was by this time beside himself, whimpering, 'Lord, what can I do? I am spent! People will not obey me. I *have* been pulling down houses. But the fire overtakes us faster than we can do it!' The city was now in full evacuation, with multitudes pushing carts, trundling barrels and carrying their possessions, either to float them away by river or to carry them along the congested streets. That evening Pepys and his wife observed from a small alehouse on Bankside: as the sky darkened, the fire glowed more dazzlingly, until it appeared as 'one entire arch of fire from this to the other side the bridge, and in a bow up the hill for an arch of above a mile long. It made me weep to see it.' So far Pepys was little more than a sightseer. The following day he would take precautions with his own property.

Vincent, reading God's wrath in the fire, recorded how, on Monday, Lombard Street, Gracechurch Street and part of Fenchurch Street were in flames, 'in the fashion of a bow'. Just as the Almighty had offered a rainbow to the justified Noah as a covenant of hope, so he sent to the City an ireful 'bow which had God's arrow in it with a flaming point'. Lombard Street, named from the Lombards, the Italian bankers who settled in London in the thirteenth century, lay at the heart of the banking community. The bankers had now bagged up their gold (there was no paper money) and carried it away to sanctuary outside the city limits. The coin that was financing the Dutch wars, subsidizing the king's household, holding the Exchequer in place, was literally in their vaults and must be safeguarded. King Charles and the Duke of York were noted for their active participation in the fire, getting their shoes wet and their hands dirty, co-ordinating the fire-fighting effort: this was seen as gallant and heartening to the populace. It was also a measure of the king's self-interest: he could not afford to allow the commercial heart of the city on which he depended to be destroyed, nor could he afford to allow riots and chaos to develop. Fire, plague and civil strife were closely aligned in the contemporary psyche.

Rumours were rife. Catholics had been seen in the act of sabotage. The conflagration was ascribed to a 'Dutch baker, who was bribed to do this work, and that the French went about scattering fireballs in the houses'. Smoke spied rising from the chimney of a Dutch baker in Westminster, a Mr Riedtveldt, aroused mob suspicion, and he was dragged out and beaten up. 'It will be a long time,' said the correspondent, 'before the people of London forget their wild rage against the foreigners.' At the end of Monday, the fire, which had now managed to leap across considerable distances from street to street, had what seemed an unstoppable momentum. It had crossed Cornhill, using the beams in clearance-sites as stepping stones, and burst from three directions in Cheapside. At night, there was no darkness, since the fire lit the desolation for ten miles around, a reminder of Milton's description of hell: 'Not light but rather darkness visible'. Evelyn thought of the 'Universal Conflagration' of Judgement Day. The sound of roaring and rattling as the fire rushed on must have reminded some of the sieges of the Civil Wars.

The effects were felt in a great radius from London. As Lisa Jardine, Christopher Wren's biographer, observes, 'When you have a fire of the intensity of the great fire of London, the effects on the environment are felt way beyond the confines of the city itself, so that three days after the outbreak of the fire, sixty miles away in Oxford, an astronomer, Mr Locke, became aware that the sunbeams shining through the clouds were tinged with a curious pink or red because of the smoke and ash that had drifted all the way from the seat of the fire.' Scorched silk was found in the Thames at Henley and burning papers were seen in the woods at Windsor.

By the end of Tuesday the fire had engulfed old St Paul's Cathedral, the towering medieval landmark which, even after a bolt of lightning had toppled the spire in the reign of Elizabeth, had soared over the capital, dwarfing the innumerable houses that huddled round its foot. It rushed up the workmen's scaffolding and caused massive lumps of stone to crash down into St Faith's Chapel, where the entire stock of the London booksellers was ruined. The merchants of the shopping centre of Cheapside had lost their costly wares in one incendiary afternoon. For the first time since Roman days, the Thames lay open to the naked eye from Cheapside. The Guildhall, with London Bridge and St Paul's Cathedral, one of the great civic symbols of the city's prosperity and pride, was gutted: Vincent saw it as a sublime 'bright shining coal as if it had been a palace of gold or a great building of burnished brass'. St Paul's had been for many years in a state of dereliction, a venerable colossus. When it surrendered to the fire, the lead melted and ran down 'as if it had been snow before the sun'; its immense timber beams and stones crashed down. The noise, like the storming of a fortress, became more deafening: Evelyn noted how 'the stones of St Paul's flew like grenados', while the pavements glowed fiery red.

Pepys, who had been up since daybreak transporting the remainder of the contents of his household to safety, dug a hole in the garden with his neighbour and colleague Sir William Batten, where they buried their wine and some documents, In the evening he dug another with Sir William Penn and buried more wine and a precious Parmesan cheese. He organized dockside labourers to blow up buildings round the Navy Office, which he saved.

On Wednesday 5 September, the king prevailed on city officials to blow up houses 'in a wider gap than any had yet been made by the ordinary method of pulling them down with engines'. At last the massive masonry buildings of the Temple and St Dunstan's Church blocked off its progress, the easterly wind abated and the co-ordinated efforts of fire-fighters in other crucial areas brought it under control. Masses of dispossessed people had been camped in Moorfields for several days, with scarcely any food or drink. Charles ordered bread distribution at markets and called for officials to be stationed in the crowded areas to ensure the safety of their belongings; he opened churches, chapels, schools and public buildings to the store of their possessions. Among the stunned population rumours still flared that foreign aliens 'were coming armed' to cut the English throats, now that they were weak and exposed: some said French, others Dutch.

Moorfields became a shanty town, as the homeless set up makeshift shelters, in which they remained throughout the winter. The poor struggled in the teeth of this new adversity while the government embarked on schemes of rebuilding on an undreamed-of scale. The catastrophe suddenly took on the aspect of a magnificent opportunity for

King Charles to possess a capital to rival that of Louis XIV's Paris, although the grandiose dream of a metropolis, on a geometrical plan with piazzas and wide boulevards, had to be abandoned as impractical and expensive. Within days of the fire, Christopher Wren, Robert Hooke and John Evelyn were putting forward schemes for the complete replanning of London, without reference to the piecemeal property rights that had existed before the catastrophe. Such plans had been mooted prior to the fire: in May of that year Wren had proposed to top the old St Paul's with a dome. The solution adopted was town planning on an unprecedented scale based on stringent planning regulations, whereby timber building would be banned in favour of brick, with wide, paved streets and markets, and conduits moved out of the main roads. A team of six architects,

The Great Fire, which raged for four days, began in Faryner's bakery in Pudding Lane and consumed over 13,000 houses and nearly ninety churches, including St Paul's, which is here seen catching light.

engineers and scientists, His Majesty's Commissioners for Rebuilding, including Wren, Hooke and Roger Pratt, assisted by master masons and wood carvers, Grinling Gibbons being one, were set to work out the plan. The city's acute monetary difficulties as a result of the fire were addressed by raising a coal tax.

The ruins were cleared, roads staked out, building begun. The Guildhall, Sessions and Custom Houses and the Royal Exchange were finished by 1671, while fifty-one parish churches were rebuilt over a period of twenty-seven years, often using the foundations of the original building and recycling the original stone. St Paul's Cathedral was the first dome to be seen in England. The king, scientific aficionado and amateur of architecture with an international perspective, welcomed Wren's and Hooke's astonishing plan: they would incorporate an externally magnificent and dominating dome with a more intimate inner perspective, by the ingenious means of enclosing an inner cone within the dome, with a hollow space between the two structures. Hooke and Wren worked as the twin lobes of one mind in creating what was at once the principal house of God in the country, a monument to the greatness and confidence of the English monarch and Parliament, and an optical instrument, demonstrating the new science. The building took forty years, during which the space for the dome could be used as an aperture on the sky in which Wren could conduct astronomical experiments. He was able to use the shafts of the building under construction to mount lenses vertically, making a massive telescope.

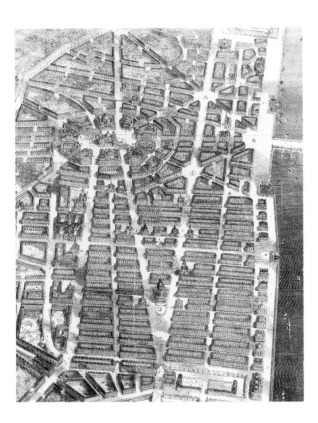

Sir Christopher Wren submitted one of many imaginative plans for the coherent rebuilding of London after the Great Fire, which showed the same rational geometry as his plans for St Paul's.

This harmony between a church which is seen as a monument to a rational God, the 'Divine Watchmaker', whose ideal is mathematical harmony, and a science which investigates the laws of the universe as a mirror of God's creation, represents the new age of rationalism that dawned with the formation of the Royal Society. In Hooke's engineering solutions to complex problems of stresses, and in Wren's dynamic concept of the modern architectural statement, the intellectual elite parted company with the mystical apprehension of the Cromwellian era. They celebrated a universe that was predictable and rational.

Yet this 'Augustan' vision had grown out of the ashes of chaos: plague and fire generated conditions for a new world that, even while it celebrated values of refinement and order, glanced round apprehensively at the turbulence in the life of the many. Out of the inordinate fire grew the cool geometry of St Paul's, which was consecrated in 1697 but not completed until 1711, incorporating the baroque principle of *trompe l'oeil* in grand simplicity which also gestures to the age of optics. This was the first of England's

Anglican cathedrals, all others being Catholic inheritances. It declares the power and centrality of God, church and king in a world that would continue to question and mock that power. The hanging of a mentally disturbed Frenchman, Hubert, for (as he suicidally and mendaciously confessed) starting the fire – which he could not possibly have done – was a manifestation of a lynch mob mentality with no concern for scientific probability. But some politicians, including Marvell and Sir Thomas Carew, continued to believe that the fire had been a plot and they nourished the flame of that idea well into the next generation.

Meanwhile, the cost in human terms was hardly counted and never compensated. Many people's lives were devastated, never to be rebuilt. The homeless, adaptable in adversity, accommodated themselves in tents using canvas from the navy yards, found new premises outside the city, or set up weavers', goldsmiths', salters' and cutlers' businesses within the precincts of St Bartholomew's Hospital, or built rickety booths to sell fish or cheese on the charred ruins of their old shops. But many never recovered, tipping into pauperdom and despair. Anthony Joyce, a tallow chandler, tried his hand at inn-keeping but lost the struggle and tried to drown himself: 'The sense of his great loss by the fire, did bring him to it.' Widows found their situation desperate. Elizabeth Peacock described how she and her husband and six children had lived in some comfort at the Horseshoe Inn in Snow Hill. Her husband and eldest son having died before the fire, she then lost everything, 'her whole stock of hay, coals and beer laid in for her winter provision and also all the furniture', leaving her with just over a pound in cash. From the charitable fund she received one guinea and a plot of land on which to build. She tried to do so but when money ran out, she and her five children, 'in a very sad and deplorable case', applied to the fund and received ten pounds. This was much more than most distressed claimants received. For such suffering, a state-of-the-art cathedral seems meagre compensation.

The gleams of insight given by the diarists of the period are arresting in their immediacy. Pepys's image of the London pigeons' reluctance to quit their roosts, hovering 'about the windows and balconies till they were some of them burned, their wings, and fell down', is a searing detail. Pepys' omnivorous curiosity is legendary, but it was shared by his generation in its comprehensive passion for things antiquarian and exotic, for the secrets of the cosmos seen through the finest lens and the gender of vegetables, the behaviour of comets and the teeming world of human quirks and foibles. Edmund Wyld, one of John Evelyn's circle of intimates and a member of the Royal Society, was described by the historian Roger North as 'a rich philosopher' with a house full of 'knick-knackery', fascinated by new inventions and greedy for all sorts of knowledge, which he and Aubrey, just as much as Pepys, did not distinguish from tattle. When the Great Fire had died down, it was realized that the monument of Dean Colet had been broken open: 'his coffin, which was of lead, was full of a liquor which conserved the body. Mr Wyld and Mr Ralph Greatorex tasted it and 'twas of a kind of insipid taste, something of an ironish taste. The body felt, to the probe of a stick, which they thrust into a chink, like brawn.' Nothing more perfectly conjures the peeping-tom mentality that viewed the world as a giant laboratory than this vignette of the two natural scientists investigating the embalming fluid from a great man's coffin by tasting the ferrous liquor

After the Great Fire, London was rebuilt on modern, classical principles. The skyline was dominated by new churches and the dome of Sir Christopher Wren's St Paul's Cathedral.

Opposite: Nell Gwyn had been a theatre orange-seller and actress, before becoming the most popular of King Charles II's mistresses. She was known as 'pretty witty Nell'.

surrounding the corpse, not content with which they poke a stick through the wood to experience the corpse's texture. The Great Fire had been, from this perspective, an opportunist's dream, clearing the ground for a new London and throwing open 'a chink', the doorway to the grave.

RESTORATION SCIENCE AND ART

In the reign of Charles I, men like Aubrey and Wyld belonged to a novel world characterized by intellectual fecundity, fraternal sociability and appetite to see, taste, know and tease out nature's secrets. Such men termed themselves 'virtuosi', meaning at that date practical scientists, savants, but also critics, amateur collectors, connoisseurs and the elite of gentlemen, who took a speculative interest in the world around them. It was within this rage for knowledge that the great scientists of the period – Newton, Hooke, Boyle, Petty, Wren, Halley – flourished, as well as the poets, Dryden, Cowley and the bibliophile Elias Ashmole.

The matrix for these discoveries was the Royal Society, which had its origins in a small Philosophical Club founded in the 1640s. Charles II gave the society its royal charters in 1662 and 1663, as the Royal Society of London for the Improving of Natural

Knowledge. Rarities and curiosities were greatly prized by the society, and, since subjects were not yet split into specializations, amateurs could hope to make discoveries and inventions alongside the more technically qualified professionals. An inclusiveness and public spirit informed the Royal Society at its best: the gardener, botanist and traveller, John Tradescant, had given his collection of rarities to Ashmole, who bequeathed them to the University of Oxford in 1682. The close relationship between science, commerce and naval foreign policy is exemplified in the support of Edmund Halley's venture to chart the heavens by the East India Company: he was allowed to use the island of St Helena to determine the position of 341 stars between 1677 and 1678, naming one of the constellations 'Charles's Oak' after the tree at Boscobel where Charles II had hidden after the Battle of Worcester. Halley's work with the Ordnance Office was to create for strategic purposes a comprehensive map of the globe.

Out of this period of royal patronage, commercial enterprise and scientific labour came a stream of revolutionary discoveries, including Newton's *Optics* and *Principia Mathematica*, Halley's *Micrographia*, Richard Lower's experiments with blood transfusion within and between species, barometers, the Greenwich Observatory, air-pumps, longitude, watches, navigational devices, diving-bells, the reflecting quadrant, vivisections, the cataloguing of plants and John Wilkins' experimental 'universal and philosophical language', a code for the cataloguing of absolutely everything. The vastness of the unknown called thrillingly to the scientist's newly awakened confidence in his own power to know it.

But there was an ethical price to be paid for the gleaning of such knowledge. Evelyn was appalled at vivisection: he watched a 'poor cur, kept long alive after the thorax was open, by blowing with bellows into his lungs, and that long after his heart was out, and the lungs both gashed and pierced, his eyes quick all the while'. Aubrey was sharply perceptive when he saw the thirst for knowledge and the desire to penetrate into the secrets of the universe as a species of concupiscence. It went hand in hand with the court's lubricious sensuality, love of theatrical and circus novelties, and the feasting of the public's eyes on the spectacle of public execution: 'Ah, 'tis the best lechery to see 'em suffer correction,' wrote Aubrey, observing with reproof his own presence at a hanging, drawing and quartering. It was this growing spirit of analysis, not just of objective nature, but of the subjective workings of the mind, that gives the period its unique flavour.

The art of the Restoration represented a flowering of comedy, particularly of comedy of manners, in the work of Congreve, Wycherley, Etherege and the first professional female dramatist, Aphra Behn, which at once satirized and indulged the bawdry and intrigue endemic at court. The French influence was everywhere felt, in the proscenium theatre with women actors and in the polish of prose that was attuned to an aphoristic brilliance and elegant superficiality, with intricate plotting. The 'improving' of Shakespeare's works exposed the neurosis of the period: Davenant polished up *Macbeth* (1674); Dryden adapted *Antony and Cleopatra* formalized according to the neo-classical rules, as *All For Love* (1678); Thomas Shadwell, Dryden's inveterate rival, set *The Tempest* as a Restoration play in 1673, with an overture of twenty-four violins, harpsicals and theorbos, and a 'noble arch' with Corinthian columns, wreathed in roses, with 'several cupids flying above them'. Figures with trumpets and angels holding the king's arms were presented in this spectacle before a painted sea with *son et lumière* effects. Gone was the sublime simplicity of the Elizabethan apron stage: ornamental artefacts and frenchified costumery displayed a new self-conscious and nervous pomp. Actresses replaced the boy actors of the Jacobean theatre.

A group of court poets, including Wycherley, Buckingham, Henry Jermyn and the nihilistically cynical libertine, John Wilmot, Second Earl of Rochester, advertised themselves as 'the wits'. Rochester, Groom of the Bedchamber to Charles II from 1666, was a brilliant satirist, who wrote inventively obscene lyrics circulated in manuscript among his coterie. He and his fellow rakehells sealed the Restoration courtiers' reputation for debauchery, duelling and drunken excesses. He died of venereal disease at the age of thirty-two, 'a martyr to sin', according to his funeral oration. His gift expresses something of the complexity of the period in the delicate beauty of some lyrics ('An age in her embraces spent/Would seem a winter's day...'), the darkly witty ingenuity of his metaphysical poem 'On Nothing', and the trenchant 'Satire against Mankind':

> I'd be a dog, a monkey, or a bear,
> Or any thing, but that vain animal,
> Who is so proud of being rational.

Rochester assaults his age's love of Reason as a will o' the wisp, leading the narcissistic thinker through dreams of optics into the abortive dark:

> In hopes still to o'ertake the skipping Light:
> The vapour dances, in his dazzled sight,
> Till spent, it leaves him to eternal Night.

Raw fear underlay man's aspirations and values: 'his boasted honour, and his dear-bought fame'. If Charles II's renowned libertinism was a veneer covering an underlying melancholy, his cultivated court, with its art of conversation and its aping of Louis XIV's ostentation, covered an abyss of cynicism, above which it played vertiginously. Charles's many mistresses, from the Countess of Castlemaine to the Duchess of Portsmouth, were gilded spiders in the web of intrigue. The ambition to appear as a great world power dominating the seas burned all the more intensely for Charles's insecurity. A popular mock-epic satire, probably by Marvell, wrote of England's 'great debauch', 'sick ships' and shameful scapegoating that followed the national humiliation when the Dutch fleet under de Ruyter breached the boom across the Medway and bombarded Chatham. Marvell offered his poem, 'The Last Instructions to a Painter', as a 'bold tube' or telescope, to help Charles view the sunspots in his monarchical sun, which 'seem his courtiers, are but his disease'.

When Charles sacrificed Clarendon as the scapegoat for the shame of this raid, he did not halt the progress of the disease. Looking across the Channel, he saw the *roi soleil* glamorously presiding at the centre of a heliocentric court, enjoying a power of absolutism he could not emulate. His heart and policies leant further and further towards Catholic France.

CHAPTER 6

POPISH
PLOTS,
EXCLUSION
AND

KING
JAMES
II

With the flight of Clarendon in 1667, Charles felt elatedly free from the sour-faced astringencies of an adviser who seemed to belong to a bygone generation. Clarendon had tutored and managed his years of exile and pontificated over his seven years as king. In the end the king threw him off like shackles. In Clarendon's wake came frenzied rivalry as ministers competed for power and influence. Charles was believed to be governing through a clique of ministers known as the Cabal ('secret faction'), an acronym of the initials of a group of ministers, Clifford, Arlington, Buckingham, Ashley (Cooper) and Lauderdale. A popular jingle queried:

How can this nation ever thrive
When 'tis governed by these five,
The formal ass, the mastiff dog,
The mole, the devil and the hog?

But in fact the Cabal was a chimera: the five ministers were neither an exclusive nor a harmonious group, especially the crypto-Catholic Arlington, supple and subtle, and the volatile, dissolute Buckingham, the son of James I's favourite of the same name and a nonconformist sympathizer; these two detested and conspired against one another. There no longer existed any individual or group capable of limiting Charles's hankering after the delicious autonomy that his cousin Louis XIV enjoyed. He set about getting this by initiating policies so cryptic and capricious as to be scarcely legible by any person of merely common sense. His left and right hands played off contrary foreign and domestic policies with perfidious legerdemain. He would acquiesce in one agreement only to double back; take counsel from one interest group while making solemn undertakings to another.

ROYAL INTRIGUES

In signing a Triple Alliance with Sweden and the Dutch in January 1668, Charles reversed a Parliament-approved policy, and feigned the desire to curb French expansionism. This policy, popular with the Protestant public, brought Louis's ambassador scampering across to negotiate and was soon superseded by its opposite. In May 1670, Charles made the secret Treaty of Dover with Louis, who lured Charles into an agreement by using the latter's beloved and dying sister, Henriette-Anne, Duchess of Orléans, as mediator. The English Crown was now over two million pounds in debt and, as part of the Treaty, France undertook to pay Charles £225,000 a year to mount a joint assault on the Low Countries. When the Dutch had been conquered, Charles would share in the spoils: he pledged the English navy, which would attack at whatever strategic point Louis should require it. Twin secret clauses promised to suspend the recusancy laws against Catholics and described Charles as 'being convinced of the truth of the Catholic religion and resolved to declare it and reconcile himself with the Church of Rome as soon as the welfare of his kingdom will permit'.

These concessions were so inflammatory as to be revealed to nobody in England except the Catholics Clifford and Arlington and the Duke of York. To cover them up,

Charles had a second, sham, Treaty of Dover signed in December, without the clauses, signed by the dissenting ministers, Buckingham and Ashley Cooper (now the Earl of Shaftesbury). This sham treaty was also kept secret. Two days before the invasion was launched in 1672, Charles issued a Declaration of Indulgence, under his own authority and without reference to Parliament, permitting Catholics to worship privately and licensing dissenting meetings. He calculated that the short-term unpopularity of these measures, and the sudden military volte-face of keeping company with the hated French, would be offset by huge long-term financial gains. Once the rival Dutch were off the high seas and English trade prospered, he would be ballasted by treasure and victory.

Louis and Charles had no doubt of the success of their combined assault by sea and land on the vulnerable Dutch, since they could not conceive of the intense determination of a little people fighting for survival on their own soil against foreign aggressors. The Dutch opened their dykes and flooded their polders, checking the onslaught of the French army. They inflicted ignominious defeats on the English navy. Off Sole Bay the Duke of York lost two English flagships and the life of the Earl of Sandwich. The failure of this third Dutch war in two decades weakened Charles's position still further, and he was constrained by lack of money to recall Parliament in 1673 and to make peace with Holland in 1674. Evelyn's was probably a characteristic response to the attempts to forge pretexts for Anglo-French aggression: 'Surely this was a quarrel slenderly grounded, and not becoming Christian neighbours, and of a religion: and we are like,' he predicted, 'to thrive accordingly.' This queasy sense of indecency towards fellow Protestants reinforced the ubiquitous dislike of the French.

PARLIAMENTARY BACKLASH

The measure of the suspicion in which the Stuart court was now held is shown by the common anxiety that the king was seeking to raise forces to suppress, as his father had sought to do, his own people. He assured Parliament in February 1673 that he found it fantastic that he had to reassure them 'that the forces I have raised in this war were designed to control law and property'. His contempt for Parliament was now pure. Its anger at his guileful manipulations, together with the Francophobia that reigned in every household in England and its conviction that he was wedded to Louis and Catholicism, made Parliament's estrangement from the Crown nearly as total. Parallels began to be current, linking the present crisis with the situation in 1641. The Commons demanded and got the rescinding of the Declaration of Indulgence, and imposed a Test Act according to which all holders of public positions must not only attend Anglican worship but publicly take the Anglican communion, and swear an oath abjuring the doctrine of transubstantiation. Whereas the 2 per cent of the population who were Catholics had been able to offer a quiet semblance of conformity by their occasional presence at a Protestant church, now they must take the Anglican wafer on their tongues and the wine in their mouths, which for a Catholic was damnable heresy. James, Duke of York, resigned from his position as Lord High Admiral. Clifford resigned from the Treasury, to be replaced by Thomas Osborne.

It now stood nakedly in the open that the heir to the throne was a Catholic, a fact that had long been suspected. The fears that had been aroused in the Gunpowder Plot, the Irish Rebellion and the Great Fire were again a livid rash on the public psyche. James's first wife, Anne Hyde, had died in 1672 and he now chose a Catholic princess, Mary of Modena, as his queen, marrying her in a private Catholic service. She brought with her priests and Jesuits. Intense pressure came upon Charles to divorce his barren wife or to legitimize his eldest son, the Protestant Duke of Monmouth. He stood firm. Thomas Osborne, to be ennobled as Earl of Danby, now became Charles's chief minister, an able economic strategist and a Protestant, anti-French sop to Parliament. The government's financial twists and turns had included the so-called Stop of the Exchequer, which Marvell called 'the Robbery at the Exchequer' whereby the Crown refused to honour its debts and many investors were ruined. Danby's financial astuteness went far to balance Charles's books – or would have done, if the king had not been so relentlessly profligate. Danby swiftly terminated the Dutch war and set about wooing the 'country' party in Parliament, with an adept application of the clientage system. He bought Charles's way towards a parliamentary majority, opposed throughout by Buckingham and Shaftesbury, and in part opposed by the king's wilful and covert intrigues.

Meanwhile, the court had taken yet more of the colour of Catholicism, with the advent of a French mistress, Louise de Kéroüalle, Duchess of Portsmouth, who, coming to court a virgin, was treated to a mock marriage ceremony for her defloration. Evelyn recorded that, 'It was universally reported that the fair Lady… was bedded one of these nights, and the stocking flung, after the manner of a married bride.' The rise of Louise de Kéroüalle, who would retain Charles's favour until the end of his life, coincided with the conversion of the Duke of York and his marriage to a young Catholic wife. When Louis XIV invaded the Spanish Netherlands in 1677, and Parliament demanded that Charles ally England with the Protestants against the aggressor before supplies would be voted, Charles simply prorogued Parliament again. But he agreed to the marriage of James's eldest daughter, the Protestant Mary, to William of Orange, who had been leading the Dutch in their resistance to Louis, a typical piece of nimble but apparently self-contradictory footwork that compromised the apparent direction of royal policy. He sealed this by proposing an alliance with the Netherlands, should the French fail to withdraw their troops. Whether he intended to mollify Parliament, pressurize Louis into making peace or was attempting to turn William, a cold, determined warrior-Calvinist, into a pawn, he did little to restore the confidence of Parliament.

THE 'POPISH PLOT'

The immemorial fear and hatred of Roman Catholicism that had climaxed at intervals throughout the century had never ebbed, though Catholics were few and peaceable, and the recusancy laws exercised leniently. But those feelings existed like magma beneath the surface of national life. The frenzy that greeted the Popish Plot was indistinguishable from the language of horror generated by the Gunpowder Plot: time and experience had no power to reduce a fear of the sinister 'enemy within' and the international enemy, in Rome, France, Ireland, imaginary armies, ready to invade. Marvell was one of many sophisticated but gullible people, convinced that the Great Fire of London was caused by

This propaganda engraving of 1680 depicts the unfolding of the Popish Plot in a sequence of twenty-nine scenes,
from its supposed inception in Rome to the executions of English Catholics.

a pan-Catholic conspiracy. That the Gunpowder Plot was real, the Great Fire an accident and this brand-new plot a confidence trick was not a distinction that the threatened Protestant mind could make.

The Popish Plot was the fabrication of a delusional maniac and a compulsive liar, speaking to an anxiety a century and a half old. When in 1679 Lord Russell told the Commons: 'I despise such a ridiculous and nonsensical religion. A piece of wafer, broken betwixt a priest's fingers, to be our Saviour! And what becomes of it when eaten, and taken down, you know…' the young man seemed to think he had invented the Protestant contempt for the literalism of the mass. In fact he was repeating almost verbatim the words of the martyrs in Foxe's account. Lord Essex had hallucinations of his children 'frying in Smithfield' and a pamphleteer recommended readers to imagine their nearest and dearest 'tied to a stake in the midst of flames' like the victims of Bloody Mary. Lord Chief Justice Scroggs remarked that the ulterior aim of Catholic priests was a thirsty intention to drink the blood of Protestants. An ingredient that had been added to the mixture by the late 1670s derived from the apprehensive vigil kept by English Protestantism on the Continent, where representative institutions in Catholic nations had been crushed by the rise of absolutist monarchs, of whom Louis XIV was the darkly lustrous model. Sir Henry Capel, repeating the contemporary cliché that 'From popery came the notion of a standing army and arbitrary power', took it a step further by claiming that tyranny could not flourish in Europe without Catholicism. It is against the background of this tenacious and primitive body of fears that we read the frenzy of the Popish Plot and the subsequent Exclusion Crisis.

Yet more potent fuel for these underlying fears was the tenor of the Duke of York's Catholicism. With only a breath intervening between this Catholic convert and the throne, it was natural that his character should come under alarmed scrutiny. He acknowledged his own reputation as 'a man for arbitrary power' and Shaftesbury directed a tirade at him as a man 'heady, violent and bloody, who easily believes the rashest and worst of counsels to be most sincere and hearty'. James was a man of action, whose great military and naval experience worryingly suggested that he would force Catholicism on England with the sword. Reinforcing these anxieties was Charles's delirious and crass foreign policies, which constantly seemed to dance attendance on Louis XIV, sometimes by capering in an oblique direction, such as his sudden decision to raise an army to fight Louis, just as his war against the Dutch was clearly coming to an end, inspiring suspicions in the Commons that he intended to suppress his opponents at home by force. Charles then capered in the opposite direction by ordering Danby to negotiate secretly with Louis.

The mouthpiece of the Popish Plot was Titus Oates. His informant was a demented priest, Israel Tonge, remembered from Oxford days by the Oxford termagant, Anthony à Wood, as 'cynical and hirsute, shiftless in the world'. An ex-Puritan, he later took a living in London, at St Mary Stayning, which burned down in the Great Fire. Apparently this unhinged him and he developed a psychosis in relation to the Jesuits, who he believed not only to be persecuting himself but also to have ignited the Great Fire, the Great Rebellion and the execution of Charles I. William Prynne, whose ears had been cropped by Archbishop Laud, boasted a similar obsession. But Tonge lived, breathed and trumpeted his, with catastrophic consequences. He devoted every waking minute to translating Catholic tracts and compiling a history of the Jesuits in a style as serpentine as his inventions were fantastical. In a sense Tonge carried the psychosis of his age: it was when he met Titus Oates in 1676 that his inflamed imagination met a sound-box capable of delivering its message to the ears of a world all too ready to accept his berserk message.

Titus Oates was a model of turpitude, a charlatan so authentic that he could credit and remember in detail all the self-begotten lies and half-baked second-hand stories he brought forth, adding embellishments on a daily basis. Oates's life-history was also one symptomatic of the age's breakdown. He was the child of the regicide year, his father being a Baptist chaplain in Cromwell's New Model Army. He had been expelled from Merchant Taylors' School and proceeded to Gonville and Caius College, Cambridge, in 1667, from which after two terms he was again expelled. Taking holy orders, Oates was ejected as a drunk who was prone in his cups to use 'very indecent expressions concerning the mysteries of the Christian religion', perhaps his father's heterodox beliefs surfacing. In Hastings he accused the scion of a gentry family of sodomy and his father of treason. Oates was charged with perjury, which he escaped by enlisting as chaplain bound for Tangier on the frigate *Adventure*. Not long after he had berthed, he was dismissed for sodomy. Back he came to London, where he haunted the seamy cellars patronized by Catholic youth, and in 1677 was appointed chaplain to the Protestant members of the Catholic Earl of Norwich's London household. After three months he was given his marching orders. On 3 March, Oates entered the Catholic Church, prompted, he later explained, by the desire to infiltrate the Jesuits and expose their evil practices. Tonge, surprised at his companion's sudden disappearance from his orbit, continued with his own life's work.

An insane Catholic priest, who had started as a Protestant, converted to Catholicism, thought better of it, and reconverted only to discover his mistake and return to the Catholic fold, admitted Oates to the Church. Richard Strange, English Provincial of the Society of Jesus, sent this choice spirit to the English College at Valladolid, where the Jesuit historian met him. His description of Oates is of a bizarre creature with a flat, discus-shaped head, a snub nose, a disproportionately large chin, and a 'strident and singsong voice, so that he seemed to wail rather than speak'. His language, said the Jesuit with disdain, was straight from the gutter. With characteristically inverted logic, Oates arrived at Valladolid just as classes were going into recess. However, he kicked his heels waiting, and when instruction resumed, his ignorance of Latin, the lingua franca of the Church, was detected, and he was sent back to England. Nevertheless, at a period when Catholicism was in decline, the ignorant Oates did at least count as a body, and he remained in touch with the Jesuits, adopting the name of Father Ambrose. Having cadged for a while from Tonge, he set off for the college of St Omers in northern France, where he shared the lessons of young boys. His obscene talk and sexual indecencies ensured that by June 1678 the over-age schoolboy was again expelled.

Oates and Tonge, reunited, composed a forty-three-fold synopsis of the invented plot to assassinate the king, and contrived to present it to Charles, who listened for twenty minutes to the farrago. It is possible that the 'Captain Oates' executed in 1664 at York for plotting was a relative of Titus and that the Fifth Monarchist Thomas Tonge,

This contemporary suit of playing cards shows the mysterious murder of Sir Edmund Berry Godfrey, which seemed to confirm Titus Oates' allegation of a sensational Popish Plot.

executed in 1662, may have been Israel's brother. Certainly Israel was a name popular among extreme Puritans, signifying the Second Coming and the gathering-in of the diaspora. Tonge and Oates were casualties of the mental furore of the Civil War period, for in a period of such instability, oscillating wildly between opposite ideologies, many floundered lost in a dream world between binary opposites. If Oates seems to have spoken on inspiration and believed the testament of his own mouth, that is only an unhinged version of the belief in the speaking at the dictation of the Spirit legitimized by extreme Puritans. Bunyan in *Grace Abounding* described phases when streams of profanities had bubbled unbidden to his lips as if he were possessed, and other times when he was 'so estranged from the things I have been speaking… that I have been as if I had not known or remembered what I have been about; or as if my head had been in a bag…' Until he came to the steadier passion of an eloquence by which 'I preached what I felt, what I smartingly did feel', Bunyan, like many other Baptists, often found himself in mental states indistinguishable from madness.

Oates and Tonge were the mouthpiece of nothing but a rigmarole of communal paranoia, in a political world that was riddled with informers. Informing and surveillance were in the seventeenth century a norm, decoys and spies being nicknamed 'trepans', from their attempt to open the skull to peep inside. What lent the two offbeat characters a terrible credibility was the fate of a magistrate in whom Oates had insisted on confiding his first depositions.

Edmund Berry Godfrey was an affluent and upstanding wood and coal merchant, a JP with a reputation for fairness and decency, quick to put his hands in his pockets to aid the needy, famous in London for remaining at his post during the Great Plague, overseeing the mass burials and keeping the peace. On 12 October 1678 Godfrey vanished, having been expressing for some time anxiety about his safety. His body was found five days later at the foot of Primrose Hill. He had been strangled and subsequently run through with his own sword. His clothes were dry, despite the rain, suggesting that he had been murdered elsewhere and brought to this spot by covered cart. The murder was popularly ascribed to the Catholics and appeared to confirm Oates's tale of a plot. The Lords requested that all papists be banished from a radius of twenty miles from London. Meanwhile, the city was in pandemonium and chains were placed across the streets, for, as the City Chamberlain said, 'I do not know but the next morning we might all rise with our throats cut.' Oates gave more evidence to Parliament, designating as plotters as many names as came to mind. He named the Duchess of Mazarin, an ex-mistress of the king, as a French spy and John Lambert, general in Cromwell's army, who had been imprisoned since 1660 and gone mad in the twenty-year interlude. These were names that brought a sensational intake of breath to the hearer, but they were meaningless.

On 26 October Tonge gave evidence to the Commons on the Catholic responsibility for the Great Fire, following up a couple of days later with rumours he had heard about another Gunpowder Plot. A deputation immediately went off to search the cellars for a reincarnated Guy Fawkes. The Lords ordered the removal of a pile of timber stored next door to the chamber. On 1 November, the sounds of 'knocking and digging' that had been heard between midnight and three were thoroughly investigated. A census was commissioned of all papists in the neighbourhood. It was now learned that a French Catholic (who happened to be the king's firework-maker) had a store of gunpowder in an adjacent street. It was thought prudent to bring in the militia to search coffins in all funeral processions for signs of weaponry. Berry Godfrey was laid to rest at the end of the month, his coffin at the head of an immense procession, led by seventy-two clergymen.

That night the Commons stated its conclusions:

> That upon the evidence that has already appeared to this House, that this House is of opinion that there hath been and still is a damnable and hellish plot contrived and carried on by the popish recusants for the assassinating and murdering the King, and for subverting the government, and rooting out and destroying the Protestant religion.

It was when Oates hit upon the name of Edward Coleman, secretary to the Duchess of York, that he scored a bull's eye, for when Coleman's documents were searched, it was discovered that he had been in correspondence with Jesuits and French agents, discussing how Catholicism might be promoted in England. This was a chance hit, probably inevitable according to the law of probability, where such multitudinous and arbitrary accusations were being thrown like quoits at any peg that came to mind. Roger North wrote that, 'The discovery of Coleman's papers made as much noise in and about London, and indeed all over the nation, as if the very Cabinet of Hell had been laid open.' It became dangerous, all but sacrilegious, to express scepticism about the plot, or rather The Plot, which had flowed on from generation to generation, a 'continuous conspiracy', as if The Plot were an article of faith, in which all Protestants must believe, a kind of Test for Protestantism. Coleman's letters substantiated in a peculiarly damaging way the fact that the circle around the Duke of York had been seeking money from Louis XIV to bribe the English government. Shaftesbury pointed the finger directly at James, as a dangerous person who should be removed from proximity to his brother. Charles engineered James's withdrawal from public life.

The public remained in a state of uproar. All around them, they saw Catholics being disarmed, often of rusty old guns and ornamental swords; they saw priests marched off to prison and they received festering rumours which became not only more frightening but generated mass hallucinations, which the paranoid Commons took seriously. A regiment of trained bands (2,500 men) patrolled the city at night. The Lords took steps to prevent Catholic terrorists poisoning London's water supply. A young Catholic spark bragging in the Black Lion in King Street that 'The king is a great heretic' and 'I would kill him myself' – in French – was brought to trial, condemned, hanged, drawn and quartered, all within a December fortnight. Mass hypnosis gripped the population. In Wiltshire, Buckinghamshire, Gloucester and Yorkshire reports came in of nightriders, armies of Catholics galloping through the darkness.

'I do accuse the Queen for conspiring the death of the King!' Oates announced. He had shot his bolt. Although the Commons swallowed this whole like an oyster and called for the banishment of the murderous queen, the suggestion was so preposterous that the Lords did not support them and Charles ridiculed it. Meanwhile, groups of Jesuits and Catholics were charged with High Treason. Justice Scroggs's peroration at the trial of Thomas Whitbread and others contained the immortal words, 'They eat their God, they kill their King, and saint the murderer.' When the jury found as instructed, he congratulated them: 'You have done, gentlemen, like very good Christians; that is to say, very good Protestants.' Oates's prestige with the public remained high and he took to hiring himself out to preach in a self-designed clerical costume, a 'silk gown and cassock, great hat, satin headband and long rose scarf', as if he had been raised to a bishopric. As the judicial murders continued, Shaftesbury, who had been attempting to stage-manage the horrific farce so as to force the exclusion of James from the succession, saw that a law of diminishing returns was setting in. All the innocents whose names had been picked out of the Oatish brain (and that of another rogue, named Bedloe) went to their deaths with dignity and no one confessed. The bloodlust began to be slaked. Concurrently, the calibre of Oates and his fellow liars was recognized. Evelyn, who watched Oates's ostentatious parade of effrontery at the trial and acquittal of Sir George Wakeman, judged Oates to be 'a vain, insolent man', making a phoney reputation out of a real plot, which he embellished by implicating the nobility, about whom he could not possibly know anything.

THE EXCLUSION BILL

Charles had dissolved the Cavalier Parliament in January 1679 to protect Danby from impeachment. What came to be known as the First Exclusion Parliament was convened in March 1679: in May, Shaftesbury introduced the Exclusion Bill, according to which the crown, bypassing the Catholic James, would go to the next Protestant heir. It passed by 201 to 128 votes. Charles dissolved Parliament in July. This punitive lash of the royal prerogative appalled Shaftesbury and the Whigs, as a recapitulation of Charles I's dismissal of inconvenient parliaments. In August Charles was ill, it was feared mortally, and James returned from Brussels to safeguard in person his right of succession. Bitter and heated elections took place for a new parliament, and the Popish Plot, its credit running low, was used by the cunning Shaftesbury to add a few last discordant chords to the Exclusion clamour. The court retaliated by dismissing the Duke of Monmouth, illegitimate darling of the Whigs, from his position as Captain-General of the army and sending him into exile. Shaftesbury was removed from the Privy Council and Parliament was prorogued. In the heated atmosphere of a London that was beginning to seem like a theatre replaying the tumults of 1641, the bishops, who had all run bleating one way at the siren call of Oates, now turned in their tracks and all ran back, remembering the fate of their predecessors a generation ago. They now professed, as the minister and historian Gilbert Burnet recalled, that they had no 'fears and apprehensions of popery' at all. Whenever they opened their mouths, the number 'forty-one, in which the late wars began' tumbled out. James had appealed to conservative fears, which lay deeper than plot anxieties, about their property and privileges, which only he, as rightful and strong-handed heir, could guarantee.

In this situation, the fulminating bishops, who previously had not evoked their 1630s and 1640s predecessors, now looked, to those still crediting the Plot, markedly Laudian. Two distinct political parties were emerging. The Whigs favoured Exclusion, backed especially by dissenters who hoped to win toleration. The Whigs had notably strong roots in the City of London and other urban centres, which had backed Pym in 1641 for comparable reasons, as guarantors of their liberties under their charters. The Tories, or 'court' party, had roots in the rural gentry and Anglican alliance, viewing the Crown as the foundation of their privileges. The Whig majority in the Second Exclusion Parliament of October 1680, came about after a period of political frenzy, which Shaftesbury had stage-managed, talking tactics in London coffee houses and in the Green Ribbon Club, where an affable mingling of gentlemanly fraternizing and business could deepen political bonds. Press campaigns kept the Popish Plot going well into the October elections. Charles, recovered, did not allow Parliament to meet, proroguing it seven times, despite a monster petition a hundred yards long, demanding a parliamentary session. The very modern campaigning methods, with agents going door to door and manipulating press and populace, belonged to a radical change in the political framework which was ballasted, in part, by the wild persiflage of Titus Oates, and the nation's readiness to credit it.

But Oates was in decline. The Whigs generated a symmetrically opposite organization in the Tories, who also met in London clubs, capitalizing on the methods invented by their opposite numbers. They became known as the 'abhorrers' on account

Titus Oates was a pathological liar who invented the Popish Plot, as a result of which many innocent Catholics were executed.

of their antipathy to the 'petitioners'. In their mouths lay always the number 'forty-one'. In October 1680, because the king could not defer his need for subsidy, Parliament met. But the Lords threw out the Commons' Bill. The language the Whigs were now using, of 'liberties and rights of the people', carried too strong a tang of the Revolution, and generated a strong backlash and Charles, who had always ultimately yielded when pushed, held his resolution. He dissolved Parliament, calling a new one at Oxford. Popular fear now swung from Titus Oates's phantasmal Pope to the ghost of Cromwell, whose lineaments were seen in the handsome face of Monmouth. The reality of civil war had cured the nation of its taste for revolution.

CHARLES TAKES THE REINS

The Oxford Parliament lasted one week before Charles dissolved it, having stationed 600 soldiers round the building. The Whigs, cut off from military support in London, dispersed. Charles did not call another Parliament during the remaining four years of his life. Whereas he had frequently acted in a maladroit way in dealing with tensions, Charles had used delaying tactics, insinuation and personal intervention in the Lords debate of November 1680, showing gifts of manipulation and timing to wrong-foot the opposition. The Whigs' disagreement as to who should be the heir – Monmouth (who had the drawback of illegitimacy) or Mary (married to a foreigner) – created disunity within the party. And, at last, Charles could manage without Parliament. Whereas he had spent decades grubbing for money and limping in a chronic state of debt, now his finances were buoyant, after reforms that allowed him to collect full revenues from booming overseas trade. He held up his sleeve the trump card of the expectation of secret subsidy from Louis XIV. He had outlived the dependency on Parliament that had tied the Stuart hands from the time of James. Now Charles was in a position to savage his enemies. Shaftesbury was arrested for treason and, though the grand jury, full of Whigs, refused to indict him, he fled to Holland, to die in 1683.

John Dryden's satire, *Absalom and Achitophel*, a biblical allegory related the Popish Plot and the rise of Shaftesbury and Monmouth into the matrix of the Revolution, in which 'a headstrong, moody, murmuring race' rises against its divinely fruitful king, perverted from its allegiance by 'hell's dire agent' Achitophel/Shaftesbury. The vignette of Shaftesbury is a merciless vivisection of a character volatile and amoral:

> Sagacious, bold and turbulent of wit:
> Restless, unfixt in principles and place;
> In power unpleased, impatient of disgrace.
> A fiery soul, which working out its way,
> Fretted the pigmy body to decay:
> And o'erinformed the tenement of clay…
> Great wits are sure to madness near allied;
> And thin partitions do their bounds divide…
> In friendship false, implacable in hate:
> Resolved to ruin or to rule the state.

George Villiers, the Second Duke of Buckingham was notorious for his debauched lifestyle.

As Achitophel tempts David's beloved and ambitious son to rebel against his clement father, he also works on the populace class by class: merchant republicans who 'thought Kings an useless heavy load,/Who cost too much and did too little good'; Puritans, 'In godly faction, and in treason bold', and all the swarm of Fifth Monarchist and Anabaptist 'dreaming saints' 'Of the true old enthusiastic breed'. The character of Zimri takes a scalpel to the Duke of Buckingham, the violently unstable companion of Charles's youth, of whom Burnet said that he 'forsakes every man and departs from every maxim and sometimes out of downright falsehood', having a 'perpetual unsteadiness about him':

> A man so various, that he seemed to be
> Not one, but all mankind's epitome.
> Stiff in opinions, always in the wrong;
> Was everything by starts, and nothing long:
> But, in the course of one revolving moon,
> Was chemist, fiddler, statesman and buffoon:
> Then all for women, painting, rhyming, drinking;
> Besides ten thousand freaks that died in thinking.

From this superb poem, whose elegant couplets anatomize the period's worst nightmares, comes not only a sequence of character sketches recognizable in any age, but a profound sense of the need for stability and the anxiety at fluctuation which was, in the end, the rock on which the Whigs and the Popish Plot foundered.

In 1683 John Evelyn sighed that: 'After the Popish-plot etc there was now a new (and as they called it) Protestant-plot discovered, that certain Lords, and others should design the assassination of his Majesty and Duke, with a general rising of several of the Nation, and especially the City of London…' This fabricated 'Rye House Plot' to assassinate Charles and James, confected and conducted on the model of the Popish Plot, brought leading Whigs to execution or exile, and resulted in renewed persecution of dissenters. Many hundreds of Quakers found themselves in prison again and subjected to an onslaught of fines and violence. Charles revenged himself on the City and brought other boroughs to heel by rescinding their charters and packing the localities with yes-men.

At his death in 1685, Charles was in a position of supremacy. He held the power his father intrigued and died for. His income tallied with his expenditure. Ireland was subdued. Scotland, under the severe regime of Lauderdale, had been kept under royal control through brutal suppression of Presbyterian meetings. In 1679 an Anglo-Scottish army under the Duke of Monmouth crushed a rising of Covenanter rebels at Bothwell Brig. James (who had a power-base in Scotland) soon reasserted Crown authority. Charles packed the judiciary with royalists such as Lord Chief Justice Kelyng, who had in 1667 expressed his devotion to the rights of the subject by calling Magna Carta 'magna farta'. Church and Crown were linked in impregnable alliance. In towns such as nonconformist Bristol, which in 1681 had had six Dissenting meeting-houses, two being Baptist, two Quaker and one of the others Presbyterian, the persecution of the 1680s was the worst in memory. Riddled with informers, every group was submitted to inhuman degradation. When all Quaker men and women were in prison, the children led meetings and felt the lash, being imprisoned, stocked and 'beaten with a twisted whale-bone stick' and with faggot-sticks. Amid braying laughter, boys and girls were forcibly baptized with 'holy water'. The heroic children continued to meet. Other sects went underground. William Penn calculated that, 'There have been ruined, since the late King's Restoration, above 15,000 families, and more than 5,000 persons dead under bonds for mere conscience to God.'

Charles died a Catholic convert, a surreptitious act, it is thought, of spiritual 'fire insurance'. The milling deathbed-watchers were mostly bundled out and the double doors locked, behind which Father Huddlestone, the Catholic priest who had aided Charles at Worcester, confessed him, 'gave him absolution, the sacrament, extreme unction, and what not', Burnet records. The aged priest managed all this in the half hour available, the doors being opened only to ask for a glass of water 'when the Host stuck in the king's throat'.

Titus Oates was still declaring his fatuities to anyone who would hear. His retribution had to wait until the reign of James II, who had him convicted of perjury, fined, unfrocked, and paraded through the Courts of Westminster Hall with a notice proclaiming his offence. Pilloried and whipped from Aldgate to Newgate, and, after a couple of days' rest, from Newgate to Tyburn, he was to be imprisoned for life, but annually on specified days he was to be brought out and pilloried. That was thought to be the end of him. But with the succession of William of Orange, Oates emerged and petitioned for a pension for his services to Protestantism. He made a life for himself in Axe Yard, Westminster, where he divided his time between the composition of religious tracts and attendance at the law-courts to watch the trials. In the end, as the century drew to a close, he received his pension in 1698, when he came full circle and re-entered the Baptist Church, drawing crowds to their chapel at Wapping.

THE CATHOLIC SUCCESSION

James II's accession passed off calmly and without the expected upheaval. There was either a decent calm in the streets or the regulation bonfires and bells. Little changed as he began his reign, except a new sobriety in the court. At fifty-two, he had been under the shadow of his cynically charming, intellectually curious brother for a quarter of a century. Never quick-witted, but not without affability, James was a man of action, happiest when in the simplified martial world of male bondings, strong and valorous rather than subtle, lacking in empathy and the capacity essential to a politician to recognize different shades of opposition, to conciliate and temper his decisions. James brought to the monarchy a resolute sincerity and determination at variance with the traditional Stuart devious subtlety. Like his grandfather, James I, he hunted insatiably. He loved dressing up in red military uniform and drilling his soldiers, enacting mock battles with mighty sound effects, and camping at Hounslow Heath with his men, in compensation perhaps for the military career he had not been able to pursue. But like his brother Charles II, James had an aggressive sexual appetite, several illegitimate children and, especially in his earlier life, a voracious eye that lit on all female flesh with indiscriminate zest.

James's character was profoundly imprinted with the manner of his father's death, believing that it was caused in part by Charles I's softness and weakness in giving way to his opponents' demands. He simplified and distorted history by imagining the regicides to have been republicans intending all along to eliminate the English monarchy. Both these beliefs and the root-system to which they attached were to prove disastrous. Yet James did not come to the throne with a desire to catholicize England by force: he believed that this would happen naturally, once there was a level playing field for Roman Catholics. Nor did he intend to suppress Protestants. Events spiralled out of control because, as Burnet observed, he 'had no true judgment'. His mind took the imprint of the advice of his private counsellors and then promoted it stubbornly. Defensively aware of his intellectual deficiencies, in an age of brilliant talkers and ratiocinators, James replied bull-headedly to contrary advice, 'Let the reasons be what they will, I am resolved not to do it.' While Charles had listened to counsel without trusting anyone to tell him the truth, so that his ministers, as Halifax remarked, paralleled 'his mistresses; he used them, but he was not in love with them', James listened and believed.

Yet in 1685, despite James's Catholicism and the past storm of the Exclusion crisis, auguries were good. Rejecting the crackpot extremist advice of militant Catholics to legitimize his bastard son, the Duke of Berwick; to force his daughter Anne to convert to Catholicism and be named heir instead of Mary; or to call in French support from Louis XIV, he instead undertook to 'preserve this government both in church and state as it is by law established'. The Tory, Anglican 'landed parliament', which welcomed him was as eager as were the nation and James himself to avoid civil war, whose memory was still sharp. Parliament voted James a supply so adequate that, with an average income of £2 million, he was the most financially buoyant monarch for over a century: in a principled way, he set himself to paying off his brother's debts. He deleted the Anglican clauses in the coronation ceremony, an alteration that his subjects tolerated. Parliament swung even further behind the king when the twin rebellions of Argyll and Monmouth arose in 1685.

Archibald Campbell, Earl of Argyll, led a small expedition to Scotland to raise support for Monmouth but found none. His rebellion was easily put down, and he was captured and executed. But the Duke of Monmouth's rebellion was a more painful bloodletting. Charles II's favourite natural son had been living in exile on the continent, in the lap and pocket of his mistress. Dryden had described in *Absalom and Achitophel* Monmouth's beguiling personal beauty and manner, his prowess and graciousness:

> Of all this numerous progeny was none
> So beautiful, so bold, as Absalom…
> In peace the thoughts of war he could remove
> And seemed as he were only born for love.
> Whate'er he did was done with so much ease,
> In him alone, 'twas natural to please.
> His motions all accompanied with grace;
> And Paradise was opened in his face.

Dryden represented him as a fallen angel, the youthful and seduced creature of the satanic Shaftesbury. But in 1685, at the age of thirty-six, Monmouth was past his first youth. As the icon of English Protestantism, he landed at Lyme Regis on 11 June, raising his standard and, as 'head and captain-general of Protestant forces of the kingdom', asserting 'a 'legitimate and legal' title to the crown. Over 4,000 men flocked to his standard in the Puritan rural countryside and clothing towns of the West Country. These were chiefly poor men, craftsmen, yeomen farmers and dissenters, who, without the area's elite, composed an untrained and ill-equipped army. They marched about in a vertiginous way through three counties, until Monmouth attempted a lightning attack by night on the king's army, under the Earl of Feversham and John Churchill at Sedgemoor. He was routed.

If Monmouth's craven behaviour after the battle had a touch of poignant farce, the fate of the naive men of the 'middling' and lower orders who had risen at his call was tragedy. A list of their names, addresses and occupations is a saddening reminder that it is those with little who pay for the aspirations of the great. Monmouth ran away, after about a thousand of his followers had been killed and half as many taken prisoner. In the company of a German who had come across with him, he galloped towards Dorset, changing clothes with a shepherd he met along the way. The pursuers found first the elegantly dressed shepherd, who was able to direct them to where the German was standing nonplussed in the road. He pointed to a heap of hay into which Monmouth had crept, hoping to remain there unseen until nightfall. Meanwhile, the yeomen and workmen had either run away or stayed on to fight with their scythes and clubs, being themselves mown down until the soldiers were weary of killing.

RETRIBUTION AND REPEAL

Monmouth now threw himself upon his uncle's mercy, ignobly begging clemency, which disgusted James. On 15 July he went to his death for treason, beseeching the executioner to do it cleanly, in one blow, but the executioner was so agitated that two or three strokes

These playing cards depict the aftermath of the Battle of Sedgemoor: the pursuit of the Duke of Monmouth, the 'Bloody Assizes' and the execution of the rebel Argyll.

were not enough to sever the head from the body. He threw away the axe in despair, until the sheriff forced him to finish the botched job. 'He was soft and gentle even to excess, was sincere and good-natured, and understood war well,' said Burnet, who saw in Monmouth a fatal moral laxness that tainted his good qualities. It ruined hundreds of ordinary people. The notoriously cruel Colonel Percy Kirke summarily tried and brutally murdered rebels. At the 'Bloody Assizes' at Somerset, Judge Jeffries presided with foul-mouthed gloating, threatening witnesses, browbeating juries and taking sadistic relish in spelling out the agonies the sentenced would have to undergo. In an age of judicial barbarism, Jeffries became a by-word for cruelty. Three hundred 'traitors' were hanged, drawn and quartered; the ground ran ankle-deep in blood. Hundreds were transported to the West Indies, a virtual death sentence. There was no public outcry after Jeffries' 'campaign', as James called it. He promoted him to Lord Chancellor, and greeted the victory as a 'providence' signalling to him, as Marston Moor and Dunbar had done to Cromwell, God's special favour.

James now embarked on the attempt to repeal the penal legislation on Catholics and Dissenters that would prove his downfall. Packing the army with Catholics, he refused to disband it, causing anxiety as to his intentions, especially in view of the eerie coincidence with Louis XIV's declaration of war on his Protestant subjects in the revocation of the Edict of Nantes, which had guaranteed Huguenots a vestige of tolerance for almost a hundred years. Huguenot refugees would come flooding into Holland and England, with stories of atrocities, alarming Protestant Europe not only at the behaviour of the French king but also in relation to the Catholic English king's swollen army. Although James probably disapproved of Louis's violent measures in obtaining the 'conversion' of the Huguenots and authorized a collection for the refugees, his attitude was ambivalent: he seems to have slowed it down, apologized for it to the French and insisted on an Anglican test for recipients, suspecting as he did that Huguenots had been involved in the Monmouth Rebellion.

James II's reign, which lasted only three years, began auspiciously. He promised to, 'preserve this government, both in Church and State, as it is by law established.'

James prorogued Parliament when they demanded the demobilization of the army and the removal of the Catholic officers and initiated what was called a 'closeting' scheme, whereby he took individuals aside and subjected them to psychological arm-locks to obtain their acquiescence in his tolerationist policies. Few submitted. He fell back on the royal 'dispensing power' to dispense with laws in specific cases. Having packed the royal judiciary with suitable judges, he tested his prerogative in the case of Godden v. Hales, in which the court decided in favour of the king's prerogative power. Thus fortified, James went to work with his prerogative, purging MPs, JPs and even the universities, notably Magdalen College, Oxford, stronghold of the Anglican educational monopoly, to whose presidency James ordered the election of a crypto-Catholic. The fellows claiming that Anthony Farmer was ineligible, James sent in another name, which was also rejected. James raged into Oxford, and confronted the recalcitrant fellows with a tirade: 'Go home and show yourselves good members of the Church of England. Get you gone, know I am your king. I will be obeyed.' Magdalen was turned into a Catholic college.

The Anglicans preached stormily against Catholicism, and anti-Catholic pamphlets flowed off the presses. The bishops were ordered to restrain their ministers and a Commission for Ecclesiastical Causes was set up, on which the Archbishop of Canterbury refused to sit. This body suspended Henry Compton, Bishop of London, from office, for refusing to eject an anti-Catholic preacher from his pulpit. James, estranged from Tories and the Church of England, moved into a parlous alliance with the Dissenters, who shared with the Catholics only the fact of their exclusion from the political nation and their persecution. James had formed a close personal relationship with the Quaker William Penn, the founder of Pennsylvania, a man of culture, luminous integrity and charisma, whose dignified gentleness of address evidently spoke to something in James's nature. In his youth Penn had visited Paris and returned a fully fledged dandy; he had luxuriated in the consumerist hedonism of the age before his final conversion and adopted the Quaker 'plain dress' with a certain rueful reluctance. Burnet thought Penn puffed up with self-importance and over-fond of his own speaking voice, but it was this background that made the socially adept Penn easy with the king.

Penn acted as unofficial ambassador for James. He accompanied him on a royal progress in August 1687: they toured Bath, Shrewsbury and Chester, returning via Oxford. On Sunday the 28th at Chester, as the Anglican Bishop Cartwright recalled, the king 'went to his [Catholic] devotions in the Shire Hall, and Mr Penn held forth in the Tennis Court, and I preached in the Cathedral'. Such threefold tolerance must have seemed a makeshift version of a longed-for paradisal toleration. For Dissenters however, as for the nation as a whole, the fact that James's Declaration of Indulgence was founded on his prerogative was a danger signal. Having suspended all penal laws against religious dissidents, the Test and Corporation Acts, he made overtures to Dissenters to accept political appointments from which he had removed Anglicans. The Marquis of Halifax's brilliant pamphlet, *A Letter to a Dissenter* of 1687, warned of the falsity of an 'alliance between liberty and infallibility…The Church of Rome doth not only dislike the allowing of liberty, but by its principles it cannot do it.' Dissenters, he warned, in a memorable image, were being used to Jesuitical ends, for their destiny was, 'to be hugged now, only that you may be better squeezed at another time'.

THE PROTESTANT INVITATION

In January 1688 James's wife, Queen Mary Beatrice, let it be known that she was pregnant with a son. How did she know it was a son? people asked. Rumours of fraud erupted, and the tale went round that a baby had been smuggled into the birth-chamber in a warming pan. Satires began to appear in March, for instance *Mr Partridge's Wonderful Prediction*, prophesying some 'bawdy project' in relation to 'buying, selling, or procuring a child, or children, for some pious use'. Princess Anne wrote to her elder sister, Mary, of her conviction that Jesuitical 'foul play' was involved. Later she confided to Mary her opinion that there was reason to believe it was a 'false belly', which the mother-to-be was being coy about allowing her sister-in-law to touch. Some women of the court volunteered their opinion that the pregnancy seemed to be growing too fast to be genuine. The Protestant nation found itself with the prospect of a Catholic dynasty.

In May, confident that the queen's pregnancy was viable, James issued a second Declaration of Indulgence, which the Anglican clergy were ordered to read from the pulpit. Archbishop Sancroft and six other bishops broadcast their refusal in a petition, indicating that the 'dispensing power' on which the declaration rested was illegal. James received the petition in a blaze of mortified anger, repeating, 'This is a standard of rebellion!' He told them that the source of his dispensing power was God, and that, 'I will maintain it.' Clearly his mind skipped back to his father's repudiation by his people, and he resolved not to yield with what he thought of as Charles I's feebleness, as he recognized that Anglicans and Dissenters were closing ranks rather than allowing themselves to be wedged apart.

When the baby, James Francis Edward, was born on 10 June, James fell to his knees and wept for hours. But the rumour was rife that there had been no pregnancy and that another baby had been covertly introduced in a warming pan. At a meeting of the Privy Council forty-two men and women were to make depositions that they believed the Prince of Wales to be the king and queen's son, statements that were then entered in the Court of Chancery and published by royal authority. The warming pan story was to be kept hot for as long as there was fear of Jacobite invasion. The Prince of Wales was sometimes pictured as the child of a priest. A young Yorkshire diarist, Abraham De la Pryme, confided that 'the Pope has sent her the Virgin Mary's smock, and hallowed bairn clothes'. It was in the

James II was painted by Sir Godfrey Kneller as a warrior-king. But when William invaded in 1688, James was a broken man.

Protestant interest that the child be suppositious, and William of Orange was to incorporate the query into his vindication.

For some time after his birth, the baby's life hung in the balance. Since the doctors' wisdom dictated that breast milk was toxic for babies and must be substituted by boiled bread, gruel, droplets of canary wine and elixirs of various kinds, the baby was ill for weeks and his life in doubt. Once a tiler's wife was engaged as wet-nurse, the boy throve.

The baby was James's weapon. Thus armoured, he pushed forward with the indictment of the rebellious bishops on a charge of 'seditious libel', in his exhilaration ensuring that the jury was packed with persons certain to be sympathetic to him.

The jury came in with a not guilty verdict. Stamping and cheers echoed round the courtroom for half an hour, spreading through London to the army camped on Hounslow Heath; bonfires lit the streets that night and bells pealed. Outside St James's Palace the crowd burned the Pope in effigy. While the public rejoiced, seven politicians – 'the immortal seven' as they were later named, including both Whigs, Tories and a bishop – sent a carefully worded 'invitation' to William, Prince of Orange, requesting him to invade. The phrasing was dextrous, representing the signatories as spokesmen for 'nineteen parts out of twenty of the people throughout the kingdom who are desirous of change', since their 'religion, liberties and properties' had been 'greatly invaded'.

William's action is therefore phrased as an invasion to cure an invasion, rather than an act of foreign aggression. William had already been planning his campaign and the 'invitation' was the work of his fifth column at the heart of English government. The declarations of intent and motivation he issued were deliberately vague, and it is far less likely that he saw himself as the champion of Protestantism and parliamentary government in England than that he was motivated by urgent strategic and European concerns. William came to England not to seize the crown but because alliance between Louis and a Catholic England (Catholic now to perpetuity, since James had male issue, displacing William's wife Mary as the next heir) threatened Dutch security. The initiative for the invasion was therefore at once religious, nationalist and dynastic: it was taken by a hard-headed militarist, nourished on the harsh milk of Calvinism and the knowledge of an international mission, on behalf of the States General.

There was no reason to think that William's invasion would succeed as neatly as it did: the venture was expensive and risky. The odds were stacked against success. It was undertaken while Louis's troops were otherwise engaged, attacking the Palatinate, and when the absence of fleet and army left the United Provinces dangerously exposed. William had constructed alliances with Protestant German princes to increase Dutch strength with battle-hungry mercenaries, to guard his rear and to expedite the English invasion.

James did not believe in the possibility of any such invasion. He failed to credit that his daughters and his nephew could be so wickedly alienated as to threaten his throne by violence. Only in September did he realize that the forces he had been watching William amass were intended for use against himself, rather than France. In a flat spin of panic, he put all his policies into reverse, to drum up last-minute support from those he despised ('some would think one kick of the breech enough for a gentleman,' murmured one Tory sceptic). William issued his propagandist declaration to the English people on 30 September, before embarkation: he promised that his expedition was designed solely to guarantee the English 'a free and lawful Parliament assembled as soon as possible', to secure the people's religion and to investigate the legitimacy of the Prince of Wales.

On 20 October his immense, freighted flotilla of nearly 500 vessels, carrying 20,000 soldiers, 7,000 horses, heavy *matériel* and supplies, set sail, to be driven back to shore by a storm, with some damage. After repairs, the army awaited an east wind. On 1 November, a keen 'Protestant wind' set in. William committed himself to it, while the English

Admiral, Lord Dartmouth, drawled, 'I cannot see much sense in their attempt.' He saw William as being at the mercy of the capricious elements, for he must go wherever the battering wind drove him, which might be straight to the bottom of the sea or into the firing line of the English navy. However, meteorological hazard had been built into William's plan: he did not know where he might land, and had followers in the north and the west waiting to meet him. On the night of 4 November the wind shifted west, pinning James's fleet off the Kent coast while permitting William to land his army near Brixham. He had fortuitously landed on 5 November, Gunpowder Plot Day, and marched his army off to Exeter, whose common people welcomed the disciplined Dutch army, though the bishop and civic leaders had fled. After an irksome wait, he was greeted on 17 November by the local magnate, Edward Seymour, and his rival, the Earl of Bath.

James's professional army was large and solid: 25,000 men. If this army were to inflict a stunning defeat on the invader, James might well have swung the situation into his favour. He joined his army at Salisbury, near to nervous breakdown, tormented by insomnia, and, as Burnet says, 'his blood was in such a fermentation that it gushed out of his nose several times a day'. Indecisive, panicked and forsaken, the man of action cracked. As William marched towards him, rumours caused James's front line to waver and partially rush back into the army like an ebb-tide: James gave orders to withdraw. John Churchill and the Duke of Grafton, Charles II's natural son, deserted; Princess Anne would leave London to join William's allies in the Midlands. Hectic with dread and rage, James went to London, and sent negotiators to William, who was now moving on London in what seemed a royal progress, breaking off to view the Earl of Pembroke's choice collection of pictures by his countryman, Van Dyck.

William stated his terms. James took fright and, in the early hours of 10 December, burning the writs for the election of Parliament and throwing the great Seal of England into the Thames, bolted, having already sent his wife and son off to France. He disbanded the army without paying it, thence letting loose a potential mayhem of looting and pillage. A fisherman later scooped out the Seal near Vauxhall. The king himself was apprehended by fishermen on the look-out for papist priests, and submitted to a body-search and rough handling. He was taken to Faversham.

That morning crowds of apprentices went on the rampage in London, demolishing Catholic chapels. A gentlewoman, Anne Mildmay, wrote to her brother that her family, seeing flames, were 'all afraid that London was on fire... the flames we saw was of bonfires made, by the gentlemen of the mob, of the mass-houses and other popish houses'. They had been torn down and the timbers carried to Lincoln's Inn, where they were torched. Apprentices seized Judge Jeffries attempting to escape in disguise. This most hated figure was subjected to the power of the mob, tossed in the air for hours amid braying of insults. He was conveyed to the Tower, with the idea that he should take his own medicine, where the mayor, appalled at the disorder, called William to take temporary control.

James's personal situation had now spiralled into tragic farce, from which however a sharper-witted man might have conjured a recovery. When the people of Faversham realized they had the disguised king in their hands, 'they changed their rough usage into all the respect they could possible pay him'. Compassion for his plight filled the hearts of all who saw him and he was brought to London fêted by cheering crowds. This renewal of sentimental royalism, such a powerful and irrational factor in relation to the recurrently exiled Stuart monarchy, embarrassed William, who would infinitely have preferred the king to have escaped cleanly. Evelyn wrote on 13 December, 'The King flies… is rudely treated by the people; comes back to Whitehall… goes to mass, and dines in public, a Jesuit saying grace (I was present).' This pithy recapitulation aptly expresses the absurdity of the moment. James was precipitated out to Rochester with a nominal guard of Dutch troops, under orders to permit his escape to France.

There was now an Interregnum, while all the protagonists pondered and wrangled on the most legal-seeming means to establish William and Mary in the effectively deposed James's place. This crisis was deepened by William's disdainful refusal to defer to a woman as mere consort in an 'apron-strings' government. The problems that beset the shifting coalition in 1688–9 were a milder version of the dilemma of 1649. Now as then there was an Interregnum; now as then, a Stuart king had been ejected from the throne by a nation with no revolutionary or democratic intent. William was an alien element that was at once the source and resolution of the problem. Halifax astutely remarked that, 'as nobody knew what to do with him, so nobody knew what to do without him'. The House of Lords contained strict Jacobites to whom the dynastic succession was God-ordained: they called for the immediate reinstatement of James II. Some favoured a regency by Mary and William, during James's lifetime, after which they would reign in their own right. The Commons threw up more radical arguments and solutions, reflecting the ideas of social contract evolved in the Commonwealth era. Whigs held that James, having violated his contract with the people, had 'abdicated the government', leaving the throne 'vacant'. However, the words 'abdicate' and 'vacant' were invalid in English law, whereby the 'body politic' of the kingship never dies. In this case, the body natural was still alive and its brain had begun to function again, for James wrote in conciliatory terms that he was willing to resume his rule, guaranteeing the security of Parliament.

The solution lay in finding a form of words that emphasized the passivity of Parliament in the face of James's active truancy. The lawyer Sir George Treby phrased it thus: 'We have found the crown vacant. We found it so, we did not make it so.' The stress on the word 'found' saved the government from seeming to go down the path towards a repetition of Civil War instability. William stood astonished and impatient at the infernal wranglings of his English Parliament, whose deliberations seemed to his driven mind the purest argy-bargy. The English were debating, in the moment of crisis, the historical events that had led up to it, shifting the weight on their corporate conscience, moving more swiftly than could have been clear to him to a consensus between profoundly opposed interests. The idea of government by social contract would be expounded by John Locke in his *Two Treatises of Government* (1690). It was an idea with which William (whose position in the United Provinces was elective rather than hereditary) had no problem but, to the bulk of English gentry and aristocracy, it was sinister.

William threatened to return to the continent if the delay continued. He wished to resume his European role, in which the English invasion formed only a single step. A Declaration of Rights was drawn up to be read before the coronation of the joint monarchs, enshrining the liberties of Parliament, the law and the subject, and declaring illegal the 'suspending' and 'dispensing' powers of the Crown.

CHAPTER 7

WILLIAM AND MARY

THE GLORIOUS REVOLUTION

The foreign prince, William of Orange, who acceded to the 'vacant' throne in 1689 jointly with Mary Stuart, was the son of Charles I's sister Mary and William, Prince of Orange. He had been born at The Hague and lived most of his life in the Low Countries. He was an international statesman and Reformation warrior, his life dedicated to the struggle against the forces of Catholic French imperialism. He had been bred for this role, and all his passions and aspirations were driven by its rigours. In 1665 he had been adopted as a 'Child of State' by the States General when his uncle, Charles II, had waged war on the Netherlands and it was feared that Charles might attempt to set him up as puppet king. A child of state was what he remained all his life. On a visit to England in 1670, William could hardly believe the time frittered in feckless chat, horse-racing and gourmandizing: he itched to get on with the business of life. The French diplomat Pomponne had noted of William at nineteen all those qualities that were to mark him as a man: 'He was naturally intelligent and his judgment seemed as great as his intelligence. He knew how to hide his feelings – dissimulation seemed to come naturally to him.' He noted the young man's diligence, reserve and politic pursuit of his ends. To the English, he seemed glacial; business was usually done in a syrup of superficial pleasure, and his taciturn, curt speech and immobile features frosted the social atmosphere with a Calvinist gloom.

But the rocklike fortitude and purposefulness of William were qualities that England could respect and use. He once told the English ambassador a parable, which stuck in Sir William Temple's mind:

> I must go on and take my fortune. I saw this morning a poor old man, tugging alone in a little boat with his oars, against the eddy of a sluice, upon a canal; when, with the last endeavours, he was just got up to the place intended, the force of the eddy turned him quite back again; he turned his boat as soon as he could, and fell to his oars again; and thus, three or four times, while I saw him. This old man's business and mine are too like one another, and I ought to do just what he did, without knowing what would succeed.

This emblem condenses the Dutch republic's experience of dogged struggle against inexorable forces, its vision of the heroic in the homely, like a genre painting by Rembrandt, where sombre colours, exact realism and unglamorous persons reveal an inner light instructive to the pondering witness. Its setting is the watery landscape of the Low Countries, webbed with manmade canals, where people live a hard, solitary life, bound by the imperatives of work. This essentially Dutch character of William's vision, in which he identifies his task with that of the citizen–peasant, drawing the moral, 'I ought to do just what he did', reveals a mind bleakly bent to the necessity of an arduous long-term project.

William was to Europeanize England. He would commit the country to costly war, for ten of his thirteen years of rule. The constitutional changes that occurred in his reign and seemed to later generations to have been its first fruits were more precisely its by-products. The close ties that developed between Parliament and Crown, requiring annual parliamentary meetings, were not dictated by the Declaration (later the Bill) of Rights as much as by Parliament's unwillingness to vote him war supply for more than a year at a time. The civil list was introduced, making the king dependent on Parliament, which also limited the monarchy by specifying the line of descent and the royal prerogative in the Act of Succession. Paradoxically, since William had no interest whatever in the tedious clamour of political parties, he simply used the factious Whigs and Tories to achieve his ends. In his foreignness and reserve, William brought a dispassionate quality to the Crown. He was infinitely less bothered about his standing and prestige than by what he could get out of his newly acquired dominion and was for long periods of each year an absentee, waging war on the continent.

THE ORDEAL OF MARY

Mary was the child of James I and Anne Hyde, daughter of the Earl of Clarendon. She had been brought up against the shifting panorama of a father's debauchery and the misery of a powerfully controlling mother. Anne, who had taken to comfort-eating in the face of James's womanizing, had died in appalling pain of cancer and been forgotten within the week. Mary, removed from her father to be brought up a Protestant, had fallen in love with the beautiful Frances Apsley, nine years her senior, with whom she conducted an amorous correspondence under the sobriquets Chlorin (Mary) and Aurelia. This fantasy relationship, the secret mainstay of her difficult early years, was constructed on the pattern of female friendship brought into poetic vogue by Katharine Phillips ('the Matchless Orinda'), who had written of ideal love between women in poems to 'Lucasia' (Anne Owen) and 'Rosania' (Mary Aubrey). Fifty-eight of these letters survive, writing to 'Aurelia' as her 'dear, dear husband' and replying in the persona of 'Your obedient loving constant wife'. This highly charged romantic intimacy continued well into Mary's marriage to William. It was an emotional training ground for the dynastic wifehood that was her lot in life, in which Mary took the role of submissive wife.

As a fifteen-year-old child, she had been aghast to find herself claimed by that extreme form of exogamy that was the destiny of royal daughters. When her father informed her of the match, she wept inconsolably. Her peace of mind cannot have been enhanced by her uncle Charles's quips during the marriage ceremony, nor by his drawing the curtains on the pair with the encouragement, 'Now, nephew, to your work! Hey! – St George for England!' Mary's distaste turned, in The Hague, to an imploring adoration, which William could not reciprocate. His incommunicative habits of mind and speech coincided with a certain automatic contempt for women, normal in a patriarchal society but intensified in a man who had invested his emotions in the role of national hero. William's long-term affair with Elizabeth Villiers, great-niece of James I's 'Steenie' and cousin of Barbara, Charles II's mistress, caused Mary grief, which expressed itself in renewed gushes of her 'wifely' passion in letters to 'Aurelia'. 'I do not now mourn a dead lover, but a false one… You wound me more than you can imagine… O! dearest dearest dearest dearest dearest dear husband, send me a letter, one kind word will give me ease.' She had looked for bread and been dealt a stone with which, in course of time, this introverted, sensitive and very ordinary woman learned to make do.

When William had established the Revolution and called his wife to join him in February 1689, she left the Netherlands with agitated reluctance on a yacht with an escort

of Dutch men-of-war. After the crossing the weather had cleared, to reveal a sea 'like a looking-glass', like that which brought Ann Fanshawe home with Charles II's fleet at the Restoration. As Mary's yacht paused beyond Margate: 'I looked behind, and saw vast seas between me and Holland, that had been my country for more than eleven years. I saw with regret that I had left it, and I believed it was forever; that was a hard thought, and I had need of much more constancy than I can brag of, to bear it with patience.'

PACIFYING UNREST

The mode of life to which she had become accustomed was essentially private and retiring, and it was nearly as difficult for Mary as for William to accommodate to a monarchy that presented itself to the public in the form of ongoing theatricals. William's sullen refusal to play his role with a good grace gave offence and disappointment. He retreated to the quiet and fresher air of Hampton Court when he could. The new reign would also patronize movements for moral improvement that sprang up in reaction to the dissoluteness of Charles's and James's courts.

In Scotland and Ireland, chain reactions of unrest and revolution broke out, very different from the constitutional pandemonium in England. The Scottish Convention Parliament of 1689 demanded the freedom of the Kirk from Anglican control, the abolition of bishops and the autonomy of the Scots Parliament. While William's instinct was to reject these demands, he soon acquiesced, recognizing his dependence on the Lowland Presbyterians to help suppress Highland Jacobite rebellion, which broke out in the summer of 1689 with a great victory under 'Bonny Dundee' (James Graham of Claverhouse, Viscount Dundee) at the Battle of Killiekrankie. William offered amnesty to the Highland clans, provided they take the oath of allegiance by 1692. One of the most notorious atrocities in Scots history occurred when the Maclains of Glencoe were butchered, man, woman and child, for failing to sign on time, by the Campbells, their hereditary enemies, to whom they had given hospitality. The Highlands became a site of Jacobite rebellion for two generations.

The revolution in Ireland ran counter to the Glorious Revolution. In February 1689 James, in a French armada funded by Louis XIV, sailed from St Germain in high seas to land at Kinsale in south-west Ireland, where he rendezvoused with 'Roaring Dick' Talbot, the Earl of Tyrconnel, who had led a brilliant campaign to plant Catholics in all administrative, judicial and military positions. By the time James landed, Tyrconnel possessed the whole of Ireland except for Londonderry and Enniskillen, and the arrival of a Catholic king on Irish soil kindled an explosion of militancy and hope. James felt no answering ecstasy, hankering only after England. The 'Patriot Parliament' met in Dublin in May, with 218 out of 224 members Catholic, asserting independence, revenging itself for Cromwell's invasion by revoking the Act of Settlement that had stolen Irish lands and reassigned them to Protestants. Jubilant, naive men had flocked to James's reluctant standard in shoeless, ragged multitudes. James's troops laid siege to Enniskillen but,

The warrior-statesman, William III of Orange, was a phlegmatic Calvinist, who invaded England only to further his Protestant war against Catholic Europe.

possessing no appropriate artillery, engineers or mines, he had to starve the Enniskilleners out. When food-laden ships belatedly arrived from England, the besieged rushed out and smashed a Jacobite army at Newtown Butler. The relief of Londonderry was effected only after thousands perished from hunger and disease.

One of James's regiments had only seven muskets between them. Many men were armed only with daggers and scythes. There was no money, no food, no discipline. The frail economy crashed under the weight of the disorder. William sent an army under General Schomberg, which found itself, like many English armies in Ireland, mired, rained on, hungry, marooned, and scourged by typhus. Half the men died without a shot. William therefore came in person, at the head of an international army containing mercenary Huguenots, Dutch, Germans, Danes and Finns, crushing the Jacobites at the Battle of the Boyne.

'It is well it came no nearer,' was William's laconic comment on the wound he sustained from a cannon ball that grazed his right shoulder, as the two armies confronted one another across the river. William's vanguard crossed waist-deep in water, and fought a ferocious hand-to-hand battle to allow 20,000 men to follow. James, whose mind was fixated on retreat from early in the fighting, fled to Dublin and on to France. The phlegmatic William expressed, according to his physician, 'neither joy nor any sort of vanity', but he permitted himself to look 'cheerful'. William continued with the campaign against the Catholics in Munster and Leinster, with great slaughter, leaving John Churchill, now Earl of Marlborough, to complete the suppression. But it was the Battle of the Boyne that was mythologized by Ulster Protestants as a providential victory to be re-enacted in triumphalist fashion each year, while to Catholics it was a crowning infamy. New-minted ballads were soon for sale, with such choruses as:

> King William's courage scares his foes.
> He conquers all where'er he goes.

Mary's husband had fought Mary's father in direct combat. The psychological burden of this conflict of allegiance was recognized by both men. James had written to her in 1688, expressing his sense of betrayal at the Prince of Orange's preparations to invade, that he knew she was 'a good wife, and ought to be so, yet for the same reason I must believe you will still be as good a daughter to a father that has always loved you so tenderly'. His letter sought to exacerbate the strain on a malleable and dutiful temperament, but later went on to recognize that she must be 'very uneasy all this time, for the concern you must have for a husband and a father. You shall find me kind to you, if you desire it.' The century that had begun with Elizabeth, a regnant single woman, answerable to no man, the humanist scholar, poet and statesman who rode in armour to inspect her troops at Tilbury, would draw to its evening in a queen whose sole ambition was to be a cipher to her husband.

Mary inspected her troops from a modest covered coach. In William's absences, she governed as a figurehead regent through ministers, abashed at her stupefaction and complaining that business 'does but break my brains the more and not ease my heart'. Mary obeyed the detailed script left by William. She exercised her interest in architecture, horticulture, charitable foundations, the Church and the improvement of public morals, areas in which she felt at home. The theatre, where Restoration court display had met public fantasy, was little to her taste and, when she ordered a special performance of Dryden's *The Spanish Friar*, she squirmed while the audience smiled with *Schadenfreude*, to find the play plotted on a queen's deposition of her own father. Nahum Tate's version of *King Lear* (1681) had brought the topic to the fore, in revising the ending: Lear and Cordelia do not die, but he abdicates in her favour. A squib entitled 'The Female Parricide' was published in 1689, in which Mary was lambasted: 'worse than cruel lustful Goneril, thou!' A sense of trespass and broken taboos haunted Mary, beside the hunger for affection that was never appeased.

William's sedulous prosecution of the war against France, conducted on the principle of the boatman striving 'against the eddy of a sluice', brought him not precisely to victory but to an eroding of the opposition through strategic defensive campaigning. At Steenkerk (1692) and Landen (1693) he held on without gain but without loss either, his armies haemorrhaging blood, but by 1694 Louis's financial resources were strained and when William retook Namur, a powerfully fortified town, France's aggression began to buckle. The war ended after Mary's death with the Treaty of Ryswyck. It was more popular with Whigs than Tories, who were in favour of a cheap 'blue water war', using the navy rather than a long land campaign.

A CENTRE OF COMMERCE

The political and religious complexion of England was changing, under the pressure of many factors, and often (as far as William was concerned) by default. Because of the need for massive sums of money for the continental war, and England's new place in international commerce, a revolution in public finance issued in the founding of the Bank of England, the creation of the national debt and the establishment of London as the financial capital of the world. The administration of finance was streamlined and affluent individuals were appointed to revenue boards, where they advanced capital, to be repaid in cash and influence. The Bank of England was a chartered corporation, composed chiefly of wealthy Whigs, which soon became a clearing house for public credit. It was to issue its own banknotes, which became the currency of the country. A capitalist democracy was beginning to emerge in embryo.

The Williamite period was a time of party embroilment, a heaving chaos of faction from which the modern party system was – with hindsight – recognizably emerging. The Triennial Act of 1694 reinforced this instability by making the bitter, bribing ferment of elections all but continuous. Party agents and organizations canvassed, party newspapers rolled propaganda off the presses and the electorate was bought beer and treated to promises and invective. There were eleven general elections during the period 1689–1715. The size of the electorate had also swollen to an unprecedented 20,000, as more males achieved the property qualification entitling them to the franchise. When in 1695 the Licensing Act lapsed, nobody bothered to renew it, allowing freedom of the press and the flowering of political journalism.

The Toleration Act of 1689 was a modest rather than a radical move, which brought a limited but real acknowledgement of individual right to liberty of conscience. All Protestants except Unitarians (who denied the Trinity, and therefore the divinity of Christ) were permitted to worship as they chose, and Dissenter congregations had to be registered with a bishop or at Quarter Sessions, while the doors of meetings had to be left wide open, so that checks could be made on whether seditions or heresies were brewing inside. John Locke saw the Act as providing 'foundations… of that liberty and peace, in which the church of Christ is one day to be established'. At the same time, the Test Acts for office holders were not abolished, thus ensuring that Nonconformists remained second-class citizens. However, this very exclusion intensified Dissenters' initiative and self-belief. The Quakers became a powerful business community, famous for business probity and hard work, while many Dissenters in the eighteenth century would become self-made men and capitalists, as well as philanthropists and intellectuals. The Toleration Act came as a disappointment to those who had not wanted toleration as much as 'comprehension', a widening of the Anglican Church so that it could have accommodated persons of many colours of opinion: to bring the outsiders in, rather than allowing them to remain unpersecuted. Conservative Anglicans saw such comprehension as sounding a death-knell to the Anglican monopoly in Church and State, and the Bill was defeated amid a deafening furore.

In 1694 Queen Mary II died of smallpox. William, stricken with guilt and belated awareness of the love with which she had surrounded him, watched over her and afterwards was prostrate with grief. As she lay dying, Mary's mind seems to have floated back to her childhood, and her bed was haunted by the spectres of her Catholic parents plotting her conversion. She pointed to a screen at her bedhead and asked that her companions search behind it. When she was told there was nobody there, she cried out, 'Look again, look again. Dr Radcliffe has put a Popish nurse upon me, and she is always listening to what is said about me – that woman is a great nuisance to me…' The age of plots and treasons, both real and imagined, drew to its close.

PERSPECTIVE ON THE CENTURY

Seventeenth-century England had been rocked by fratricidal conflict, born of the aftermath of the Reformation that had divided Europe. It had seen a bloody civil war, the execution of a king and the brief establishment of a republic, followed within decades by the eviction of a Catholic king. The 'Glorious Revolution' of 1688 had perhaps solved little, in a direct sense. But during the 1690s, a new accommodation between Crown and Parliament had emerged, limiting the royal prerogative and extending the powers and function of Parliament, so that a new balance was achieved. In 1701 the Act of Settlement sought to seal that balance by establishing that the crown should pass from Mary's younger sister, Anne (whose nineteen children all died), to the House of Hanover, descended from James I's daughter, Elizabeth, 'the Protestant line'. The Act excluded any Roman Catholic from occupying the throne of England. From now on, with the Crown's power curtailed and the role of the wealthy elite strengthened, the danger of civil war receded. It was replaced by the war of words, often violent but never mortal, of party politicians debating across the floor of the Commons.

The gulf between the wealthy and the abjectly poor remained as immense in 1700 as it had been in 1600. The landless poor, working as wage-labourers, remained

Mary' II's accession as joint monarch with William III was at the price of seeing 'my husband and my father personally engaged against each other'.

perilously close to subsistence and, if they ate a little more meat than they had at the turn of the century and a little less adulterated bread, their lot was just as arduous and insecure. Manufacture was still chiefly cottage industry, but, with improvement in transport and agricultural methods, stabilization of population and a revolution in commerce and finance, there was a great increase in national wealth. In 1700 England was becoming urbanized as great towns such as Liverpool, Bristol, Norwich and Nottingham developed into 'little Londons', with their own civic sense, assembly rooms, exhibitions and coffee houses. England faced outwards to world markets, with the confidence of an international power.

Page references to illustrations or to captions are in **bold**

PICTURE CREDITS

ACKNOWLEDGMENTS

I owe my friends, Barb and Steve Garner, thanks for their generous help throughout the writing of this book, both in terms of technical expertise and the support of friendship. My agent, Jane Bradish-Ellames of Curtis Brown, has been a source of strength, for which I am most grateful. I thank Robin Brooks-Davies for his help and humour, Frank Regan for being there for me, and Barbara Prys-Williams for all her encouragement.

Dick de Ruiter
Danny Becher
Marjolein Berkvens

Sounds like
OM
Universal
Primeval Mantra

Singing the sound OM is like stepping into
a pleasant, warm bath of sound.
A most beautiful song in your head...
– *Dick de Ruiter, 2005*

Text Dick de Ruiter
Voices Danny Becher, Marjolein Berkvens

"Aum" painting on page 8 by Pieter Weltevrede (www.sanatansociety.org)
"Sri Yantra Reflections" painting on page 26 by Menno Dijkhuys
(www.sanatansociety.org)
"Sri Yantra" picture on page 33 by Maria Strutz (maria-strutz@zen.co.uk)
Photography Dick de Ruiter
Editing Valerie Cooper
Layout Jaap Koning

First published in 2006 by Binkey Kok Publications – Haarlem/Holland
www.binkeykok.com/E-mail post@gottmer.nl

ISBN 90-78302-04-6
© 2006 Binkey Kok Publications
Binkey Kok Publications is an imprint of Altamira-Becht BV and member of the Gottmer
Publishers Group in Haarlem/Holland.

CONTENTS

1   PLEASED TO MEET YOU

The existence of inner sounds cannot be denied. Just look at your own breathing. Even the activity of your nervous system has its own sound, if you know how to listen. This inner sound is not something the Mahayana Buddhists have made up. It is the scientific reality of your inner being. Even babies say "aah" when they cry. Actually, the sound AH exists already, even before it comes out of the mouth; it is there already, at the level of your nervous system.

— Lama Yeshe

In this book, we spell the mantra as it is most often written: "OM". The way it is sung, however, is as the sequence of vowel sounds, that is "A-O-U-M".

The many scriptures about the OM sound call it the mantra of all mantras, the primeval sound from which all other sounds emerged. In this first chapter we will acquaint ourselves with the mantra concept, and its function in meditative practice.

As far back as we can remember, the ancient Eastern practice of meditating with mantras and mudras has been very common in religions all over the world. Even now this continues to be part of the daily routine in many people's lives.

A *mantra* is a word or a phrase with a certain meaning or value attributed to it by its user, and which is used as an aid during meditation or religious rituals, but also as an anchoring in daily life. A person can choose a mantra individually—a word he or she appreciates or values. But traditionally an initiate receives a mantra from a spiritual teacher or master. The mantra is energetically "charged" with a special power according to the initiate's religious background. This power is transferred to the initiate through his or her continuous repetition of this personal mantra.

The most commonly used mantras have been the same ancient "holy" words or sounds that practitioners have used throughout the ages, but within some systems the given mantra is specifically attuned to the initiiate, which makes it very personal and more effective.

The sound OM is considered to be the "mantra of all mantras." Traditionally, this sound is viewed as the mother sound, the source of all other sounds, or even the origin of creation. To many of us, this may be a symbolic point of view, but the fact is that the sound does have an extremely pleasant, physical and mental effect. That is why in this book we will go further into the individual experience, the personal practice of chanting the OM sound, with or without the use of mudras. Some of the effects of such a practice include:

- a calming effect caused by regulated, slowed-down breathing;
- facilitates the attainment of the first stage of meditation by drawing your attention from the outside looking in;
- a pleasant, harmonic sound massage for the chest, belly, spine, and head;
- improved organ function;
- improved concentration and other brain functions;
- an indescribable feeling of well-being, peace, and harmony that can only be experienced to be properly appreciated;
- last, but not least, it provides an ideal introduction to several kinds of meditation and spiritual practice.

So, there are plenty of reasons to further investigate the unique sounds of the OM mantra! In the next chapters we will get acquainted with the basics and history of chanting OM, both the symbolic or mystical values, as well as the mere physical effects of the sound vibrations. Finally, we will learn how to put these options into practice, including the use of the CD belonging to this book.

In the beginning there was only Silence
And from this Silence, the Word emerged
And the Word was OM

The origin of the use of mantras and the first application of the OM mantra have been lost in the mists of time. The image shown on page 8 is a Sri Yantra, the visualized expression of OM. Dating from the 17th century, it provides palpable evidence that the OM sound was known in those days. But this knowledge actually goes back much further in time, to the blossoming of Indian culture, long before our era. The oldest-known Sri Yantra has been dated at 3,000 years B.C.E.

In the heat of August 1990, in a dry lake bed in the wilderness of Steen's Mountain, east Oregon, a very peculiar variant of what we usually call a "crop circle" appeared out of the blue, covering over 13 miles, with a circumference of over a mile. Each trench in the diagram was 3 inches deep and 10 inches wide. This image (on page 10) was an exact replica of the Sri Yantra image, an ancient Indian symbol that represents the OM sound.

At first, four jokers laid claim to having created the image, but after attempting to reconstruct their story, it appeared to have been utterly impossible to have performed such a task. These people would have had to haul heavy equipment for several miles into the desert wilderness refuge, where vehicles were prohibited. Furthermore, the work would have taken several days and they would have surely been observed going to the site. The elements of the yantra were so accurate that even with professional measurements and digging equipment, it would have taken them many days to finish the job. Pilots flying overhead on a regular basis, however, reported noticing the appearance of the image overnight.

The only remaining "explanation"—which many people still wave off as nonsense but fail to come up with another idea—is that these and many other images, appearing regularly all over the world, could only be made by a technically advanced alien civilization.[1]

THE SYMBOL

The Sanskrit lettering of OM contains the following symbolism:

The lower curve of the "3" on the left side of the symbol stands for the material world, the waking consciousness (*vaishvanara*).

The curve on the right represents the subtle body, the unconscious, and the world of dreams (*taijasa*). The upper arc of the "3" symbolizes the original, the subconscious, and deep sleep (*prajna*).

The dot on top, also known as *bindu* (mustardseed), and also appears as the central point in the Sri Yantra, represents the "fourth state," the absolute or superconscious, which is all-embracing and brings the three other states together (*turiya*). The dot is also a symbol for the "third eye" (the sixth chakra) and Atman/Brahman, the higher self.

The half-moon carrying the dot symbolizes the separation from this fourth state of consciousness, although it still is connected to the other three. The aim is to penetrate through *bindu*, in order to access the higher spiritual regions.

•

Symbols: Humanoid or Divine Inspiration?

Sanskrit is one of the most ancient languages. It has been called the "language of the gods." The component strokes of OM written in Sanskrit are beautiful examples of this symbolism.

The symbolism of the Sri Yantra

A yantra is a complex geometric diagram, a *mandala*, which is used in spiritual practice as an aid during meditation, or to direct the attention from the outside world to one central point and, eventually, inward. The word *yantra* comes from the root *yam*, meaning knowledge of the essence of an object or concept. The syllable "*tra*" is a conjugation of *trana*, which means liberation from bonds. *Yantra* also means liberation (*moksha*) from the circle of birth and death.

The Sri Yantra consists of two series of triangles surrounded by lotus leaves and circles. The four triangles pointed upwards represent the male Shiva element, the intense spiritual longing for the subtle worlds, and the fire element (*agni tattwa*). The five triangles pointed downward stand for the female Shakti element, the symbol of the inexhaustible source of the Universe, and the water element (*apas tattwa*).

The ever-intersecting triangles represent the forces which, when joined together, are more powerful than the separate shapes. Every intersection creates new triangles, a total of 43 altogether, ever varying in size and angles.

Often there are characters inside these triangles, for accompanying mantras.

The outline of two intersecting triangles makes a perfect six-pointed star, the *Shatkona*, which we know as the Star of David. This represents the unification of *purusha* and *prakriti* (or Shiva and Shakti), which was the origin of all creation, according to the ancient scriptures.

The dot in the center of this yantra, known as a *bindu*, is the central focal point. Many monasteries practice the technique of drawing these yantras, making the creative process of drawing them a very special kind of meditation. Westerners were mesmerized by the Tibetan Buddhist practice of making such figures with dry colored sand when the Dalai Lama performed the Kalachakra initiation in the United States for the first time in 1981. This requires the utmost control and concentration.

The circle, *chakra*, is the logical expansion of the central *bindu*. The point draws a circle around itself, symbolizing the range in which the individual awareness can manifest itself.

The chakra circles are symbols of *shristi* (creation), *sthiti* (preservation), and *samhara* (merging into the all that is).

After the point and the circle, the triangle is the most simple geometrical shape. In the Sri Yantra, the nine intersecting triangles are the balanced framework around the central point. The lines around the yantra symbolize the function of preservation, preventing the loss of the magical powers represented in the central pattern. They also are supposed to enhance these magical and subtle energies.

The edging of lotus leaves symbolizes arising purity. Lotus leaves in a yantra point to a perfect protection from negative and disturbing influences from the outside. The outer square represents the earth, the central point of which is the ethers. From the outer material world, the spiritual journey directs one to the inside, to the ethereal worlds and spheres within.

3 YANTRAS, MUDRAS & MANTRAS
Incantations or exact science?

We are living in a world of chaos. So many impressions, images, millions of invisible but ever-present sound vibrations, and electromagnetic fields surround us. These impressions are continuously affecting us, whether we like it or not. We are literally being bombarded by these chaotic waves. We can take certain measures to counterbalance this chaos, just as we would protect our ears as much as possible against damaging levels of noise, or avoid these in our own living environment. Today there is even certain advanced equipment that can protect us against negative energy fields.[2]

And, now and then, we can also utilize special sound fields in order to harmonize our whole being. As such, the OM sound is one of the most suitable holy tools; holy in the most literal sense of the word, that is: wholly, whole, healing, harmonizing.

YANTRAS
In the Far East, yantras were—and still are—used during the practice of singing mantras. In this book you will find several examples of the *Sri Yantra*,

the visual image of the OM sound, which is used in conjunction with the OM mantra, as described in the previous chapter. Yantras are generally used during open-eyed meditations in order to direct one's concentration to one-pointedness, and to stop or at least slow down one's inner dialogue. Thus it is the preliminary stage of meditation with one's eyes closed, when the mantra is repeated inwardly, in order to eventually arrive at the utter and absolute silence within.

MUDRAS

A *mudra* is a kind of posture or body movement that one carries out while chanting a mantra. The Muslim praying posture, kneeling down toward Mecca, could be considered a mudra, as is making the sign of the cross during Christian prayer. In the Eastern religions, mudras are always connected with devotion or prayer, with opening up to the sacred. In yoga, the word *mudra* pertains to certain postures that cause a flow of energy to specific body parts.

MANTRAS

There are two kinds of mantras. First, there is the endless reciting of a specific "sacred" mantra—like *hare Krishna*—with the belief or conviction that this represents a certain power or deity, for the benefit of some specific purpose. Obviously, this mantra type has a religious connection and obtains its powers or effects through *faith*.

In Islam and Sufism there are the mantras *la ilaha il'alla* (there is no God but Allah) and *subhana'llah* (praise to the Lord). The *dikr* is the Islamic way of saying the mantras, the continuous remembrance of God, by repeating His holy name and other proverbs. While reciting prayers, the Muslims use the *tasbih*, which has 99 beads and is completed three times during a service. With each bead the name of Allah is praised, and it is said that at the hundredth name, one will enter paradise! In India a similar string of beads, the *mala*, is used (in Tibet it is called the *tengwa dorje*), and the prayers (such as *om mane pame hum*) are always initiated with the first bead, known as the *guru bead*. Our word "amen," by the way, probably has a connection with OM through the Proto-Indo-European language.

The second kind of mantra consists of very specific sound structures known as *bija* (pronounced "bee-ja" and meaning "seed") in Sanskrit, that have direct physical and psychological effects upon us, by way of their vibrations, pitch, and vowels. No matter what religion one follows—or not—*bija* have direct physical and psychological effects upon us that are clearly measurable and verifiable. We will explore this kind of mantra more at length here. We will get acquainted with various applications and singing methods, and how to sing along with the sounds on the CD enclosed in this book.

The effects of Sri Yantra

Concentrating on a geometric figure like the Sri Yantra activates our left brain hemisphere, while the singing a mantra stimulates the right hemisphere. These combined activities balance the energy in both hemispheres, resulting in a calm and concentrated mind—the first and most important condition for meditation.

For the Westerner, whose lifestyle typically stimulates the left brain hemisphere more than the right, this method is an ideal and very practical way to balance the hemispheres, and thus to function better and achieve more in daily life.

However, the way this works can be explored much deeper. "Shape-energy" is a concept that has yet to be accepted by Western science, but in the Far East, they like to explain it this way: By *resonance*, a certain kind of energy in the practitioner's *microcosm* will resonate at the same wavelength as a similar vibration of endless energy in the *macrocosm*, the kind of energy that is expressed in the Sri Yantra.

By way of *kinesiology*, or muscle testing, one can easily demonstrate how the Sri Yantra works. If someone, for whatever reason, appears to test weak and then just looks at a Sri Yantra, he or she will immediately test strong. Incidentally, this will happen likewise when using the "Western yantra" designed by psychologist John Diamond (see p.19), who claims that by just looking at the picture, one's thymus gland will function better and produce more antibodies in one's bloodstream, resulting in a simultaneous higher production of hormone-like particles in the brain, such as serotonin, making one instantly feel more comfortable, even happy.

The intention of a word

When we use a mantra, it is important to couple our own *intention* with the word or words of the mantra. A matter of faith? Perhaps. But the power of intention—in other words, the direction and intensity that you will give to your thoughts—is demonstrably effective!

Masaru Emoto, a Japanese scientist, performed many experiments with plain water. This water was divided among several petri dishes. Emoto then had a number of words written on labels that were then attached to these dishes of water, and then these were frozen. The ice crystals in each petri dish, viewed magnified with a microscope 200 to 500 times actual size, appeared to be completely different, although they were all from the same "batch" of water. Apparently it was these words attached to the water that made the difference. In this manner, over a period of four and a half years, Emoto took about 10,000 photographs of ice crystals, also showing, for instance, the influence of different sounds on the water.[3] Pleasing sounds and words with positive intention produced geometrically balanced and beautiful crystals while harsh noises and words seemed to cause the crystals to form chaotic shapes. Because we humans primarily consist of water, it's not so far out to assume that the sounds of a mantra, combined with our personally-set intention, will also have a direct, positive effect upon all of our cells!

Still, it is not only the energy that we ourselves combine with the yantra that will determine its effects. The shape by itself also contains a definite influence. Again, using *kinesiology*, you can energetically test various geometrical shapes. Just try it out: draw some very simple figures—such as a circle, a triangle, and a square—on different pieces of paper, and let someone else do the muscle test on you, while you look at each figure in turn. You will see that you will react differently with different symbols. You will even experience different muscle strength in these tests when you for instance remove one of the sides of a triangle!

As said before, the Sri Yantra always tests strong in *everyone*, regardless of education, race, or belief. One hundred percent! The same applies to chanting the OM sound. This shows clearly that belief in the symbols and sounds is not a prerequisite for gaining their benefits.

In the 19th century, Ernst Chladni (1756 – 1827) experimented with dry sand on metal plates in square, circular or other shapes, which he vibrated with a fiddlestick, causing the sand to form geometric shapes. Hans Jenny (1904 – 1972, pioneer of *cymatics*, or the study of wave phenomena and inventor of the tonoscope) and later on Barbara Hero continued and expanded upon these experiments, and concluded that all harmonic sounds, with all overtones in harmonic sequences, will also show geometrically perfect images in the resonated matter.

One of the most special discoveries in these experiments with sound and computer-generated imagery was that when the vowel sounds of OM are sung into the microphone, at first you will see a circle, and when the whole mantra has been sung, the complete Sri Yantra will be visible on the screen.

Yes, exactly the same image that has been pictured for ages in stone, on linen, and paper! We can only guess where the ancient wise men got their knowledge from, but we can presume they knew a lot more than historians would have us believe…

These are but a few ways in which modern science is confirming ancient wisdom and knowledge. The OM sound gives us literally a harmonizing vibration, resonating in the whole of our bodies, while lifting our spirits to another level.

This we can best experience by putting it into practice. This practice is described in the last chapters, including the use of the CD as an important aid.

Affirmations are sentences or words, repeated over and over again, aloud
or just in thought, or in writing, as a literal remembrance of a certain positive thought or impression. They can also be recorded on tape or CD, to
be played daily, to help us shift our consciousness into a healthier place.

The OM mantra can be used in a similar way, as a self-affirmation or,
if you will, as an affirmation of the Self.

The use and practice of affirmations can be traced back through the ages.
Certain prayers are nothing less than positive self-affirmations in religious
words. Mantras are repeated endlessly in order to grasp and live in accor-
dance with their meaning or contents.

But in principle, the old-fashioned method of writing out the same sentence a hundred times, as at school, is also a kind of affirmation, with the
purpose of literally drumming the values and beliefs into your brains, never
to be forgotten! And the ever-repeated television and radio commercials are
another boring (and somewhat demeging) example of drilling a message into
our minds...

A more positive application nowadays is the use of affirmations in so-called positive reprogramming on CD, or even on video or DVD. There are various ways and "tricks" with specially engineered sounds and images to get messages into the subconscious. Because that is purpose: deprogramming the old, negative self-image from the "hard drive," the subconscious, and replacing it with a positive and effective new program. And indeed, one can experience tremendous results using this method to get out of a negative vicious cycle, to then choose a new, positive direction through one's own effort. It is an effective way of self-actualization. You should be careful to choose only sentences or phrases with a positive setting, so words like "not" and "no" are to be avoided.

It is of course important here to know and understand what enters your mind, because this programming can also happen subliminally, by evading the conscious mind.

As early as the 1950s, scientists in the Soviet Union used a method of "sleep programming," playing repeated propaganda all night long during sleep. Today we know this as subliminal programming, which can also include the use of tiny image flashes in movies, or almost non-audible words in music, anchoring the suggestions directly into the subconscious mind.

Everyone from health professionals to educators use subliminal programming nowadays. Many athletic programs, sales organizations, government agencies, retailers, and particularly the Internet use subliminals.

In a similar way, you can utilize the positive energy of the OM sound, with the matching positive energy from the Sri Yantra, by continuously repeating the sound while keeping your gaze upon the picture. You do not even need to understand how this energy transfer exactly works. Likewise, we don't need to know exactly how electricity causes a lamp to light up; it's enough to know where the "on" switch is!

Below is an example of a Sri Yantra / OM meditation. You'll find more methods in chapter 7. According to the Indian tradition of *Vastu*, comparable to *Feng Shui*, the art of arranging one's living space harmoniously, the Sri Yantra should be hung on a wall facing north or east, at eye level when sitting in front of it.

Sit in *sidhasana*, the prescribed meditational "lotus" sitting position, or in any other comfortable sitting position, keeping your back straight. If necessary, use a solid back support. Of course you need to take your time, and you do not want to be disturbed during meditation.

Meditation with the OM sound and Sri Yantra

Begin by breathing calmly and evenly: In through the nose, out through the mouth, between slightly opened lips. This causes the mind to be drawn inwardly.

Gaze at the center of the Sri Yantra picture, trying to blink as little as possible. You do not want to look at the details of the image; you just take in the whole, while focusing on the central part.

Now breathe in deeply, open your mouth to a wide AH, and begin singing the OM sound at a comfortable pitch, or sing along with one of the CD tracks, while you keep your focus incessantly on the picture in front of you. Try to keep your body as relaxed and motionless as possible. Between each singing of OM, keep a silence of at least three quiet breaths.

After a while, you may close your eyes and try to picture the Sri Yantra in your mind. Don't expect this to be perfect in your first efforts. Now and again you can open your eyes to see the image again, and then try once more to inwardly visualize the yantra. Eventually, sound and image will mingle into *one impression*, a very peculiar experience. Yet, as a beginner, you do not want to sit and wait for this experience to happen, because this expectation will just block the process. It will come at its own pace and time, so do not focus on that.

In the last phase of your meditation, you will stop singing the sound, but inwardly it will continue to reverberate by itself.

You may notice that in one moment this meditation will be a lot easier and smoother than in another, but that is normal. It depends on so many factors in your daily life. Still, in the long run, and with daily practice, there will emerge a constancy, allowing you to remain in this same calm, focused state of mind, which is the purpose of your meditation.   •

Although the sequence of experiences while singing OM is very subtle, by practicing it while automatically letting your attention go inside of your head, this experience can be observed very intensively, up to the moment when the sound itself becomes "the hand that rocks the cradle." From that moment on, you do not need to make any effort at all anymore, because the sound will "repeat itself." This is the point from which the actual meditation departs.

It need not take years of practice for this exceptional meditational experience to be yours. And of course you do not necessarily have to use the OM sound; there are other ways and methods as well. But with the use of the OM mantra this experience may take place uniquely—in the most literal sense of the word—and eventually lead to the ultimate silence within, from where the journey through the inner realms may begin.

In essence, we are all connected by an invisible umbilical cord with these inner worlds, our source and origin, even though most people are no longer consciously aware of this. But if we choose to, we may make use of this age-old method in order to once again reconnect with this awareness.

Chanting the OM mantra is a wonderful mechanism that in fact utilizes a typical property of our mind. Just think of a popular song that you just heard a couple of times on the radio and now is re-playing itself inside your head. The whole day you keep on humming it over and over again, sometimes *ad nauseam!* The same principle, of course, is used by commercials. The well-known slogan is: *repetition is the key!*

This mental mechanism of the mind is what you'll use in order to have the mantra eventually "repeat itself" inside your head. You repeat the mantra over and over again until it automatically becomes like a song inside your head. A most beautiful song…

The repetition mechanism brings you into a kind of timeless realm, not to doze off or dream away, but to experience freedom and a profound, peaceful, and quiet space that cannot be described. Add to this the direct effects of the OM sound itself, to be felt physically as well as mentally, and there you have a simple but nevertheless very effective method that can enrich your life so much.

The OM sound, with or without the accessory Sri Yantra, will eventually lead to a place within, from where the inner journey home can begin.

How the Sri Yantra originally came into our world will always remain an intriguing matter. It is really not as important as the answer to the question: What effects can the Sri Yantra and the OM mantra actually have on us when we know how we can use them? That is what this chapter is about.

Effects of the Sri Yantra

What looking at and concentrating upon the Sri Yantra can do for you is beyond description. In chapter 3 we attempted to fathom the secrets behind it. What remains is simply a matter of practice: just do it and wonder! The practice of singing the OM mantra, described in chapter 7, will only be enhanced by simultaneous concentration upon the Sri Yantra mandala.

OM – Physical, psychological, and spiritual effects through vibrational resonance

The effects of the OM mantra are extraordinary indeed. These effects also can hardly be explained in words, because it is a matter of pure experience. Still, we shall try to describe an analysis of these effects.

1   Sound vibrations and resonance

As we all know, our body consists mostly of water. Water can easily be set into motion with sound vibration. Just as a pebble thrown into a pond causes a circular wave pattern on the water surface, *every sound has a direct effect on our body fluids*. Naturally, the heavy sounds like a passing truck or a heavy church bell are more easily perceptible in our bodies than the more subtle vibrations like a refrigerator or a musical instrument. But these vibrations still do affect us as well, depending of course on proximity, frequency, intensity, and, most of all, how long we are exposed to the sound.

Apart from this direct physical influence upon our bodies, these kinds of sounds also have a direct influence on our mind and our awareness, mainly—but not only—through our ears. The sounds affect the brain waves in such a way that our state of mind is constantly subject to change. Using earplugs or locking ourselves in a soundproof room in order to resist the daily bombardment of sound frequencies is not always possible or desirable for most of us. This is one of the reasons why it is so lovely to retreat in nature for a while, to be alone with the silence, or listen to the relaxing sounds of the wind rustling in the trees or the murmuring of a brook. But we do have a choice: as a counterbalance to all these daily noises we have to endure, we can opt for the silence of a church, a park, or forest . . . any quiet place.

We can also consciously choose yet another dimension, that is, taking in perfectly harmonic sounds, harmonic in all their aspects of pitch, resonance,

volume, and above all, their overtones. Often, singing bowls are utilized for this purpose, but the human voice can also serve this purpose, provided certain conditions are met. The advantage is that you always carry this instrument with you, and you can harmonize your own voice with some regular training.

The vibrations of the vowels (A, O, and U) and the consonants (M and N) all have their own resonance area in the body. Obviously they all resonate inside your larynx, mouth, and trachea. But there are still more specific parts of the body in which you will clearly sense the resonance of each sound. When this coincides with the right pitch for a particular body area, you can feel the vibrations even better, and the effects will be deeper. You may even visualize or use certain colors—in colored lights, painted walls or plates, tinted or stained glass, cloth or clothing—that correspond to the chakra(s) in the part of the body you want to treat.[4]

These correspondences of the OM sound are listed below:

A – Resonates in the chest area, heart, shoulders, upper back; corresponds with the fourth chakra, the *heart chakra*; the pitch is F and the colors are pink and green.

O – Resonates in the upper belly, the first part of the digestive track with all its organs, including the stomach, liver, gallbladder, spleen, pancreas, duodenum and small intestine; also the solar plexus nerve center; corresponds with the third chakra, the *solar plexus chakra*; the pitch is E and the colors are gold and yellow.

U – Resonates in the lower belly, the last part of the digestive tract, including the kidneys, large intestine, colon, rectum, and the ovaries or prostate; corresponds with the second chakra, the *sacral chakra*; the pitch is D and the color is orange.

M – Resonates in the entire spinal column from bottom to top, *and* in the head. Low M tones obviously have more effect in the spine, while higher-pitched M tones resonate only in the skull, mainly the brain. *As above, so below!*

N – Resonates only inside the head, mainly the forehead, and face, including the eyes, nose, and mouth cavities, as well as the inner ear. So, when you sing, with mouth shut, the M and the N simultaneously, your whole head will resonate. The pitch with this combined M-N may be A, belonging to the sixth chakra, the *brow chakra or third eye*. The colors to visualize with this sound are indigo and purple, up to a very light lilac and clear sun-white in the seventh chakra, the crown chakra.

2 *Slowed-down exhalation*

One of the essential characteristics in Hatha Yoga is the fact that while practicing the *asanas*, or yoga postures, the pace of your breath will be slowed down, coordinated with the slow yoga movements. Actually, the movements are being adapted to the slower breathing. This naturally results in more relaxation—physically as well as mentally—because the breath can be seen as the collective mirror of both our body pace *and* our state of mind. When we are physically or mentally stressed and excited, our breathing will automatically be restless and faster. Yoga practitioners are able to slow down their breathing and let it flow in a more relaxed manner, resulting in a better overall state of mind and body.

By chanting the OM sound, your breathing will become slower as well, so the same effects will be the result.

Of course this needs to be cultivated. Initially you may find yourself out of breath all of a sudden while still singing the U, so you do not get to the M at all. The singing has to be apportioned according to your lung capacity: if at first you do not have such a long breath, you need to move faster from A to M, in order to be able to sing a long MMM in the end.

3   Regular exhalation

During the process of chanting, exhalation will not only become slower, but also more regular. Sometimes this also requires extra training—just as in a professional singing lesson where one has to learn how to control one's exhalation —but eventually you will be able to obtain perfect control, in order to get a *long, even tone,* without jerking or straining.

4   Complete exhalation

The third aspect of the exhalation during OM singing is the completness of exhalation. It is a sounding, to be literally long-winded, as long as possible within one's limits. During the first part of the exhalation the ribs lower, the chest relaxes, and at the end of the breath, your belly muscles are even a little contracted, so the last bit of air is pushed out of your lungs. After that, the belly muscles relax once more, allowing the new breath to come in on its own.

You do not need to be an experienced yogi to be able to sing the OM mantra, but of course training yourself in *complete yogic breathing* will come in handy.

5   Combination of 1/2/3/4 = *mastering the breath and complete relaxation*

The sum of the parts appears to be more effective than the separate effects. When the aspects of 1 to 4 are combined in this one OM sounding, we have here a perfect method for experiencing the treatment effects even stronger. Another leading aspect is the period of silence that follows. It feels like this silence is almost palpable—an extraordinary experience!

6   The dispeller of thoughts

Although the above discussed effects are mainly effective on the physical level, there is also an undeniable effect on our mind and sense of well-being; the calming part, the spatial feeling, letting go. . . But there is more. With the singing of this sound you will be able to stop the treadmill of your thoughts.

In the first stages of singing OM, there is no other way but to keep your focus on the sound and your breath control, otherwise it will go wrong. This is in itself a fine way to redirect your attention from the outside looking in. The whole day long, from the moment we open our eyes, we are used to being focused on the outside world. Most of us hardly ever give a moment of attention to the inside, what we think and feel. So this is a new habit formation for which we need time to adapt; this is not a one-day effort. Singing the OM sound is just one splendid way to realize this. Because you need to completely direct your attention inwardly and listen to your own singing voice, your thoughts are automatically calmed down. For this reason it is also a good thing to perform at night before going to sleep, to become restful and centered and thus able to fall asleep more easily.

7   Spiritual effects by attunement to the realms within

Except for the physical and psychological effects there is still another realm, the attainment of which is the ultimate aim of the OM meditation practice: to enter a meditative state of being. In this way, OM chanting is the first stage in meditation: the vocalization of the sacred sound, or just listening to the chanting, and then repeating the mantra inside as part of the actual meditation, with the ultimate goal of becoming a traveller into the inner, spiritual realms, to be guided by a Master, who has already travelled this road.

During initiation by the *(Sat)guru,* the initiate will be connected with the "radiant form" of the Master, who will guide the initiate all the way onto the inner path towards enlightenment.

A complete description of this process falls beyond the limits of this book, but as they say in India, "When the pupil is ready, the Master will be there."

In this chapter you will find a number of ways you can use the OM mantra at home, alone, or in a group. You may listen to the sound on the CD, or sing the sound by yourself, with or without the help of the CD. After regular practice it will eventually be clear to you which method appeals to you most.[5]

The practice of singing the OM mantra

The recommended sitting position is the already-mentioned *Siddhasana* (half lotus), but the kneeling position is also very useful. For many people, it is easier to keep the back aligned and straight in the kneeling position, which is crucial in this exercise. Ideally, the heels are kept apart, with the toes of both feet almost touching each other, so there is a natural kind of support for your buttocks. If this fails, you can always use some pillows, below the insteps of the feet and between your feet and buttocks; better still is a low meditation bench, with the feet free below it. If you are not able to bend the knees that far in these positions, just sit on a chair with a straight back.

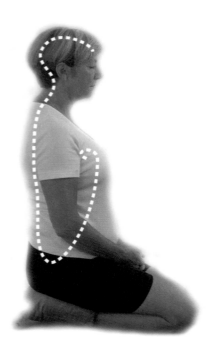

First, you may practice and experience where in your body you feel most of the sound vibration. Just sing the vowels apart from each other, one by one. Feel that the **A** will resonate most in the stomach and chest area, and in front and center of the mouth cavity. The **O** resonates in the whole upper belly and more in the back of the mouth. The **U** vibrates very deep, in the lower belly and lower spine, and almost disappears into the gullet. Feel also the different ways in which your tongue shapes these sounds.

You will feel the **M** sound mostly throughout your entire spinal column and inside your head. Try experimenting with the **M** and the

N separately. By humming the **NNN**, mainly your forehead, your entire face, and sinuses will resonate. The **MMM** resonates more inside your skull and brain. So when you simultaneously sing the **M** and the **N**, with the tip of your tongue behind your front teeth to your palate, your entire head will resonate. When singing the OM mantra, do this as well, for a more complete resonance inside your head.

Try to use about half of your exhalation for the **A-O-U** vowel series and the second half for a prolonged **M/N** sound. *You can sing along with tracks 2 to 5 of the CD.*

• • •

The next two practices are simple ways of combining the OM sound with a graceful yoga movement.

You are supposed to sing the OM sound in one elongated exhalation. This means you must pace your sound-making with your exhalation so that you will have enough breath to sing all the way to the M! This needs some practice but you will quickly learn how to regulate your breath. The art is to eventually do it effortlessly and naturally. Then, sound, breath, and movement will become as one. You can also do these movements while listening to track 6 of the CD.

2 UNIFICATION

1. Stand with your feet a little apart and your knees loose, arms relaxed alongside your body and your shoulders heavy and relaxed. Take a few quiet and deep breaths and sigh out loud. Center yourself. With another deep breath—let it go all the way deep down into your belly—you open

your mouth as if you are already taking in the A-sound.

2. Now begin singing the **A** while spreading your arms wide open, like opening yourself to embrace the sound in the space before you.

3. While you seamlessly transform the sound into the **O** and the **U**, you gradually bring your arms together in front of you, like you are taking something very precious into your hands. Visualize something that is round and radiating light.

4. As the sound now changes into the elongated **MMM**, your hands are moving together with their precious, radiating treasure, toward your chest, to your heart chakra.

5. In the following silence you lay both hands upon your chest and breathe quietly, while a smile enlightens your face.

You may repeat this sound movement a few times, always with a pause of a few quiet breaths in between. This is a very special, calming, but simple sound movement that brings your attention from the outside inward.

3 SURRENDERING

1. Sit on your heels, with a bolster or pillow in between your heels and bottom, if needed, knees a little apart for balance. Again, you may begin with a few deep breaths to concentrate.

2. Then, while breathing in slowly and completely, stretch out your arms above your head, while looking up. From there you start singing a nice, mouth-wide-open **A,** while very gradually bending forward with arms and torso.

3. The A transforms into the **O** and the **U**, and meanwhile your arms

move sideward and back, alongside the body, while your head comes closer to the floor in front of your knees.

4. During the long **MMM**, your head lies heavily on the floor, or on a prop if you cannot touch the floor, and your arms and shoul-

ders lie relaxed and heavy. While kneeling, you are supposed to keep your bottom on, or as near as possible to, your heels.

5. Breathe a few times quietly in this relaxed pose, then return slowly and with a rounded back to the upright position. Ideally, you repeat the sound movement 3 to 5 times.

If you are not able to do this on the floor, you can do it sitting on a chair. You then just hang your upper body over your legs, with your head between your knees.

This is a pose of surrender, of letting go. It's a perfect exercise before going to sleep, as a kind of closure of your day. These exercises 2 and 3 combined make a fine 'five minute session' for more concentration, clarity and relaxation in between work shifts.

•••

4   BEING AWARE OF THE EFFECTS

Seated in a meditative position, you can sing the OM mantra while concentrating on the effects in your body as well as in your mind. Meditate on the effects during long silences between the chanting of the sounds.

You may sing along with tracks 6, 7, 13, or 14 of the CD.

5   SILENTLY REPEATING THE MANTRA WITHIN

Now it gets interesting: after you have sung OM several times aloud, you continue "singing" the same sound internally, in your mind, so you imagine singing OM, only without using your voice (this is known as *madhyama*). It is just like when you first concentrate on an object, and then with your eyes closed, try to "see" the same object in your mind. At first you can do this while the muscles of your tongue and jaw still make the same movements, and in the same rhythm as your gradual exhalation. After a long time of practice, you'll reach the stage when the mantra will repeat itself, as it were—or could we say here repeated by the Self?—without any conscious effort on your part.

A variation could be that, while repeating the sound internally, you imagine that with every breath you are singing the sound one pitch higher. If you find this too hard, you might start over again with the vocalized sounds. But the good thing about this meditation is that when you do this internally you will be able to get much, much higher than if you were to use your actual voice. The effect is very special, but also very hard to describe—you just have to experience it yourself.

The sound will repeat itself by itself, and your consciousness will be one with the sound (*pashyanti*). The final stage will be that the awareness enters the inner realms of being, which goes beyond the limits of this do-it-yourself practice, because these realms can only be entered by an initiate, under the guidance of a Master.

The first three stages, though, are quite safe, when they are acquired gradually, but if you feel insecure yourself, you may have an experienced friend or teacher supervise you. The result will be a complete stilling of the mind, a delicate, deliciously relaxed awareness in which you can remain as long as feels good for you.

At first you can listen a few times to tracks 11, 13 or 14, and sing along if you like (you don't have to; you can also just listen). You will concentrate on the resonance, where the sounds are most perceptible, in your body and head.

Then, stop listening to the CD (the best way to do this is to program your CD player so that it will turn off by itself) and you sit in silence while repeating the mantra internally, as much as possible the same way you just did by singing or listening. At this stage you won't have to do this repetition in concert with your breathing. Let your breathing continue naturally, by itself.

As long as this concentration can be maintained without effort, you may keep doing this internal process. There will be a signal from within when it is enough. Breathe deeper, feel and move your muscles, and become aware again of your body.

6 REPEATING THE MANTRA WITHOUT SOUND SUPPORT

You may start with singing along with a mantra on the CD for a while, just like you did in exercise 5 (see above). Then, stop the CD and continue singing on your own, as long as it feels pleasant and effective. This method has a lot of possibilities: you can, for instance, direct your attention at trying to make very long and smooth sounds, or at the long pauses between the sounds. You can try out different pitches and feel the difference in resonance and effect. You can make the **MMM** sound last extra long.

And here also, you may, after a few times having sung it aloud, repeat the OM in silence inside your head, as described in exercise 5.

7 CONCENTRATION ON THE THIRD EYE

The "third eye" is another word for the brow chakra, two finger-widths above the point right between the eyebrows and also somewhat behind the forehead, inside the skull. While concentrating, you do not need to tense any muscles in your eyes or eyebrows. Just try to simply be there, with your attention in this one point, without any strain.

As a start, you might sing along with, or just listen to, track 13 and/or 14 of the CD. But after this introduction, there is no need for any sound from the outside; you will completely block any outside sound out, because your attention is only directed at this one point within your head, while you constantly repeat the OM mantra.

After a while, when you are able to keep the concentration completely within, in the chakra point, you will notice that the sound will repeat itself, without any effort on your part. The sound has become part of you and you have become one with the sound. As long as you can stay alert, you can remain in this position and just observe, being in the here and now, until even this observing becomes autonomous, or merges into pure silence.

A signal from within will tell you when to return to ordinary consciousness. Breathe deeply, feel and move your muscles, and become aware again of your body.

• • •

Then, finally, there is also the practice of singing OM in a group. Humming the **MMM** sound can be very equalizing, for instance, during heated discussions or meetings, when feelings are running high, to calm down and create room for new ideas and possibilities. I have heard many beautiful stories like this from my own students, who put into practice what they had learned in the yoga class.

Singing OM in a group is increasingly being done by therapists, at the beginning of therapy sessions and group meditations. It can create a beautiful transition into the sessions, and can help direct an intention. It creates a sense of peace and harmony.

CD MANUAL

Listening to the CD is an experience in itself. Here you will find an overview of the 15 tracks that can be used for several purposes. A couple of these possible applications have already been described in the previous chapter. You can probably come up with other possibilities yourself. Now you will read some impressions of the various soundtracks.

For listening to the CD you need a good sound system. The speakers ought to be preferably 50 watts or more, and a surround-sound system would be nice, so you can bathe yourself in the sounds all around you.[6]

1 OM singing with the tambura as accompaniment

Although in this book we have been using the complete A-O-U-M sound, on this track you will hear an **OOOMMM** sound, with the beautiful accompanying instrument known as the multichord. The track lasts long enough (7 minutes) to be used as a spiritual practice. If needed you can program the track on repeat, so you may continue as long as you wish. You can hear the beautiful harmonic overtones in the voice.

Tracks 3-6 are meant to be voice and sounding exercises, with the purpose of obtaining more control over your voice. But they also constitute an excellent healing practice, since these vowels and tones are direcly applicable and effective specific body areas. At the beginning of each track you will first hear the right pitch on a chime.

2 On this track you hear the **A vowel**, sung in the pitch of F, associated with the *heart chakra*. This sound will be mostly perceptible and effective in the chest, lungs, and heart. This vowel endorses reaching out to the world outside, feelings from the heart, and the feeling of making more room, space.

First try to sing along with the sounds you hear and afterwards practice by yourself, always with ample silence between each toning. Be here and now, an observer of what is.

3 On this track you hear the **O vowel**, sung in the pitch of E, associated with the *third chakra* in the stomach area. This sound will be mostly perceptible and effective in the digestive organs. The kidneys also get their share of balancing energy. This vowel endorses the awakening of a better self-image and feeling of identity, individuality. I am!

First try to sing along with the sounds you hear and afterwards practice by yourself, always with ample silence between each toning. Be here and now, an observer of what is.

4   On this track you hear the **U vowel**, sung in the pitch of D, associated with the *second chakra* in the center of your belly. This sound will be mostly perceptible and effective in the intestines, kidneys, adrenals, ovaries, or prostate. This vowel endorses a feeling of grounding, solidifying, feeling more present in the body. It makes you feel secure and calm.

First try to sing along with the sounds you hear and afterwards practice by yourself, always with ample silence between each toning. Be here and now, an observer of what is.

5   On this track you hear the **M consonant**, sung in the pitch of C (low and high!), associated with the *first chakra* in the base of the spine, but also with an opening and connection to the spiritual world, from the *seventh chakra* upwards. This sound will be mostly perceptible and effective in the area of the lower belly and lower back, including the coccyx. Like the U, this sound is also grounding; it draws excessive energy from your thinking head into your body and its contact with the earth. It literally gives you more head room, balance, and a feeling of harmony.

First try to sing along with the sounds you hear and afterwards practice by yourself, always with ample silence between each toning. Be here and now, an observer of what is.

6 OM meditation for the root chakra

This track is extremely suitable for self-practice, for instance as a preparation for a long meditation, in order to direct your attention inward. But it is also very effective for those people who tend to keep most of their energy inside their heads instead of in their bodies. These sounds are "grounding" because they vibrate in the pitch of C, corresponding to the *root chakra.* In the background you will hear the deep sounds of a singing bowl. The meditation lasts an ample 9 minutes.

You may sing along with the performer on the CD. It does not matter so much if you cannot sing as long as the performer. The pauses in between sounds are ample enough to take a few deep breaths before the next sound begins. You will be able to feel the resonance of the sounds inside your lower belly and pelvis area. You might want to visualize a clear red light there. Also, feel your breath reaching as deep as possible inside your abdomen. Breathe freely, release all tension! Try to keep your back as straight as possible (if needed you may lean against a wall or the back of a chair), but do this also without any excessive strain. Still, these sounds create a direct connection with the seventh chakra and the spiritual realms. An opening, but a safe one. You will remain connected with your body and the earth.

Experience the feeling of space in the sound. Also, perceive the utter silence after the sound, for at least 1 minute. For convenience, you may program your CD player so you may sit in silence for a longer time.

7 OM meditation for the heart chakra

In the background you will hear the sound of a quiet heartbeat, providing an extra calming effect. Here, the OM sound is sung with clearly audible overtones, in the pitch of F, corresponding to the heart chakra. This effects a very liberating feeling of happiness. Do not be surprised when emotions will come up. Just let them be. Embrace them. And release them. In between sounds there is room for one extra breath (10 seconds). The heart chakra is the exact centerpoint between the lower and the higher chakras. It creates a connection, using the force of universal Love. This meditation lasts about 10 minutes as well. Here also is a minute of silence after the sound.

*The next 5 tracks all contain three voices, combined in a **triad,** in particular intervals with very specific effects.[7] Of course you cannot sing three parts by yourself, so just listen and experience the sound, or sing along with the keynote of the triad, which is printed in **bold**. These tracks are also being opened by the keynote of a chime and last about 3 minutes each.*

8 OM Triad C major (triad: **C**/E/G). Connects the 1st chakra (red) by way of the 3rd (yellow) to the 5th (blue).

Affirmation: *I am relaxed and in balance. My head is clear.*

Works on obtaining clarity and problem-solving abilities. Balances extremes like too much tension/relaxation and thinking/feeling. Aids in maintaining the body temperature. Improves strength and activity in the muscles. Works with all head and brain problems: migraine, headaches, eye trouble, neuralgia, coma, undefinable fear and anxiety.

9 OM Triad E major (triad: **E**/G sharp/B). Connects the 3rd chakra (yellow) by way of the 5th (blue) to the 7th (violet).
Affirmation: *Balance. I see the Light.*
Clarifying the balance of earthly/bodily and spiritual matters, this triad is excellent for dreamers who need to get their feet on the ground. Shines a light in the darkness of a negativity spiral. Benevolently influences the blood circulation and the blood itself, all heart conditions, problems of the spine and the nerve fibers. An especially useful triad for spiritual teachers.

10 OM Triad D major (triad: **D**/F sharp/A). Connects the 2nd chakra (orange) by way of the 4th (green) to the 6th (indigo).
Affirmation: *I allow myself ample space in every aspect of my life.*
Gives much clarity in consciousness of your inner self and feelings; promotes a feeling of strength, of being on top of things; deepens the breath. Fortifies the nervous system (brain and spinal fluid), especially the cerebrospinal nerves; integrates the brain hemispheres. Affects the speech center, throat, vocal cords, the inner ear, and the hearing canal.

11 OM Triad a minor (triad: **a**/c/**e**). Connects the 3rd chakra (yellow) by way of the 1st (red) to the 6th (indigo).
Affirmation: *I open myself for new developments.*
You are realizing your own view of life; the triad also contributes to other inner processing. The chord resonates with the longing for the unknown, spiritual aspirations. Provides good ambience during meditations.

12 OM Triad b minor (triad: **b'**/d/**f sharp**). Connects the 4th chakra (green) by way of the 2nd (orange) to the 7th (violet).
Affirmation: *My body and soul are one. There is but one Source!*
For people who live in an inner struggle and always find themselves having to choose between the material or the spiritual. Awaking of immortality of the Self. Through purification and suffering to realization of the Light.

13 OM meditation with women's choir (third eye)
Here you can sing along with a women's choir. The OM mantra is chanted in the pitch of A, connected to the *sixth chakra* inside the forehead. This sound could be an ideal introduction to a silent meditation: after the audible chanting, you turn off the player and silently repeat the mantra internally, while your concentration is upon your third eye. Again, you may choose between singing along with the choir, or just silently listening and experiencing. This track lasts 5 minutes.

14 OM meditation with male choir (third eye)

This track has the same purpose as the previous one, and is sung in the same pitch as well (in A, here also with a clearly audible overtone in C, makes you feel grounded and safe), only with men's voices. Just try to use both tracks several times, so you may choose the one you prefer. This track lasts an ample 6 minutes.

15 OM meditation for the crown chakra

This meditation starts and ends with the clear sound of a temple bell. This is an experimental recording of a whispered OM sound, like the wind, where you can hear the M only as a continuous undertone in the background, in the pitch of B of the crown chakra, transferring into the high C pitch, representing the higher spiritual realms. Towards the end the pauses in between the sounds are getting longer. In a three-dimensional sound environment you will hear birdsong, angels singing, and a beautiful wind chime. Processed is also a heartbeat, almost inaudible. A very special meditation that lasts 9 minutes.

CD Contents

1 OM with multichord (CCFFF) 7:30
2 AAA in F 2:10
3 OOO in E 2:20
4 UUU in D 2:30
5 MMM in C 2:10
6 Elongated OM with 15 seconds silence in between, in the end 1 minute silence in C (first chakra) 9:00
7 Heartbeat and OM, normal breathing pauses, audible overtones, in the end 1 minute silence, in C (first chakra) 9:50
8 OM Triad in C-major 3 voices 2:30
9 OM Triad in E-major 3 voices 3:15
10 OM Triad in D-major 3 voices 3:10
11 OM Triad in a-minor 3 voices 3:00
12 OM Triad in b-minor 3 voices 3:00
13 OM women's choir in A (brow-chakra) 6:15
14 OM male choir in A (brow-chakra) 6:20
15 INFINITE SPACE (crown-chakra). Basic M-tone in B. Whispered OM with spaceous effects and nature sounds 9:30

Total playing time 74 minutes

NOTES

1   *UFO Magazine* 6 no. 3 (1991).

2   See website of Real Health: *www.realhealth-online.com*

3   See the Reading List for further information about Emoto's work.

4   All these connections are described in detail in the book & CD *Chakra Delight*, also published by Binkey Kok.

5   Some of these practices are also mentioned in the book & CD *Yoga & Sound*, also published by Binkey Kok.

6   You will find an extensive description of a "sound bath" in the book and CD *Chakra Delight*, also published by Binkey Kok.

7   A complete explanation and a whole series of 24 healing triads can be found in the book & CD *Yoga & Sound*, also published by Binkey Kok.

Reading List

Donna Carrey and Marjorie de Muynck, *Acutonics®: There's No Place Like Ohm: Sound Healing, Oriental Medicine and the Cosmic Mysteries*

Randall McClellan, *The Healing Forces of Music: History, Theory & Practice*

Hans Cousto, *The Cosmic Octave*

Deborah Van Dyke, *Travelling the Sacred Sound Current* (book & CD)

Masaru Emoto, *The Water Crystal Oracle* and *The Hidden Messages in Water*

Jonathan Goldman, *Healing Sounds: The Power of Harmonics*

Gray Henri and Susannah Marriot, *A String of Prayers*

Hans Jenny, *Cymatics: A Study of Wave Phenomena and Vibration*

Caroline Myss, *Anatomy of the Spirit: The Seven Stages of Power and Healing*

Russill Paul, *The Yoga of Sound: Healing and Enlightenment through the Sacred Practice of Mantra*

Eldon Taylor, Ph.D., *Subliminal Communication: Emperor's Clothes or Panacea?*

Lillian Too, *Mantras and Mudras: Meditations for the Hands and Voice to Bring Inner Peace and Calm*

Other titles in this Book/CD series, see: www.binkeykok.com

DANNY BECHER (1953) has been a musician since his twenties, and studied Eastern classical music and singing in India for eight years. Since 1981 he has been living and working in the Netherlands as a gifted singer, musician, and teacher. He holds a degree in Western classical music and is also a qualified choirmaster. He has performed in concerts in many countries with singing bowls and overtone singing.

MARJOLEIN BERKVENS (1967) has been a vocalist since 1997, instructing adults as well as children. Apart from learning a repertoire and general musical cultivation, a central theme in her lessons is to discover and develop the sound of one's own voice. She is also active as a choirmaster, as a visiting teacher for voice education, and as a soloist.

DICK DE RUITER has been a yoga teacher since 1969, and has specialized since 1980 in the harmonic possibilities of sound. In the 1970s, he introduced new age music to the Netherlands with his mail order business Sono Music of Silence, and has offered numerous workshops about the effects of sound and special music in daily life. He writes and translates books on yoga, sound, and related subjects. www.maisondesmiracles.nl.